WITHDRAWN
HARVARD LIBRARY
WITHDRAWN

THE STRATEGY OF CULTURE

The strategy of culture

*A view of the changes taking place
in our ways of thinking and living today*

C. A. VAN PEURSEN
*Professor of Philosophy
State University of Leyden*

Translated by H. H. HOSKINS

1974

NORTH-HOLLAND PUBLISHING COMPANY
AMSTERDAM · OXFORD
AMERICAN ELSEVIER PUBLISHING COMPANY, INC. – NEW YORK

© North-Holland Publishing Company 1974

All rights reserved. No part of this publication may be reproduced, stored in a retrieval system, or transmitted, in any form or by any means, electronic, mechanical, photocopying, recording or otherwise, without the prior permission of the copyright owner

Library of Congress Catalog Card Number: 74–81325
North-Holland ISBN: 0 7204 8024 8
American Elsevier ISBN: 0 444 10749 5

Originally published under the title *Strategie van de cultuur*, by Agon Elsevier, Amsterdam

Translated from the Dutch by H. H. Hoskins

CB
19
.P47I3

Publishers:
NORTH-HOLLAND PUBLISHING COMPANY – AMSTERDAM
NORTH-HOLLAND PUBLISHING COMPANY, LTD. – OXFORD

Sole distributors for the U.S.A. and Canada:
AMERICAN ELSEVIER PUBLISHING COMPANY,
52 VANDERBILT AVENUE, NEW YORK, N.Y. 10017

PRINTED IN THE NETHERLANDS

Contents

I A model of culture
The development of our contemporary culture   7
The three phases model   12
The strategy of culture   19
The function of the model   24

II Mythical thinking
Myth as human potentiality   29
Some functions of myth   32
Man and world   41
Magic   45

III Ontological thinking
Ontology as a means of liberation   50
Some functions of ontological thinking   54
Man and world   65
Substantialism   69

IV Functional thinking
The transition to functional thinking   78
Aspects of functional thinking   83
Man and world   97
Operationalism   103

V From technology to organization
Technology as a function of the body   112
Technology as a function of the mind   121

Man's activity as organizer 131

VI Culture as a programme
Culture as a learning process 142
Inventiveness 148
The brain and culture 158
Vegetating, producing, consuming 169

VII From knowledge to ethics
Knowledge, technology, ethics 185
Natural, biological and cultural sciences 190
An ethics of interaction 200

VIII Possible and impossible worlds
The world's structures 212
The blind spot 217
A programme for the future 222

How to use this book 238
Literature 242
Illustrations, list of sources 251
Index to illustrations 252
Subject index 254
Name index 257

I
A model of culture

The development of our contemporary culture

A very great deal has been written about the essential character of human culture. One can understand that; for culture is the deposit of an activity typical of man, so that any question about culture at the same time bears upon the questioner himself. Yet in very recent years we have seen this theoretical interest in the 'essence' of culture diminish. It is the more practical issues, relating to the actual cultural programme, that are now coming to the fore. Teaching, scientific research, intensifying the output of industry, town planning, the ordered use of space, recreation, air pollution, habitual conduct on the roads, psychic stress, decoration, the way to handle the communications media – these are just a few of the many terms which every day provide a theme for projects or a topic of conversation in the Press, in educational activities, in the protest movement among the young, in political discussion. It used to be the case that people would prefer to start by thinking through the question of culture at a more theoretical level, thus making it possible for some practical consequences to be drawn – often enough by somebody else! Nowadays the preference is for working out and putting in hand a practical policy, a programme, and afterwards, within that context, examining such questions of a cultural-philosophical nature as may arise.

What we have touched on here in outline and propose to explore more exhaustively in subsequent chapters of this book might well be described as the instrumentalizing of the whole question of culture. The problem of culture is not an end in itself for theoretical reflection; but the analysis of it must be made to help bring into being a policy for culture, directed toward and focussed on the future. This instrumentalizing is presaged in the shifts that have occurred in our understanding of culture. Two of those are worth mentioning briefly here. The first has to do with the enlargement of the concept of 'culture'. Initially, the term 'culture' covered various expressions of the higher reaches of man's intellectual and spiritual life, such as religion, art, science, statecraft. One feature typical of that idea of culture was the distinction between 'culture peoples' (with a very advanced civilisation) and 'nature peoples' (the more primitive peoples). This way of envisaging culture has long since been discarded. Culture is regarded nowadays as the expression of man's mode of living – not any more within a purely natural milieu but as a mode of intervention, of making inroads into that natural milieu. Man's living encounter with nature, with death and life, with sexuality, his way of providing himself with food, his cultivation of the soil, hunting, manufacture of tools, of pots and dishes, clothing – all this is as much part and parcel of his culture as are art, science and religion. It is precisely from the 'nature peoples', so called, that we learn the extent to which agriculture, fertility, the whole realm of the erotic, artistic expression and religious myths constitute a single, inextricable whole. Thus it would be impossible nowadays to reckon up the number of books by cultural anthropologists, phenomenologists of religion and philosophers of culture, in which we find documented in great detail this broad conception of culture.

A further shift has to do with a more dynamic interpretation of 'culture'. The term is treated more as a verb than a noun. 'Culture' is not meant primarily to embrace such objects or products as tools, pictures, works of art, and still less museums, university buildings, tax offices. It refers in the first instance to man's activity in the manufacture of tools and weapons, to the ritual of dance and incantation, to the multiple range of behaviour patterns as they relate to eroticism, to hunting, to the preparation of food. One aspect of culture is tradition – the handing on of effects and of rules – but that tradition is subsumed within the variety of man's activities and within the countless possibilities of change and development presented by existing patterns of culture.

Culture is the heritage of history, like Rembrandt's 'Night Watch' in the Rijksmuseum in Amsterdam, as it is also the nightly occupation of that museum by the protesting artists who in illustration 1 (p. 17) would seem to have stepped straight out of the celebrated canvas. Thus the meditation of the Buddhist monk belongs to the realm of culture, but no more so than Rodier's fashion models, silhouetted tautly against the background of Brazilia's modern architecture (ill. 2, p. 18).

The accelerating pace of history which man is experiencing today has no doubt helped to amplify and dynamize our notion of culture; but it is even more important that culture is no longer something which man 'undergoes' as a kind of fate – not, at least, to the extent he once did. In fact he is trying to take control of the forces it brings into play. The purpose of this book is to make some contribution to that enterprise through a serious attempt to instrumentalize the issue of culture and work it out on the basis of a scheme or model. That model must not be envisaged as an ideal conception of culture but on the contrary as a very restricted scheme; and such a scheme can be taken to be a sort of guideline for the practical cultural programme referred to at the beginning of this chapter. The model employed will also have to be a developmental one. This entails our envisaging culture not as a state of affairs already attained, a status quo, but as a historical process, with contemporary culture a phase in that process.

In the first place we shall have to explore a number of problems which a developmental model of this sort inevitably entails, and in so doing we should be able to elucidate the function of the model itself. A developmental model goes along with an explanatory method usually described as 'genetic'. Some development of a given phenomenon is then traced in outline, with a view to shedding light on the question as to why that phenomenon occurs in that particular way. At the same time this may result in our being able to exert an influence upon it: insight into the *modus operandi* of the thing can often make it possible for us to help guide the course its development will take. That all this is true with respect to culture, for example, will constitute the argument of this book. The aim of a genetic model, therefore, is to offer not just a descriptive account of certain historical developments, but also a critical appraisal of the process as a whole.

In the process by which human culture evolves factual event and evaluation are inseparably connected. The chronological course of events in culture is never accepted by man – either modern man or primitive man – as being simply self-evident or self-explanatory, but is always evaluated in a particular way. When it comes to the actual course of events (the *'quaestio facti'*) man raises the question whether it was a good thing, or not, that the cultural process turned out as it did: the question therefore of its legitimacy (the *'quaestio iuris'*). Thus Solon, two and a half thousand years ago, describes the history of mankind as a kind of judicial action of cosmic dimensions; and indeed the demand that criteria, standards of some sort, be applied to the actual course of events and to natural relations within human history is a typical feature of every culture. It is of the essence of culture, says Kant, that man should be his own instructor. Culture, therefore, is that activity of man which never stops at what is given, either historically or in the course of nature, but presses on with the quest for improvement, change, reformation. Instead of merely asking how a thing is, man asks how it should be. In that way he is able to break through the determinate condition (immanence) produced by the processes of nature or of history, by postulating norms that reach out beyond what actually is (transcendence).

The development of living entities from the simple, unicellular organism right up to the most highly organized animals constitutes a lengthy process of biological evolution, exhibiting laws it is the job of science to discover and to scrutinize. Those laws (rules) are implicit in nature and have a part to play in the life of man as well. But in his case a whole new dimension starts to operate, as it were, because man subsumes all the 'rules' of nature within normative rules. This applies not only to the so called higher functions, such as learning how to do science, acquiring modes of behaviour, responding to moral ideals, staking one's all on this or that social or religious belief. More biological functions too (those, for instance, of nutrition, sexuality, breathing, the aggressive drives) are in their ultimate effect determined partly by norms prevailing in a particular culture. One thinks, for example, of the ritual associated with cooking, various culinary refinements, the exigent (or, alternatively, execrated) custom of belching, the historically so very mutable art of eroticism, control of breathing through meditation, direct and indirect, the exercise, armed and unarmed, of aggression, and so forth. The distinction between the rules of nature and those of culture is chiefly that the former just have to be kept (it is a case of physical necessity), whereas the latter do not have to be followed, even though it may be proper to comply with them (a case of moral obligation). Indeed, there are times when a man does not simply fail to observe the rules of propriety out of weakness or negligence but contravenes them deliberately, because he holds them to be inadequate and is seeking to have the rules revised. The business of positing standards and applying them forms the transcendent dimension that breaches natural immanence in such a way as to require recurrent acts of initiative, a fresh start, on the part of individuals and groups. This it is that provides the dynamic element in human history.

Contemporary culture is in process of rapid development, and modern man is well aware of the fact. A sensitive concern with a critical evaluation of the existing culture is perhaps more evident today than in most other periods of human history. Elucidating one's own course of development against the background of previous phases can be a means to evaluating and restructuring, in practice, one's own culture. What is more, such a developmental model of culture not only serves to disclose, within the limits of such a model, something of the divergence but also of the common factor in human culture, namely, the question men raise regarding the legitimacy of such developments as do actually occur. C. Kluckhohn speaks of the 'anthropologically sensitive world' in which we now live – because the cross-links between all cultures, whether past or present, are now so numerous that man today is becoming more powerfully conscious of a universally shared humanity. This is bound to have certain consequences for the practical organization of industry and international relations.

To sum up: our concern must be to establish a developmental model that will take into account various phases of culture. These are not to be envisaged simply as a chronological scheme; for the basis of this kind of model will not be historical curiosity but the critical evaluation of what is happening here and now. One might also put it like this: every culture can be regarded as programmatic, a guided course of activities. This is the theme to which chapter VI will be devoted. In earlier times man's way of grappling with the great issues of his existence was not the same as it is today. Any model which is intended to schematize culture – or rather the several phases of its development – must therefore be seen as first and foremost a representation of varying forms of 'policy' or strategy. Such a policy, programme or strategy of culture in fact functions in the context of the developing historical process but is not finally subsumed in it, because it also entails a response to the question about the legitimacy, the proper evaluation, of all that happens in the life of men.

The three phases model

What is happening today can best be typified by setting it against the background provided by earlier phases. Of course, to represent the historical growth of human culture in all its diversity is an impossible undertaking; but what one can do is try to highlight, by bringing them into a concise scheme, a few striking transitions in the continuing process. That we propose to do in the next three chapters by dividing it into three characteristic phases which bring out some salient differences of cultural policy, although naturally one can recognize many more phases than that in the actual course of history. The phases in this model are: the mythical, the ontological and the functional. The mythical phase is marked by a particular stance or attitude in which man has the sense of being engrossed by encircling powers. As yet he is incapable of distinguishing himself from what surrounds and enfolds him. Indeed, he participates directly in it, is part of it, at any rate at the climactic moments of his existence, as we shall seek to show in chapter II. A second phase, however, poses quite explicitly the question as to 'what it all really is': ontology is strictly speaking the systematic study of all being. Here man is no longer directly participant in the forces that surround him, but in distancing himself stands over against them. Whereas mythological thinking is the specific hallmark of primitive cultures, ontological thinking makes its appearance in those ancient civilisations where speculative, and in some instances even scientific, thought is able to flourish. The third phase – that is, the functional – entails a mode of acting and thinking in which the focal point, as it were, is neither man's separation from his environment nor his sense of being directly engrossed by it. It is more of a referential kind of thinking, where instead of participation and distance the central feature is relation. In a sense each phase is the expression of a programme, of a procedure calculated to control the relation between man and the normative forces; but in functional thinking this relation becomes a salient feature of man as well as of the powers (meaning the divine, social structures, ethical standards, and so on).

Our developmental model involves something more than a number of diverse psychological or even cultural viewpoints. E. H. Gombrich provides an example of the latter when he invites us to contemplate the same landscape as depicted by people from differing cultural milieus: Derwentwater in the Lake District, sketched by a Chinese artist and by a European one (ill. 3 and 4, p. 18). As we shall see later on, both these pictures represent the scene from the ontological standpoint, to which they belong. The difference is of a *structural* kind, however, in the case of the next two pictures, representing what is basically the same action: a man flinging a stone at birds. The first is on a Greek vase and represents Hercules; the second is a work by the modern painter, Miró, and is entitled 'person throwing a stone at a bird' (ill. 8 and 9, p. 36). The early Greek picture gives us the 'ontological' representation: that is to say, it reproduces the stylized aspect of man and animal, and the very action becomes part of the stylization. In Miró's picture on the other hand it is the action that so to speak absorbs the substance, the concrete aspect of what is depicted; so that of the standing figure he reproduces only what is functionally relevant, namely, point of support (in particular the foot) and point of vision.

Within these broad contours we shall introduce in the next three chapters various finer points of distinction, one of which might be mentioned straightaway. Cultural development is never of a kind that leads inevitably to a better state of affairs. Therefore no phase is superior to the one before it; it is simply that the programme it forms is different in kind. Admittedly, there is discernible progress (science, technics, the achievement of personal identity); but this is ambiguous, because it can also have a negative outcome (technocracy, individualism, and so on). That in turn links up with the fact that every phase has a negative component. There is in man an urge to dominate which is liable to disrupt the regulative system in any culture-situation. In the context of the mythical position magic is to be characterized in this way, in the ontological phase substantialism, and in the functional approach operationalism; we shall be expatiating and elaborating upon these negative components in subsequent chapters.

There is nothing new in describing the history of culture as a process of development in three phases. Two examples of this, very different from each other, are worth mentioning here. In the last century the philosopher Hegel embedded the development of culture in a scheme comprising thesis, antithesis, synthesis. First comes the thesis, the self-evident truth, as given expression in direct experience and the settled forms of life manifest in the natural-cum-moral realm. A second stage is constituted by the contrast or antithesis in which the mind bifurcates, as it were, and there emerge two opposite worlds: this world and a higher reality. A third stage is the synthesis of opposites, in that mind, at work in men and in their culture, discovers itself in both realms: that of the experiential world and that of the higher values. For Hegel this is an idealist philosophy, a coming to consciousness and a process of growth on the part of Mind, of which mankind, culture and nature are a manifestation. Here then is an ideal evolution, reaching its culminating point in the idealist philosophy.

Operative at about the same time as Hegel, in the first half of the 19th century, was the French philosopher Auguste Comte. His positivist philosophy was the opposite of Hegel's idealism. Mind is not something given absolutely; but it has to be analyzed in the relations posited by the sciences between phenomena and in the structuring of social relations. Although a complete opposite of Hegel in that respect, Comte nevertheless projected a scheme of the development of man's knowledge in three phases. The first stage is the 'theological' one: here the knowledge man forms of the world goes hand in hand with the formation of fictions, that is, with discourse about 'powers' which are conceived of by analogy with man's own activities and behaviour. Animism, polytheism, monotheism, Comte assigns them all to this primary stage. A second stage is 'metaphysical'; here the anthropomorphic fictions are replaced by abstractions: forces at work in nature, the essence of things and values, substances as vehicles of visible properties. A third stage is the 'scientific', which Comte also calls the positive stage: here we do not talk any more about personal powers or, for that matter, about absolute forces and energies, but about scientifically explicable phenomena, positive data. An encyclopaedic classification of the sciences, culminating in sociology, then serves as preparation for the practical application in society of positive ideas, which may be envisaged as a kind of victory over preceding stages. One finds influences of this positivism in the work of Lévy-Bruhl, who ascribes to primitive man a pre-logical sort of thinking. We shall be going further into that in the next chapter.

The three-phase model, which we take as our point of departure in this book, differs fundamentally from the ideas expounded by Hegel and Comte. In the first place, we make no pretension here to be describing the actual course of historical development; we are only providing a model of it. Later on in this chapter we shall consider what the basic limitations are of any model. Secondly, there is no question of a development that one could interpret as an ascent to higher levels; it is more a matter of there being diverse trends of cultural policy, which whilst they are of course successive are not for that reason to be understood as 'progress' or as 'overcoming' previous phases. Thirdly, this implies that metaphysical reflection, religion and the like are not restricted just to certain phases and do not get left behind by the human race; nor do technological pursuits and logical reasoning occur only in the so called higher phases. All man's cultural activities and stances come into play in every phase, even if they are realized in each phase in a new way. Fourthly, in the model provided here we make constant allowance for a negative component. Indeed, it is not a question of proffering an idealist or positivist utopia, but of facing up to the real tensions and conflicts, the reality of evil and of the inadequate compromise.

To sum up: the really outstanding difference between the ideas we have been discussing and the model we propose here is that the latter subserves the comparability of cultural patterns, whereas Hegel and Comte wanted to give us an account of a real progress in the history of culture. This comparability means that we can see the three phases – there may in fact be more than three – as distinct trends or directions on which human culture has embarked in the course of history. Of course, they do usually occur in fixed succession; but it could well be that in the course of its actual development the mythical position passes abruptly into the functional, sometimes exhibiting from the outset markedly operationalist tendencies. A rapid transition of this sort must be taking place at the moment in a number of developing countries. Then again, of the three phases each will involve an emphasis on particular aspects which as potentialities are implicit in every human culture. There is a common basis, as it were, a background against which certain tendencies emerge in sharper outline.

This means that we shall discover functional elements even where the main tendency of a culture is mythical or ontological, just as our modern society itself is not entirely without its ontological and mythical aspects. It will often be necessary, in the context of a modern functional viewpoint, to give a more or less functional account of certain features of the mythical or the ontological world picture. When that happens, it must not be done in order to smuggle our own ideas in among those of the past (interpreting, as it were, by hindsight), but simply as a method of translating, with the aim of making clear to people today what the case was for such a way of looking at things and such a pattern of living in times past.

Quite a number of writers (Dilthey and Jaspers, for instance) have supplied a typology of various schools of thought and ways of envisaging the world; and they have often started from a nexus of ideas rooted in psychology. The present model entails more of a structural than a psychological analysis. This means that the actual course of events is run down to a few salient features offering possibilities of establishing certain rules of policy or a strategy; for it is our purpose, after all, to consider within the context of what happens in fact (*quaestio facti*) the question of legitimacy (*quaestio iuris*). The phases of thinking to be outlined are therefore not tied to a particular disposition of the psyche. Each phase does of course evince a typical contrast, but this is not so much psychological as ethical in character – a contrast tallying with what is nowadays described as an 'open mind' and a 'closed mind'. This contrast is provided by the negative tendencies (magic, substantialism, operationalism) within the various phases. To some extent this also corresponds to an older method of categorization developed by Grünbaum, namely, that of 'dominating' (negative: closed attitude) and 'cherishing' (positive: open attitude).

A material point of difference from all the schemes so far discussed is that the model employed here is intended in the first instance to help us arrive at a critical assessment of the present situation; and that will entail our regarding both the preceding phases as a kind of background picture making the present strategy of culture more readily discernible. Thus they are framed, as it were, in a 'flash-back'. This in its turn implies that our developmental model will be focussed on the future: contemporary culture, envisaged as a strategy in process of development, presents various opportunities for concentrating in its programme upon the future – which is not to say, however, that it is to yield a descriptive account of that future. Speculations about the future and what its character will be are not to the point. Our proper concern must be with a right view of the present, since it is only this that can furnish a reliable backing for a responsible policy. That is why the question of what a fourth phase might be like is a speculative and senseless one. Such a

Culture: artists' all-night 'sit-in' at the Rijksmuseum in Amsterdam (in front of the celebrated 'Night Watch').

2 Culture: a fashion display by Rodier in Brasilia.

3 Chiang Yee, Derwentwater (1936).

4 Anonymous, Derwentwater (1826).

question might actually distract us from attending to the urgent problems and tensions of the moment. The whole model is rooted, therefore, in the contemporary situation and should moreover be regarded as a practical model, not a piece of speculative description.

The strategy of culture

The emphasis accorded to this or that phase has to be looked at against the background of a tension between man and the 'powers', as we put it earlier on. Only in the last four chapters of this book will it be possible to set out this fundamental relationship in somewhat greater detail, when we come (especially in chapter VI) to investigate more closely the learning process which man undergoes in his culture and to consider strategy as giving shape to this learning process. What we can do here and now, however, is point to a few things that may help to explain or exemplify this strategy of culture or, better perhaps, culture as a strategy.

We have already made some reference in earlier passages to the terms 'transcendence' and 'immanence'. Immanence denotes the closed, determinate character of the world of human ideas and action. Man, it would seem, is liable to settle down in existing traditions and resign himself to the laws with which nature confronts him. As it turns out, however, this leads again and again to fixations the effect of which is not merely to freeze human society into rigidity but actually to disrupt it. There is no such thing as natural innocence; and those who – like Rousseau, for instance – propound a doctrine of life according to Nature do so more in order to apply their norms to the existing culture, or even to condemn it, than to surrender their critical responsibility as men in favour of an automatic, tensionless, 'natural' mode of being. All this suggests that immanence is repeatedly being broken through by transcendence. Transcendence refers to what comes from without, that is to say, to what cannot be accounted for within the terms of a purely natural existence. In that sense every discretionary act, every evaluation and every application of a norm involves our going above and beyond the unquestioning and natural acceptance of all that is, as it is.

The demonstrators who appear in our first illustration felt that the prevailing regulations were too immanent; and so they wanted to break through them. Their action was at any rate designed to ensure the application of a transcendent norm, thus a break-through out of immanence. Other demonstrators in behalf of transcendence are the group of figures representing Sumerians at prayer. Their rather queer, even comic, posture and expression surely reflect something of the lofty smile of the Powers gazing down upon them (ill. 7, p. 35). In Christian art too, of course, people have attempted to give expression to the Transcendent. The tension in this case is most clearly detectable – sometimes even sublimely so – where the transcendent is not represented in isolation but as a dimension of the immanent. This is brought out in Andrea del Castagno's fresco (15th century), in which a number of saints, including Jerome, are portrayed standing beneath a symbolic representation of the Trinity. One striking feature is that the figure of the crucified Christ is shown hovering above the earth on the cross, in a not entirely successfully foreshortened perspective (two angelic figures near the loins serve to conceal the imperfection of the drawing). Because of this horizontal position the cross, in other instances depicted vertically within immanent, earthly dimensions, takes on a transcendent dimension. It is startling to see the same technique and the same effect employed in the portrayal of the crucified Christ by the modern surrealist painter, Salvador Dali (ill. 11 and 12, p. 38).

This tension between immanence and transcendence can assume very diverse forms. Always the question at issue relates to the right ordering of human existence and of society. This or that way of envisaging the world, social rules, ethics, art, but also practical policies, the legal system, work, technical skills, the mode of intercourse between people, all these follow rules which are not in the nature of things fixed or constant and may therefore vary from one period and culture to another. Furthermore, in all these areas the confrontation between man and 'powers' assumes a particular form. To these powers a religious, cosmic, social, political or organizational character is accorded, depending on the fields in which man happens to be operating. For the most part the various fields are integrated within a fundamental position, a posture which may be ethical or religious or rooted in some overall view of the world. Norms and standards are created because man lays down certain rules regarding social behaviour, attitude to life, dealings with nature and so forth. They are always experienced, and can only be described, as a response to man's environment. Precisely how this response is interpreted will depend on a given world view and on individual or collective convictions. There are many shades of difference on this score, ranging from a more biological-cum-behaviourist view – man as a creature who in the struggle for existence adapts himself through learning-processes to his world, as best he may, or even attempts to dominate it – to a religious view according to which man is the image of God, and his existence a response to God. In all these interpretations, however, it would appear impossible to reduce everything to a natural process wholly explicable in terms of biological science, as is argued, for instance, by Dobzhansky, Simpson and Waddington. In one way or another man's cultural activity always evinces a transcendent dimension.

This basic condition compels man over and over again to reach a new awareness of his situation; and this awareness is assuredly not just at a theoretical level. Even those systematized world views which look to be more speculative and theoretical – the sort of thing produced by the great philosophies of India and China, for example – turn out to have a thoroughly practical function. The questions men ask about the meaning of life and the proper ordering of society affect every aspect of man's existence and pervade speculative reflection as much as they do artistic expression or practical conduct. This imbues every culture with an extremely dynamic tendency. The response which a group of people make to a given situation may be adequate to the needs of a particular age, but may later on become useless. Man lives not in a purely natural world but in a historical one; which is why he has to be continually striving for renewal, if he does not want to be caught in the immanent toils of pure tradition or of rules imposed by nature. Then again, man has a more pronounced individuality than other living creatures; and this ensures that at any given period quite different responses can be made to the circumstances of his environment.

All this is closely bound up with man's ability to influence a whole variety of processes, in nature but also in his own society. Laws which at one time lay beyond his sphere of influence – such as those described by physics or those which govern heredity, and even some which operate in the mental realm – man is able to bring within the scope of his own technical capacities. All culture, not excluding the culture of the most primitive races, may be regarded as man's way of imposing form upon the forces around him. A primitive culture would appear to be rich, even very rich, in this respect, because the confrontation with transcendent powers evidently makes it possible to introduce norms into such very disparate areas as hunting, land cultivation, the manufacture of weapons, decoration, ritual sacrifice, education, moral prescriptions, organization of tribal interrelationships.

One of the fundamental characteristics of man's mode of being is the sense he has of time. Part and parcel of this is his habit of reflecting on life and death – something which implies a process of transcending, of reaching above and beyond, what is given in nature. This pinpoints one of the differences between man and the higher animals, a difference that we shall be discussing at greater length later on. Even so, this is a good place at which to quote from Jacquetta Hawkes' work on the subject of pre-history: "A great deal has been made of the role supposed to have been played in the evolution of man by the hand and the opposable thumb. That role is certainly an important one – but only as it subserves the awakening brain. The hands of the large apes would be perfectly suited to performing the most delicate operations, if their mind were to move in that direction: the apes could have been clockmakers, had they but developed a notion of time." Now human culture is pervaded by this sense of time. One illustration of that is provided by the 'intihuatana' (seat of the sun) in the ancient Inca culture. Hewn out of a great block of stone, this seat of the sun fulfilled the function of a sun-dial; but its role in telling the time went hand in hand with the religious worship for which this 'high place' (on which we shall have more to say in chapter II) provided the opportunity (ill. 10, p. 37). Time, centred now around the idea of transitoriness, is also the theme of the painting by Jacob Ruysdael, entitled 'Jewish cemetery'. In some respects this work anticipates Romanticism and even surrealism; and it achieves a peculiar effect by means of the contrasting details (splash of light on tombstone, dead tree silhouetted against branches in full leaf, the stream coursing along between the fallen gravestones), so that nature itself participates in the message of transitoriness (ill. 13, p. 38). Thus nature is brought within the compass of the values and the norms which man applies and of his relativizing activity.

All this can happen, as we said before, in a whole variety of ways. The total system of rules thrown up by any given pattern of culture can be understood, therefore, to be a kind of policy. It is a particular strategy in respect of the relation between immanence and transcendence, which it is the business of human culture to regulate. By a 'strategy' we are to understand a general rule à propos of which particular rules and actions acquire their justification. The term has been in use for a long time now in, for instance, military science and the game of chess and today is often employed in organizational science and in games theory. It can happen that one sees somebody make a move on the chessboard and then concludes that this is not only a wrong move but a meaningless one, because no purpose whatever can be assigned to it. In such a case an expert might point out that this move is meaningless only if one goes on thinking about the play in terms of the strategy initially pursued by the player, but that the move is very meaning*ful* when one realizes that in making it the player is going over to a different strategy. The strategy therefore indicates the inclusive rule or boundary within which the several moves and the procedure are justified. Strategy coheres with the perspective afforded by the rationale of the separate processes.

All this holds good in a wider context as well. Anyone, at the time of the discussion between Newton and Huygens, who postulates that light could consist of waves (Huygens' theory) as well as of particles (Newton's theory) is saying something that during the period in question was meaningless; for the physics of the period was as yet unfamiliar with a strategy within which the complementarity of 'wave' and 'particle' is a meaningful thing. Strategy as the delimitation of what is and is not meaningful is also to the point in the case of culture. It is precisely here, after all, that the question of justification, of applying standards and norms, arises. What is given *de facto,* including natural processes, man subsumes within a strategy of culture; and such a strategy consists in the way in which a group of people responds to its surroundings. Man is for ever transforming the natural and so evaluating nature by means of his cultural activity. What man perceives as 'natural occurrence' has to be viewed within the dimension of transcending, overstepping the bounds of, the natural – the dimension, that is, of a responsible strategy. There is a well known story about Socrates, which Plato tells in the *Phaedo:* the explanation of why I am now lying in prison, says Socrates, cannot be supplied by an account of the movements made by my legs, muscles and so on. And indeed the significance of these things, these actions, only becomes evident in the total strategy of Socrates, which for Plato becomes a paradigm (exemplary illustration) of the relation between transcendence and immanence.

The model of a developmental process in three phases is to be interpreted in this way: it is a pointer to three kinds of possible strategy and thus to culture as a means of giving variegated form to the fundamental conditions in which man is conscious of being situated. The model is not meant, therefore, to supply a factual account of a historical development, although our purpose is of course to illustrate the model with this and that historical transition. But the idea is to exhibit, in a simplified form, some strategic boundaries within which patterns of human behaviour can be held to be meaningful or meaningless. Thus the terms 'mythical', 'ontological' and 'functional' serve to register the changing boundaries set to the unchanging question as to what has point and purpose in it for human existence.

The function of the model

The model should be regarded as instrumental, that is, as a means to concerted activity and to making possible a still more practical orientation for the culture of today. Therein lies the model's limitation as well as its usefulness. To explain this more clearly one could point to the role which models fulfil more especially in the natural sciences, but to some extent in the social sciences too. From the copious literature that has appeared on this subject it can be shown that a model sometimes is an interpretation of a more abstract, formal system, sometimes it consists in marshalling graphic or visual elements in order to exemplify a more general theory or to expand a theory still in process of development with the aid of some concrete examples. The former case occurs primarily in sciences such as mathematics – for instance, with the aid of ordinary numbers it is possible to elucidate, fill out, certain algebraic rules ('suppose that for "a" we put "3" '). The latter case arises when by using wire models one illustrates atomic structures or tries with water models to elaborate certain theories regarding electric current. In all these sorts of cases the models resemble one another in this respect, that they make no claim to represent reality at all, as *is* the case with an older idea and still in ordinary discourse, even now ('model-building' as a hobby); nor is it a question of setting up a kind of ideal image; this meaning of 'model' also occurs in linguistic use, for example, 'model husband'. No, a model is more a 'curtailed version' of actual data or of a theory, designed to illustrate a particular order, relation or development.

A model may be highly abstract: for instance, a mathematical model of economic processes. Quite often, however, a model will enshrine a considerable number of graphic elements. We must not let ourselves be misled by that into thinking that this reproduces the real state of affairs. After all, the very purpose of the model is to give prominence to a specific lay-out or arrangement – in the case of our developmental model in this book, to certain possibilities of a strategy of culture. This entails that for the sake of clarity and usefulness the real state of affairs will sometimes have to be drastically distorted. A simple example may serve to illustrate this. In the Piccadilly Line of the London Underground there is a model indicating the stations in their correct sequence as well as the various other lines with which those stations happen to connect. It shows us the Piccadilly Line traversed at two points (South Kensington and Gloucester Road) by another line called the District Line. Are there really two different lines, then, with the same name? No. Admittedly, on the instrumental scheme indicating where it is possible to change we do find two points at which this line cuts across; but the comprehensive plan showing all the lines of the Underground system reveals that there is just one line, which for a certain distance runs side by side with the Piccadilly Line. This plan gives a more real picture of the state of affairs, but it in turn is a tightened, utilitarian model representation of the lines as they actually run. That is evident enough on a geographical map, which of course is itself a simplification of the *de facto* situation (ill. 18, p. 56). Even a very ancient map of Roman roads uses a model-forming technique which in the effort to achieve an efficient presentation goes further, almost, than the modern plan of an underground railway network. The routes are pulled taut and indicate only the main staging-posts; the terrain is sliced into bits and pieces and displayed in sections lying one below the other; consequently, the seas bordering Italy appear as narrow channels, and so forth (ill. 17, p. 55). Precisely because of the high degree of abstractness intrinsic to a model it is possible to represent the same datum by models very different from

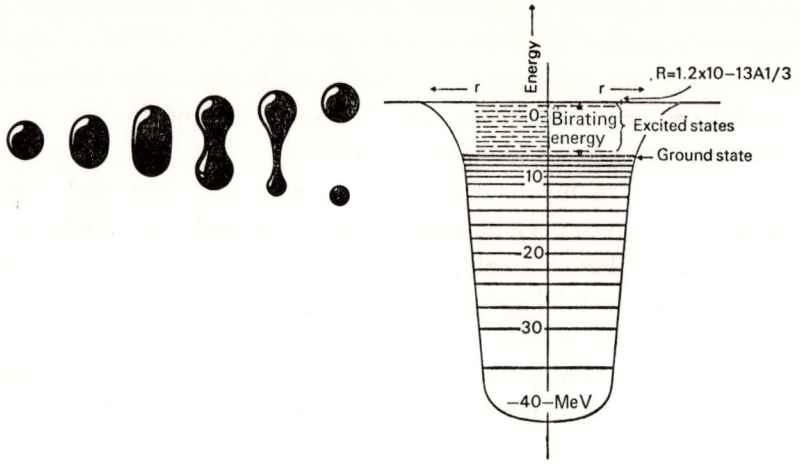

5 *Above*: the 'drops' model of atomic fission: *right*: the 'layers' model of the levels and discharge of potential energy.

one another, yet each serving to structurize a certain aspect, as is often done in modern physical science (see ill. 5) with two complementary models: the 'drops' model of atomic fission and the 'layers' model of the discharge of potential energy. The model of a culture will yield similar misrepresentations: for instance, exhibiting as a single phase a process which in reality includes a large number of finely differentiated transitions. For instrumental purposes, however, the model representation is more to the point than is a direct description, better suited to a study devoted to cultural history.

A railway timetable also serves to illustrate the function of a model. It shows the arrival and departure times of the trains, along with other particulars about train connections and how to use them correctly. Thus trains have numbers which sometimes change, even though the train may still be the same one (generally, another train is involved, and then one has to change) in cases where, on an instrumental view, coaches leave the main line: operationally, the train then becomes a different one. The timetable is put together in such a way that it meets the demands of proper and efficient use and thus furnishes information. We must not take the departure times to be descriptive, but regulative: a mishap, a stoppage, that sort of thing have not been taken into account. One always has to remember the limits within which the timetable can be handled to good purpose. Anyone who within a particular country wants to launch an enquiry into social conditions among the railway employees should not proceed to use the timetable as a source of information, because he would be posing a question that has no meaning within the rules of that document. We can only handle a model well if we ask the right questions and always remain aware of the discrepancy with the fulness of reality.

We may take this even further by defining a model as a transformation of real data. Wittgenstein referred to the model as a component of a science's symbolism; and indeed the elements from which a model is constructed do have a symbolic function. They do not, primarily, describe things but arrange and marshal them within an instrumental scheme. A water-model of electric current does not refer to water; but the water is there as a symbol of electrical processes. At the beginning of this chapter we were talking about the instrumentalizing of the whole question of culture. Our culture-model enshrines some descriptive elements; and certain factual developments will sometimes correspond thereto. Even so, description as such is not its purpose; but these descriptive elements function as symbols, as guidelines for the direction and control of such developments as are occurring here and now. Thus the model should not be regarded as conformable with earlier epistemological theories, which envisaged human knowledge as a reflection of some encompassing reality. More recent insights into the nature and function of man's knowledge stress rather its practical and instrumental character. No doubt there is such a thing as knowledge which 'reflects', a mode of enquiry concerned with unprejudiced insight into the essential nature of the world about us; but this kind of knowledge must be isolated from man's total pattern of reaction to reality. Man does describe phenomena which present themselves to him; but in so doing he aspires, above all, to regulating them, because he wants to intervene and incorporate them into what he recognizes to be meaningful. His concern is always, in fact, to find the adequate reaction, a right adjustment to and control of such phenomena. Therefore even descriptive knowledge gets integrated within this human orientation, whereby man's symbolic activities, in religion, art, science and practical, day-to-day affairs, are all the time transforming and reorganizing the world around him.

We shall be dealing at greater length with this particular tendency in chapter VII, where it will appear that even descriptive knowledge may lead to this or that application, and so to technical procedures; and further, that this again raises the question as to whether those procedures are good or bad, raises, that is, the ethical issue. Many forces in nature, in living phenomena and society are felt in the first instance to be alien and disastrous; but eventually, through scientific, medical and other modes of knowledge and action, they are brought under control. Along with that, man's responsibility increases. Evidently, he does not achieve utopia. On the contrary, new tensions and questions as to what is a justifiable policy keep arising. That is true of all culture. It is no longer an impersonal power, outside of man, working itself out in history. Modern man is coming to realize that humanity is moving toward an all-embracing world culture which does not just happen of its own accord but has to be continuously directed, steered by man himself. More than ever before, culture today is a human strategy; so that we have to envisage the model of contemporary culture not primarily as descriptive but as a means of identifying strategies. For the same reason this book ought not to be taken as an argument for a contentious theory about the fundamental nature of culture. It stakes a more modest claim: to stimulate the sort of discussion that may assist modern man to become conscious of his own liability vis-à-vis the directives he is going to put into action in whatever cultural policy he may devise.

II
Mythical thinking

Myth as human potentiality

The mythical world of the primitive cultures exerts a powerful attraction. On the one hand the mythical world with its fascinating forms of expression in art, its arcane rites and its direct ties with surrounding nature has about it something of a paradise lost. On the other hand that world is much akin to ourselves, because in it modern man is able to discern the basic features of a universal humanity. Yet the exotic as well as the familiar in the mythical mode of experience is seen in a different light, when in the wake of contemporary enquiry and research in cultural anthropology we take note of the stresses and tensions which for primitive man assumed at times even demonic dimensions.

It is no part of our purpose to provide an analysis, or even just a description, of the mythical world. For that there are more competent authors to whom the reader should turn. However, we do intend to use material which such writers have already analyzed, in order to say something about the pattern of mythical thinking. This in turn is necessary in order to provide a background to those processes of change which our own culture is undergoing at the present time.

A propos of all that, the first thing needed is to single out once more – for it has been done by a lot of writers already – a number of common errors. The term 'primitive' in particular is one that could give rise to a quite false idea. Primitive peoples are no simple 'savages', either in the romantic sense so evident in Roussseau's time or in the pejorative sense that they lag far behind peoples with a highly advanced civilisation. The more romanticizing view sees the mythical world as a very mysterious one, where supernatural forces are continuously at work and where everything is 'inspired'. Yet primitive man would seem to know very well that a stone is ordinarily a stone, a spear is a spear.

Nor are his rites to be regarded as so many methods of conjuration. They often have a matter-of-fact function as a means to mutual encouragement, helping people to be better prepared, mentally and spiritually, for the natural course of events (sickness, drought and so forth). Those forms of expression which we nowadays call 'art' are again not invariably to be regarded as a magical way of influencing nature or as an expression of some deep religiosity. Thus certain Eskimo drawings depicting a whale turn out to be nothing more than a story, a record, of the spectacular discovery of a whale. Primitive peoples are also unmistakably possessed of ordinary technological skill and understanding. On all these points modern research is presenting a continuous flow of material which we may take as a reaction against the more romantic – and till recently so very widespread – interpretation of primitive culture.

That is not to say that on all these scores there do not also emerge some marked differences from the contemporary pattern of culture, partly because sometimes explanations are given that are thoroughly supernatural; yet bearing in mind the connection between mythical and modern culture, it is only right that these more down-to-earth observations should be made first of all. There is more to the issue than that. As we said before, within the context of this book we are concerned not with a detailed analysis of primitive culture but with the character of mythical thinking in its broad outlines. Now this thinking has long been represented as something different in kind, as indeed 'primitive', not so far logical thinking. Sometimes this might be done with a romantic enthusiasm for the way in which the intellectual faculty finds expression in the first instance in myth, as the philosopher Schelling described it in the last century. It could also be done more negatively, as with the scholar, Max Müller, who toward the end of the last century called mythology an infantile phase and even 'a disease of language'. In this century such a viewpoint, embodied in the compendious work of the Frenchman, L. Lévy-Bruhl, has come to be very influential. He speaks of a *'mentalité primitive'*, which he calls a pre-logical *(prélogique)* mode of thought and to which he attributes as one distinctive feature the various ways in which such primitive thinking participates directly in the surrounding world *(les lois de participation)*.

Very often, however, so-called primitive man would seem to be capable of ordinary, logical reasoning; and if he sometimes thinks in quite a different way from a modern man, that still does not mean that his mental outlook is beyond comprehension. It is much to the point that Lévy-Bruhl saw this himself and emphatically acknowledged it. In his posthumously published *Carnets* he declares that we must stop describing primitive man's thought as pre-logical, because the logical structure of mind, which expresses itself in language and in social patterns, is everywhere the same; and that the unmistakably mythical or, as he says, mystical element in this thinking is also present in the modern variety.

This affords a link with a great many ideas current today. The contemporary French cultural anthropologist, C. Lévi-Strauss, for instance, argues that phenomena of a social (e.g. matrimonial regulations) and an economic nature (e.g. the exchange of goods) would appear to be the result of permanent rules not restricted to one particular cultural milieu. He actually talks about the play of laws which are admittedly veiled, but nonetheless universal. Every culture has of course a character of its own; but this is because, in any given culture, of the total fund of potentialities inherent in human culture only a limited number can be realized. Thus we describe primitive man as 'childlike' in his behaviour and view of the world; yet there are primitive people, Lévi-Strauss says, who find modern man extraordinarily childish because, for instance, when something is explained to him, he keeps on asking questions.

If all cultures may be regarded as realizations, in this or that direction, of certain fundamental human potentialities, we can get a better understanding of our own existence as human beings precisely through this process of concerning ourselves with very different kinds of civilisation. We then arrive at a variety of patterns of culture (R. Benedict). There are, however, more far-reaching lines of enquiry. Might we not be able to see right through the several patterns of culture, as it were, and so discover something of the common factor in human existence? There are many anthropologists, such as Margaret Mead, whose work is tending in that direction and constitutes an attempt to use fundamental insights of this sort to regulate modern society. C. Kluckhohn actually speaks of a common 'logic' as the ground of all cultures, meaning by this certain very general forms in accordance with which man interprets the interrelationships between phenomena. C. Lévi-Strauss has tried to establish general structures, a kind of universal trellis-work, which can be filled in with elements from any primitive or modern culture whatever, so that the relations constituted by the trellis-work turn out to be totally constant.

In the present book what is universal in human culture is treated more as a development-model. Thus it is limited in its purpose, because the point at issue is not the disclosure of any basic pattern of human culture but rather the background to our own culture of today. Furthermore, we take one particular aspect only of that culture: the dynamic tendency to development, with its accompanying tensions. The mythical world must itself, therefore, be presented, albeit in outline, as a universal human potentiality, so as to make such a genetic model feasible: myth is both the country of origin and the enduring (if mostly latent) travelling companion of the contemporary pattern of culture. Thus our special concern is to portray a structure, the structure of thinking as an expression of the forms of life crystallized into cultures.

This mythical thinking is not, finally, to be equated with immediate, lived experience, with the *'expérience vécue'* represented by many philosophers (Merleau-Ponty, for instance) as the subsoil of every experience that has been rendered explicit. Myth is not irrational experiencing or a wordless undergoing of whatever happens to occur. A culture of pure, non-verbal experience does not exist; and every human society has its tensions, triumphs and developments, which are equally observable in the world of today. The dynamic structures referred to are expressed in symbols. P. Ricoeur speaks of a primal human experience which is never immediate but is expressed via symbols. In their turn these symbols are then subsumed and embodied in myth and also in speculation. This would at the same time imply that at the primary level of the symbols the separation of what later came to be known as art, religion and science is as yet hardly present.

Some functions of myth

The most characteristic thing about myth is the participation by man in the world around him which it serves to accomplish. This can also be done by means of magic; but magic is described below as a secondary form, even a negative form, of myth. This participation is not, however, any kind of pre-logical thinking, but more a relation between man and that which lies about him, which again is realized in a different way in later thought-forms, in ontological and in functional thinking. Some of the functions of myth are outlined in brief with a view to elucidating this central and typical feature of myth.

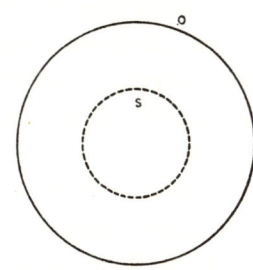

6

As a simple scheme indicating the structure of the mythical stance we make use of the above diagram, which shows how the environing world, the 'object' (O) (one can only speak of an 'object', in the proper sense, in the ontological stage) permeates the subject (S). The subject, that is the human being or the tribe, has as yet no self-contained individuality; and the functions of myth, such as the manifestation of various powers guaranteeing that certain activities will proceed smoothly, are produced from this structure.

One of myth's primary functions is the overpowering manifestation of something. This we might call, with M. Eliade, the 'ontophany', the appearing or manifestation of Being. Myth affords us a sight of strange powers. And then it is not simply a question of becoming acquainted with those powers, but of experiencing their creative effect on nature and on tribal connection. One might even put it that in myth nature is identical with the supernatural. This does not imply that primitive man is reckoned to live in an out-of-the-way, supernatural world, possessed and actuated by peculiar powers – we have dealt with that already in the preceding section. In the mythical world itself, even, there is an evident distinction between profane and sacral occurrences, a distinction which, as R. Caillois has argued, carries with it practical and social consequences, among others. What we do find repeatedly in the mythical world are points of interconnection between the natural and profane order and the supernatural, sacral one. There are Indians whose tribal spear bears the name of a living creature. Is this some kind of pervasive animism? No; for the other spears are not thought of in that way, and the tribal members apparently have a very technical and matter-of-fact approach to spears and to other material. But it is possible for strange energies to manifest themselves in a spear. Among the early Greeks too one comes across the notion of powers that can find a dwelling in people as well as things. B. Snell, for instance, makes the point that when we read in Homer's Iliad of the 'bloodthirsty urge' which impels a spear through the air, this is not simply a metaphor, but an awareness that impersonal forces can take possession alike of people, animals and things.

We repeat, therefore, that this is not pre-logical thinking in the sense that primitive man declares things to be what they are not and so comes into conflict with the logical principle of the avoidable contradiction (*principium contradictionis*). In West Africa questions were put to a 'leopard society' who on occasion had killed people in such a way as to leave clearly visible on the corpse the imprint of a leopard's paw. Did they think, at the time of such a ritual murder, that they had actually turned into leopards? No; they were themselves – and yet were spurred on and possessed by the same force that manifested itself in the leopard. Some Indian tribes identify themselves with a totem animal; but it turns out that they feel no special affinity whatever with that animal as it is encountered in real life; they are concerned with it as it once used to be in some mythical, primaeval age. If the animal has a role to play, it is not so much as a zoological datum, but as a symbol. E.O. James speaks of a sacramental view in terms of which the symbol and what is symbolized come to be identified. One is not the animal, not the symbol; and yet one does, via the symbol, participate in what through symbol and through myth is manifested as energy.

From that flows a second function of myth: myth serves to guarantee the present. Many writers, among them G. van der Leeuw, have put the whole emphasis on this function. When a piece of land is being taken over for cultivation, the story is told – or is sometimes represented in dramatic form – of the first time that the gods set about tilling the land in the primaeval age. This repetition of the story renders present once more what happened of old, provides a basis for the current enterprise. In some parts of Indonesia during the period when the fresh rice is being planted, a whole series of stories, continuing day and night,

7 Sumerian praying figures.

8   Hercules slinging a stone at birds (greek vase).

9   J. Miró, Person throwing a stone at a bird.

36   10   Sense of time: 'throne of the sun' - the Incas' sun d

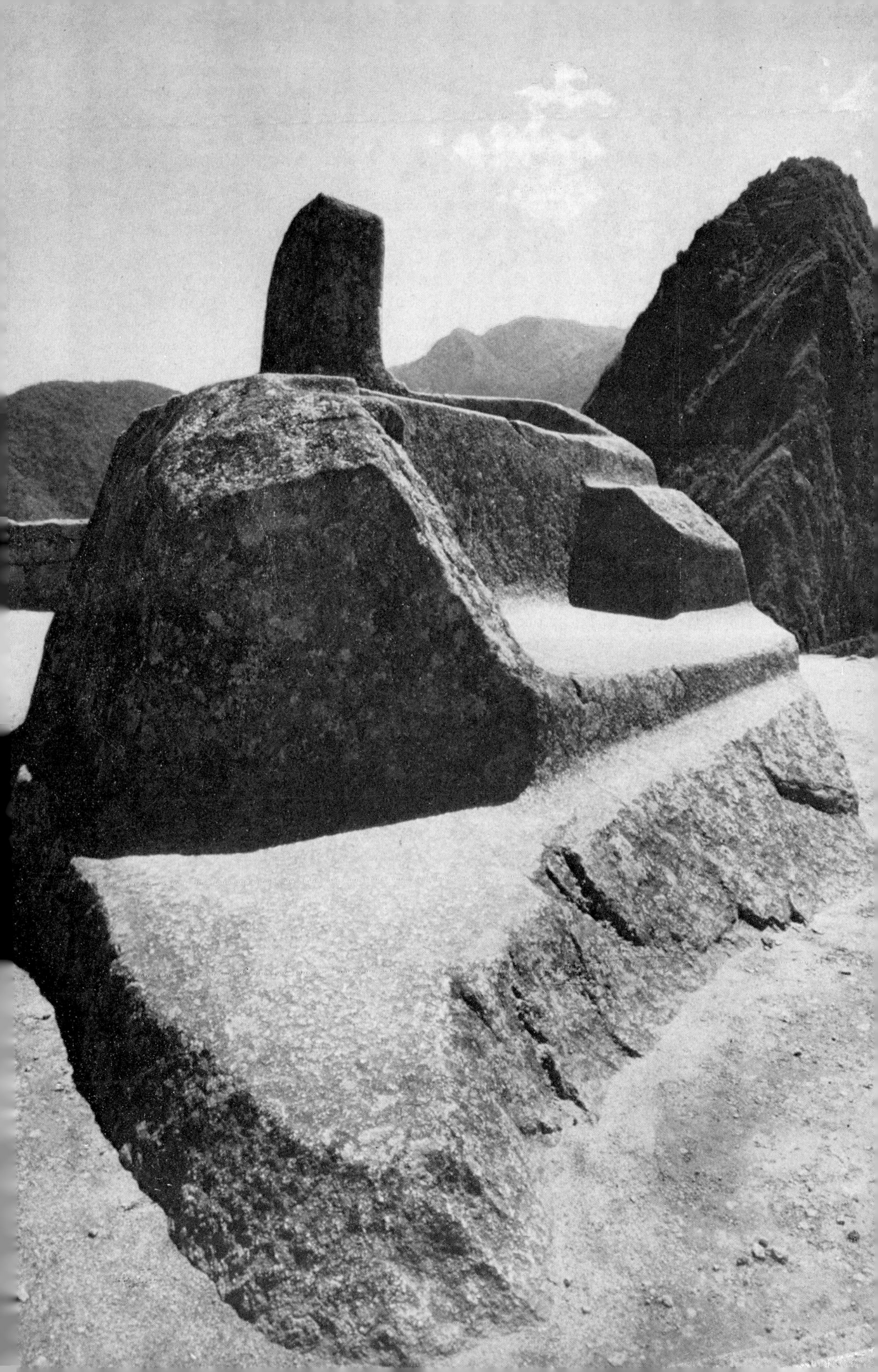

11 Castagno, St. Jerome and the Trinity (fresco).

12 S. Dali, Christ of John of the Cross (Glasgow Art Gallery and Museum).

13 Sense of time: J. Ruysdael, Jewish cemetery.

are told, all of them having something to do with fertility. Here again, it is not done just to while away the time, but in order to ensure that the plants will grow. According to M. Eliade, when certain desert tribes take possession of an oasis, they sometimes enact a story from their prehistory, when the gods wrested their living-space from demons. For the moment the wild animals of the surrounding desert are the representatives of those prehistoric demons. Thus there are countless occasions – settling a locality, marriage, the hunt – when by means of story, rite and cult the symbols of myth make efficacious the contemporary life-pattern. Here, as indeed in the case of the other functions of mythical activity and experience, a major role is fulfilled by the dance: divine powers take possession of the dancer, who in this way is enabled to secure a future course of action against risks. In Africa today one can still come across dances associated with the change of seasons and with transition-rites like those for girls in Ghana (ill. 20, p. 58) or those that were probably danced under the direction of shamans or priests in Tlatilco (Mexico) some three thousand years ago. A remarkable statuette of this kind of female dancer (some say she is actually a goddess) has two faces and so offers a good parallel to the work of Picasso (ill. 21, p. 58).

From these brief references it will be obvious that whether we have to do with rock drawings, the ritual of the dance, the use of animal skins, the decoration of weapons and utensils, the arrangement of huts, or whatever, the same things cannot always and everywhere be interpreted in the same way. Sometimes it will be simply a matter of decoration or story-telling, sometimes of an ordinary matter-of-fact utilizing of objects, sometimes of the supernatural interpenetrating the natural, either incidentally or more continuously. Of course, myth is always more than just story or colourful speculation; but the fact remains that as a third function of myth we most certainly have to note that of 'knowledge of the world' (Jensen). After all, myth does offer explanations; and it is able to satisfy inquisitiveness. Quite often expounded in it are the origin of heaven and earth (cosmogony) and of the gods (theogony). In the case of long-standing traditions, for instance in the arsenal of stories available to the present-day African medicine-man, this knowledge-function may even become predominant, so that the purpose of myth is then more or less exclusively that of speculative knowledge. This of course in turn lends some degree of importance and status to the story-teller and helps him to make his practical work – for example, prescribing herbs in case of sickness – that much more effective.

Several functions of myth have been presented here in outline, so as to put us on the track of a key feature of mythical thinking; for this is bound to throw into relief the structure of modern culture. For that very reason we have eschewed a detailed analysis and concentrated our picture of the mythical culture-pattern in one characteristic term: central to mythical thinking is the experiential discovery *that* something is. In experiencing, knowing and acting, the mythical world has its centre and focus in the 'that'. There is no distanced observation of the surrounding world; rather, man is obsessed by that world. That such and such a thing is, the very fact of the existence of the surrounding world as well as of one's own tribal connection, constitutes a vital power governing all thought and action. Man looks for the sources of the life-process, the springs of existence. Ancestor worship, symbols such as the tree of life, the primaeval ocean – all these point to a surplus value implicit in the givenness of existence. This symbolic value and presence of existence entails that the symbols which express it may be regarded as the unlocking or disclosure of a transcendent dimension, *'des ouvertures vers le transcendant'* (M. Eliade). Up to a point the gods themselves are such a symbol, because they appear as lustrous figures among mortal men (W. F. Otto). Even an animal can in many respects manifest this life-presence. So it is the 'that', the very fact and the preponderance of existence per se, that is the core of mythical thinking.

That something is – the overwhelming power which this constitutes affects man's own existence as well as that of the world around him. This existence of his is not to be envisaged in individualistic terms; it is more the existence of the clan, the tribe. Furthermore, as will appear later on, we cannot press home very far the division between what is one's 'own' and what is alien: the structures and energies proper to one's own clan are likewise to be encountered in the world around. Some, following in the tracks of the positivistically inclined French scholar, E. Durkheim, whose influence was particularly strong at the beginning of this century, have even tried to explain primitive religion as a means of perpetuating the cohesion of the group. But nowadays more attention is paid to both aspects: the group cohesion and the surplus value (the symbols' transcending function) of the surrounding world. Both stress the significance of the 'that' for mythical thinking.

Man and world

Within the realm of mythical thinking no sharp division exists between man and world, subject and object. In fact it is hardly possible to speak at this stage of a human subject, because man has not yet acquired a self-contained existence and only with some considerable effort is he able to identify himself. Man is subsumed within, and almost absorbed by, the cohesive relation between tribal bond and cosmos. Various people have written of the 'socio-mythical orbit' in which man moves.

The literature of modern cultural anthropology and the phenomenology of religion offers innumerable illustrations of this, which do not lend themselves to loose generalization. We know, for instance, that an individual who for one reason or another has been turned out of his tribe will often appear to have forgotten his name; for it was his name that bound him to the tribal community, and his expulsion has rendered him nameless. In many cases that will also mean that no further prospect of living remains: the outcast dies, even though others may adopt him, because the vital link with the 'that' of his existence has been severed.

This is also brought out by the way in which a man will talk about himself. M. Leenhardt refers to certain tribes in Melanesia who frequently use a word which denotes 'I' in direct relation to an important congener, for instance, 'I-with-maternal-uncle'. Again, when a story is being related, the terminology will change: for example, like this: then I came to a river, then he crossed the stream, then that man saw a tree, then I climbed into it, and so forth. It is as if the man's own identity is still only partly there and as if, to use Leenhardt's expression, the concept of the person is nothing other than a fulcrum for the role which the man in question has to fulfil in social life, within the socio-mythical sphere.

Any division between inner and outer worlds is in some respects simply not present. The 'soul' does not have to be domiciled in one's own body; for a modern concept of the soul is not entailed here. It refers rather to everything that exerts power. An oddly shaped stone, a corpse, a mask, moonlight – all this may be referred to as 'soul'. Here again there is no absence of a matter-of-fact kind of thinking. In practice a thoroughgoing distinction is sometimes made between, for instance, organic and inorganic nature. Only at certain crucial junctures in life and at points of climax – sometimes even in the literal sense of 'cultic high places' – in the socio-mythical sphere do the frontiers between the supernatural and the natural disappear and with them the possibilities man has of marking himself off from what environs him. One's own soul can sometimes grow, eat and be eaten. It may reside in a particular body, even to the extent that each organ may have a 'soul' of its own (as with certain tribes of Eskimo) but also outside the body, for example, in a tree of life; or again in the image of an ancestor, like the one made of chalk that comes from Melanesia (New Ireland) (ill. 22, p. 58).

A man's own body is not all that sharply demarcated, either. The vegetation outside him is sometimes regarded as an extension of his own intestines: what is recognized is one and the same world, one and the same field of vital, organic forces and forms. In modern art we find this idea worked out in Wilfredo Lam's (Cuba) picture of the jungle (1943) (ill. 19, p. 57).

This interpenetration of man and cosmos also finds expression in man's relation with the gods or with divine powers. Primitive man has a down-to-earth, practical grasp of a profane world; but there are moments when it is as though divine powers take possession of him. All the while he is dancing, the leader in an African rain-dance becomes the rain-god. In many Asian religions gods are able to manifest themselves in human beings; and we find this also in the early Greek world. W.F. Otto gives a classic example à propos of the story in Homer that the goddess, Pallas Athene, laid her hand on Achilles' arm, just as he was about to lift his sword against his comrade in arms: such sudden circumspection falls outside the pattern of normal human conduct and is therefore attributable to the influence of a divine being. When we read elsewhere how 'fear' seizes the warriors, this is not (according to Snell) a way of referring to a psychic impulse, but a vestige of the belief in the fear-daimon, a not much more than impersonal divine power, which takes up a position next the warrior and causes his hair to stand on end. At a later stage (in the Odyssey) we find a transitional form, when it is said of an idea occurring suddenly to Telemachus that either a god had prompted it or it had arisen within himself. The mental life of man is not yet a firmly demarcated, inner domain, but, as H. Fränkel has it, a terrain lying open to the influences exerted by divine powers.

At the same time the gods give form to the values regulating society. The power of sexuality, fertility, parenthood, is often venerated in extravagant forms: fertility-figures, erotic temple-rituals and so on. Yet this never implies sheer licentiousness or anarchy. On the contrary, even the most spontaneous, uninhibited behaviour is canalized in prescribed rules and the limitations imposed by sacred times and places. Similarly, the giving and taking of women is tied to complicated, almost logically structured rules which have been studied and mapped out by such investigators as Lévi-Strauss. See the plan of kinship and affinity the structure of which Lévi-Strauss interprets in his *Structures de la parenté* (ill. 14). Structurally most artistic is the grouping of female figures on the door of a granary in Mali (ill. 23, p. 58).

It would appear that values invariably function within a broad area of alternatives, where what is admissible is carefully marked off from what is obligatory.

Values and norms are for the most part directly related to issues of life and death. Man's relation to death is minutely stipulated: in myth

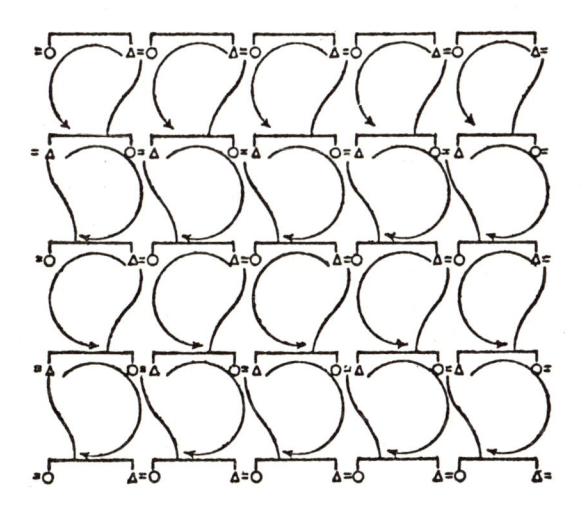

14 Structure of a pattern of matrimonial contract, namely, with the daughter of the sister of the father (from: C. Lévi–Strauss, *Les structures de la parenté*).

through stories of the gods, and in rite through the burial ritual we find being practised even by prehistoric man. Sometimes the boundaries between life and death are very fluid: the outcast loses his name and is in fact dead, whilst the departed tribal chieftain continues to live and govern the community from his place of burial. This close relation between the living and the dead is something that one comes across in widely separated cultural milieus: among the early Etruscans, but also among, say, tribes in Africa. These few examples serve to demonstrate how very difficult it is precisely to identify and localize the norms and values present in mythical thinking. The values are not made explicit but are interwoven, as it were, with a view of the world and with social structures. The sway exercised by one's kith and kin, by tribal chiefs and so forth amounts to an expression of value-systems which can be inferred only indirectly from the mythical behaviour-pattern.

Primitive society was governed first and foremost by laws of kinship, not as yet by the circumstances of production (Lévi-Strauss). This has an important bearing on the capacity of values for change, for undergoing transformation, or to put it another way, on the role played by history. Of course revolutions may occur in a primitive society: one has only to recall Margaret Mead's studies of instances of abrupt change, more especially in primitive societies that come in contact with modern technical civilisation. In a period of quiet, however, the social structures are thoroughly static. Although the sense of history is not wholly absent, it is certainly not dominant, either. In many respects there is even a noticeable contrast between mythical thinking, which is a-historical in its orientation, and the modern mode of thinking, so markedly conscious of history. A society based on production is what it is to a large extent because it is managed by people whose role in it depends, not on the value assigned to the natural and stable ties of kinship but on the value attaching to their technological ideas and their organizational abilities – both factors related to rapid historical change. Van der Leeuw says that mythical thinking is grounded entirely in the primordial event, in prehistory, and so remains cut off from the dimension so very characteristic of historical consciousness: the future. M. Eliade points out that there is a myth embodying the idea of perpetual recurrence, which is reflected in the primitive sense of time, but also in that of post-primitive cultures – those, for instance, of proto-Asia and even of the Greeks. By way of contrast we find in the thinking of the ancient Hebrews a much more linear, and therefore historically orientated, notion of time. Lévi-Strauss concludes that the mythical world does reflect an awareness of history, but as something more stationary or at the very most a fluctuating process. The whole life of modern society, on the other hand, is based on the realization that new potentialities can always be added to existing ones; and so it is conscious of history as a cumulative affair. Scant possibilities of personal self-identification, values which it is almost impossible to demarcate, interwoven as they are with the regulations imposed by patterns of natural kinship, as well as a restricted sense of history – these together form a single, basic structure of mythical thinking: man and the world around him, the one pervading and interpenetrating the other.

Magic

It was long ago recognized that magic is part and parcel of the way primitive man goes about the practical business of living. Magic is not primarily a matter of spells and charms, but of immediate, experiential facts, as K.Th. Preuss pointed out some time ago: facts of experience in the sense of mishaps, to counter which certain measures can and should be taken. In a way, therefore, magic is a means of applying preventive measures (Preuss), is centred around a variety of 'reassurance rites' (Van Baaren), which one might compare, up to a point, with modern insurance procedures. Thus it is not a question of sheer superstition, but is usually related to something that forms an integral part of a religious view of the world as a whole.

Of course, there will be a noticeable difference of emphasis, depending on whether one is dealing with religious myth as such, or more especially with the practice of magic. We have earlier on referred to mythical symbols as windows onto the transcendent, to use what is more or less Eliade's phrase; myth has to do with a transcendent reality (R. Pettazzoni). But magic is centred more on the immanent. Primarily, it serves to ward off calamity and to bring influence to bear on natural forces and on other human beings (for instance, one can harm one's enemy by destroying an image of him). This is not to say that magic has no connection with myth. On the contrary, magical practices, including spells and implements, often derive via one of the medecine-man's progenitors from the activities of a god. Yet the object is not so much to maintain contact with a primaeval age and with the world of the gods as to make use of such contacts in order to control the world around.

The mythical and magical stances differ, therefore, in their forms of manifestation; and that too is a distinguishing factor. As will appear in subsequent chapters, a similar difference is to be noted between, respectively, ontological and substantialist thinking and in the second instance between a functional and an operationalist approach. To illustrate this, in each of those chapters we show the human female form and that of a building as they are severally manifested in the two pairs of categories aforementioned. The portrayal of woman within the realm of myth is something we encounter in many cultures, right down to the most primitive. Thus we have a cave-drawing, possibly with a ritual function, which depicts a number of running women. With a few stark lines – and not until one tries to copy the figures does it become clear just how taut the run of the lines really is – this early Australian caveman has created a silhouette which in some respects resembles modern functional art. See illustration 15 and compare with it the collage by Henri Matisse (ill. 16, p. 47). Mythical too is the delicately shaped figurine of a mother and child which comes from a temple at Shango (Nigeria) and was set up there in honour of the fertility-god (ill. 25, p. 75). Designed entirely to exert a magical influence, on the other hand, is the celebrated and grotesquely erotic statuette from prehistorical Europe, known as the

15 Cave-drawing of women (prehistoric).

16 H. Matisse, The green stockings (1952).

Venus of Willendorf (ill. 26, p. 75). Mythical and magical trends in architectural style are to be found, for example, in the temple belonging to a sect in Africa, reproduced as illustration 27 on p. 75.

Magic might perhaps be described as one of the many components of mythical thinking. Nonetheless, magic has a character all its own; so much so that in our projected model of the thought-phases within human culture magic sticks out, so to speak, calling for mention as a distinct feature, in various respects contrasting with myth. M. Mauss, for instance, draws a sharp distinction between rites that are religious in character and rites which have a magical function: the latter are not associated with a particular religion and cult, and their effect is to augment power and authority by means of some occult doctrine. Van der Leeuw actually contrasts the religious function of myth with magic: religion implies service, magic involves domination. In magic the subject endeavours to master the object, so that magic involves the 'Will to Power'. The same antithesis is drawn by J. Wach. We call those techniques magical, he says, which are the outcome of a wish to master, control and apply to one's own purposes the powers that one knows from experience. One of those to whom Wach makes reference is R.R. Marett, who in his address on 'The Birth of Humility' (1910) argues that every time vital energies are released – in myth, but also elsewhere, in modern culture, for example – at a particular moment this leads to presumptuousness. In the primitive world it is magic that is the typical expression of this kind of arrogance. Again and again, therefore, an attitude of humility is required to cleanse and purify these vital energies.

These various expressions of view have an important bearing on the structural design given in this book of the shifts and changes occurring within contemporary culture. Each and every culture brings to birth certain broadly human possibilities. Every culture is in part a confrontation of man with the powers that surround him. In each phase of development, then, however much they may differ the one from the other, it is possible to distinguish two components, as it were, of a single line of force: the struggle to find a suitable context within a proper, meaningful relationship of man and the powers, and the endeavour to grasp at power for oneself.

If the magical attitude to things makes any substantial headway, then mythical symbols, values and even the gods come to be little more than marginalia, a mere endorsement of magic ritual or of a system of magical knowledge. In the oldest parts of the Vedic writings we find a sacrificial ritual which is extremely complicated. The numerous cultic actions and incantations occupy such a prominent position that scholars have come to the conclusion that the only role still left to the gods is to serve as a reason or excuse for performing the sacrifices. The sacrificial rites have then become an end in themselves; and H. von Glasenapp points out that this in turn enhanced the authority of the priests, because only they could still be masters of the ritual, down to the minutest detail of every part. In that way a hereditary priestly class became the highest caste.

In a cruder form one finds the social consequences of magic exemplified among various African tribes, where the medicine-man sometimes exercises a real dictatorship over the rest. In magic man attempts to get the powers under his own control. As regards the world around, this implies that the subject is going to dominate and rule the object. But who is that subject? Not as yet the individual human being; for the person, after all, has not so far acquired his self-contained identity. Perhaps one could say, therefore, that the subject is the tribe and that a priest or a medicine-man, for example, is an exponent of the tribe's power. Magic has a coercive character; and for that reason it narrows the horizon of mythical thinking. There is a part of transcendence, that is to say, a dimension which it is beyond man's capacity to manipulate, which magic shuts away. Immanence, that is, the range which actions and words in themselves possess, comes to the fore. That is why the magical posture entails the lopping off of alternatives. Stiffer action to affect society, a more self-centred, self-orientated (Van der Leeuw says 'autistic') way of thinking and a fixed attitude to decisions once made are typical of magic – and not of magic only but of all forms of decline which turn up as component elements in the basic trend of this or that particular culture.

III

Ontological thinking

Ontology as a means of liberation

One primary mark of the mythical way of thinking is an attitude of fear and trembling toward the primordial powers of life and the cosmos. One might think of it as a whole variety of ways in which a group of human beings tries to arrive at an accommodation and tries to find the right attitude to adopt toward the powers surrounding it. In this activities of a practical kind, such as ritual, and more theoretical speculations, such as stories regarding the origin of the universe, will have a role to play. The main distinguishing feature of ontological thinking is the understanding which man sets out to obtain of the powers and energies he is able to detect outside him and within. He begins to stand back from his environment, feels less constrained by the world around him and even becomes in some respects more of a spectator. At this stage the practical pursuits involved are such things as craftmanship, art and technics, along with more theoretical considerations including, for instance, theories about the visible (physics) and the invisible world (metaphysics).

The movement from mythical to ontological thinking has been characterized as a shift from 'mythos' to 'logos', after the title of one of Nestlé's works, in which he describes how Greek philosophical thought came to develop and to stand on its own feet. It has been objected to this that the Greeks were not the pure rationalists and intellectualists that earlier centuries sometimes made them out to be; for irrational forces, social aspirations and a deep religious sense quite evidently had an effect on their philosophical view of the world. However, this movement from myth to logos is something we can certainly endorse so long as we interpret the ontology of the Greeks – and for that matter of other cultures like those of India – not as a kind of purely speculative or theoretical thinking but as the reasoned presentation of interconnected factors, with a practical end in view. That end is liberation from the inscrutable powers of life and death, coming to be and ceasing to be, act and destiny, guilt and grief; and such liberation strikes home all the more where step by step mythical thinking has fallen entirely beneath the petrifying spell of magic. It was as though in magic above all else the more demonic component of the mythical world had had its own way; and this had led to a sort of dictatorship within the social patterns. When man proceeded to enquire systematically as to the reason for suffering, the reason for the cosmos and the reason for language, it was possible for fear and bondage to disappear. In Greek thinking, therefore, the term 'logos' often signifies 'sense' or 'reason': to perceive the 'logos' of an action is to understand why that action must be carried out in such and such a way; to comprehend the reason for what is is to grasp why the course of history and the order of things are as they are. Perception, understanding, has a liberating and even redemptive character.

Gradually, the purely theoretical aspect became detached from all this. Knowledge was not just a means of deliverance; it was also an end in itself. Ontology means: the theory (science) of what is. Everything that exists – things, animals, people, values, gods, laws – can be named and known for what it is. To ontological thinking, therefore, doubtless belong speculations about Being such as appear in the great philosophical systems of India and of the Greeks and have continued to exert an influence down to the present time. Yet the greatest thinkers and seekers after knowledge have always affirmed that whilst of course this knowledge existed in its own right, nevertheless it had ultimately to be related to the right moral attitude and to man's freedom: Plato, the Stoics, Descartes, Kant are all agreed on this very point. Knowledge already has within it, in fact, something of a liberating nature, because as one begins to penetrate to the order of things, so one is able to eliminate the irrational, the refractory, the baffling. Thus knowledge which is a result of the ontological approach to things brings about an enormous enlargement of the mental horizon – an enlargement which takes place not only at a theoretical but at a practical level too, in the discovery of nature's laws, of strange countries and customs, of possible ways of using technics to transform the world.

The liberating aspect of reflection upon Being comes out very strongly in the Indian systems, whether it be in the various schools of orthodox Hindus or in heterodox movements like Buddhism and Jainism. For that reason, of course, this thinking has been contrasted with Western philosophical thought. Yet these bodies of teaching about deliverance, release and so forth actually provide the context in which an obviously ontological type of reflection has developed. The focal point, as it were, shifts ever more emphatically from the old Vedic religion with its stress on ritual and the observance of outward rules to an inwardness stressing redemptive insight and the repudiation of an illusory, external and transient world, so central a feature of Hindu philosophy but also of the heterodox systems aforementioned. Hiriyanna points to the magic element which got the upper hand in the later period of Vedic religion, so that "priest and prayer henceforward become transformed into magician and spell". There is then a reaction against that, entailing reasoned reflection upon Being, with among other things a tendency at once highly regulative and monistic (leading back to a single principle). Here are to be found the sources of later Indian philosophy as a whole.

This habit of reflecting upon Being manifests itself in a multiplicity of religious ideas and philosophical speculations. It is impossible in a few words to map out even in part this wealth of viewpoints. From the many studies which competent scholars have devoted to constituent parts of this Indian mode of thought one gets the impression that at all events 'salvation' involves a growing insight into true reality as the absolute – sometimes lying beyond every opposition, like that of subject and object, being and not-being – which implies detachment from all that is relative, changing, transient. This then leads to very explicit ontological systems, in which the processes of knowing and reasoning are analysed with great care. Thus within the Hindu tradition one finds schools like that of the Nyaya-Vaisesika (17th century, deriving from documents of the 2nd and 4th centuries) and the later schools of the Vedanta (5th century, et seq.), where all forms and categories of existence are closely related with modes of knowing. A whole range of categories of thinking and of being, with the most subtle logical ramifications, functions in the context of one saving insight: that all is one within the Absolute.

This ontological consciousness is typical also of the West. Thought and reality are closely correlated; and on matters of detail we find a correspondence with ideas in Eastern philosophy: for instance, space and time, because they are recognizable individually, are sometimes regarded in both traditions as self-subsistent. Again, Western philosophy enshrines a whole variety of subtle distinctions in this area: for example, that space and time exist only in the non-absolute order of coming-to-be and ceasing-to-be (Plato, Plotinus), or that they are indeed absolutes, but in relation to physical phenomena (Descartes, Newton), or that they are not so much categories of being as of thinking (Kant, Schopenhauer).

Yet there are evident differences between Eastern and Western thinking; it is as perilous, almost, to deny them as to attempt to specify them. It must suffice for us to point to the less monistic tendency of Western philosophy, which because of a more direct orientation on reality as presented is in many people's eyes less spiritual, not so immaterialist, whilst others would call it for that very reason more relevant and less other-worldly. The development of science and technology occurs primarily within a context of Western ontological thinking; and the present cultural transformation is one which now embraces the whole world and has been very much determined by modern science and technology in the process.

The development in Greek Antiquity from myth to ontology is of outstanding importance, because its effects continue to operate to a great extent in the present-day scientific view of the world and of society. In ontological thinking the powers are not abjured, but they are certainly transformed. Man no longer acknowledges the powers because their presence takes him unawares and fills him with fear and trembling, but only as and when he acquires an insight into their true nature. The gods of early Greece are at first indeterminable, impersonal forces; but they assume a recognizable shape and their toil provides analogies with his own. As the world sprang into being, the procedures adopted by the gods were not so very different, perhaps, from those of the Greek craftsmen: sculpturing, working with metals, building houses. It is fair enough that the early Greek philosophers, in seeking to explain how the world came into being, should so often have explained it, therefore, in terms of the techniques of smelting, cooling, blowing, artistic production and so forth.

It is even possible that one factor in all this – as Ricoeur has argued – was disillusion with the gods. The great Greek tragedies, attended dozens of times by many people and still closely allied to cultic observances in that respect, taught men a blind acceptance of destiny and of uncomprehended guilt. To this philosophy there was some sort of reaction: understanding alone liberates. That is why philosophy attached so much importance to clarifying the relation of man to the transcendent, of existence to guilt, of time to eternity. Thus a theogony (mythical doctrine about the origin of the gods) became a metaphysics, cosmogony (doctrine about the origin of the world) became philosophical physics(for instance, in the *Physics* of Aristotle) and inner purification in the face of destiny ('catharsis') developed into ethics. The total world process is recognized as being one great judicial action; and many writers (Fränkel, Jaeger) have pointed out how from Solon and Heraclitus on, this theme runs through the whole of Greek thought: science and philosophy reveal how there is a just order that exists throughout the cosmos.

All this calls for an entirely novel and fresh posture to be adopted toward the familiar, dependable and yet mysterious world. First and foremost it demands a noble effort on man's part to use his powers of thought, because he now proceeds to set himself over against what is going on, in order to take stock of it and map it out. Albeit to a lesser extent than in the Indian schools of thought, we do of course encounter, even in the thinking of the Greeks, the fusing together of subject and object; but still, even in this case, there has to be a prior and very clear contrast established between subject and object, man and the surrounding world. Ontological thinking gains its freedom from the power of myth through the tension created by such distancing.

Some functions of ontological thinking

A basic feature of the ontological attitude of mind is the disjunctive posture assumed by man in respect of the world around him. That disjunction, that distancing, acquires a very pronounced character in the particular mode of thinking which we will be referring to later on as 'substantialist'. As will appear, it leads to isolation – an isolation of man and also of that from which he differentiates himself: ideas and values, for example. But this is to be presented as a negative component of ontological thinking, which does not in itself entail isolation at all. The

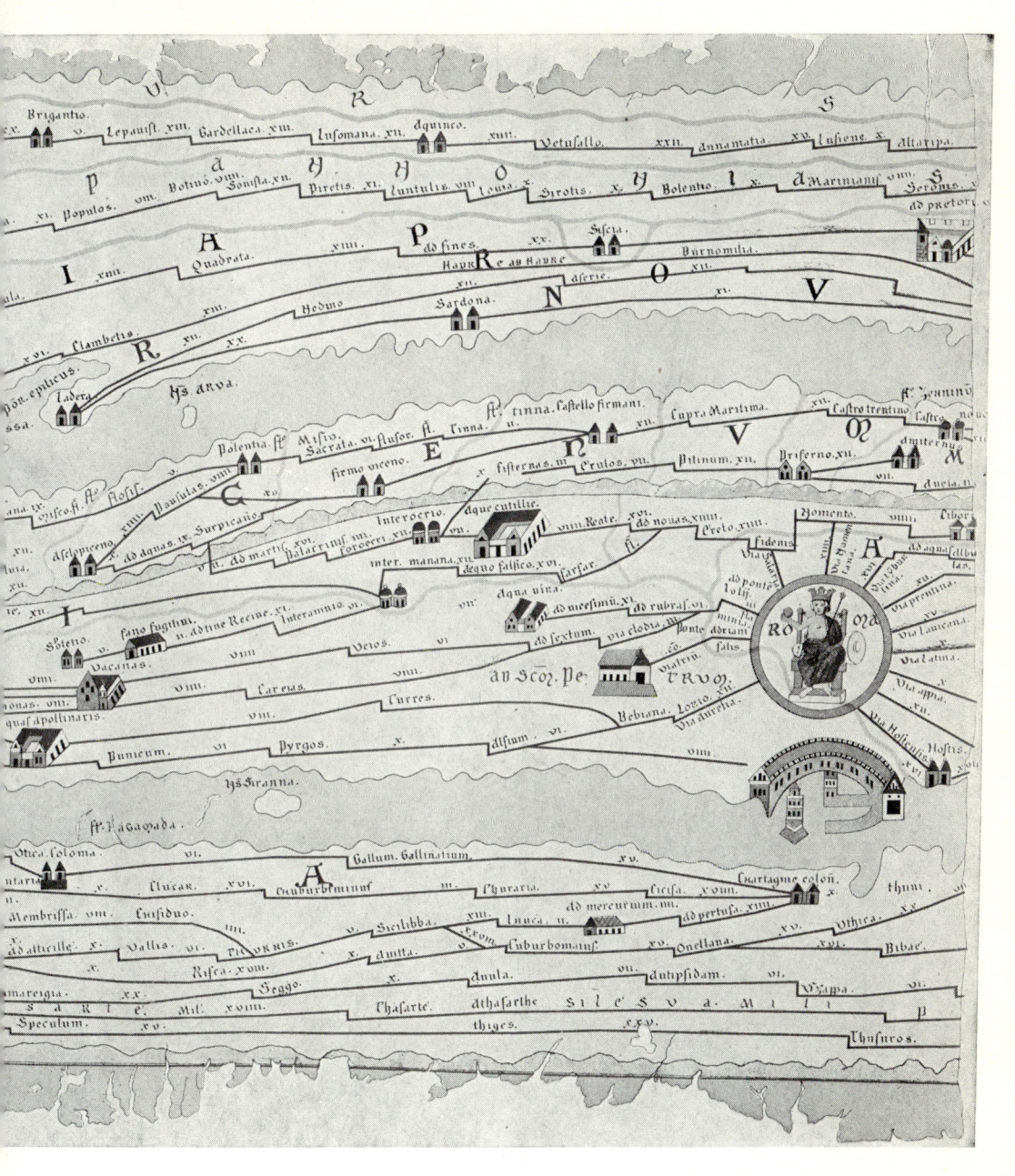

17   Plan of roads on a Roman map.

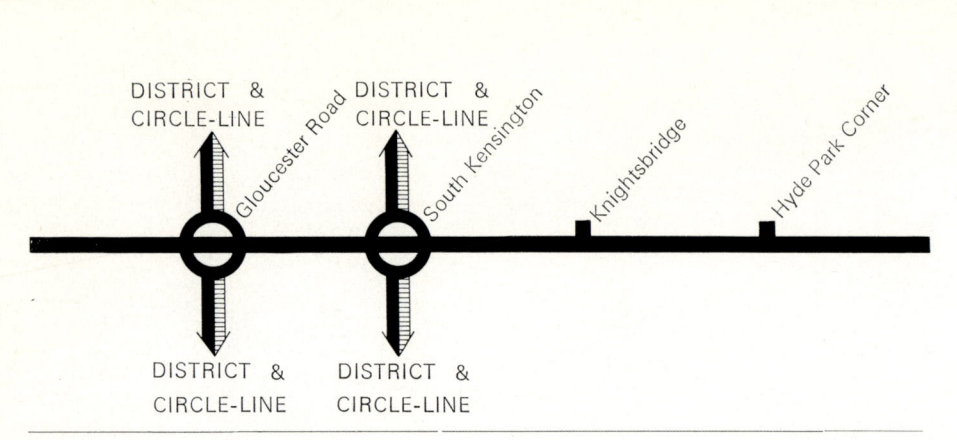

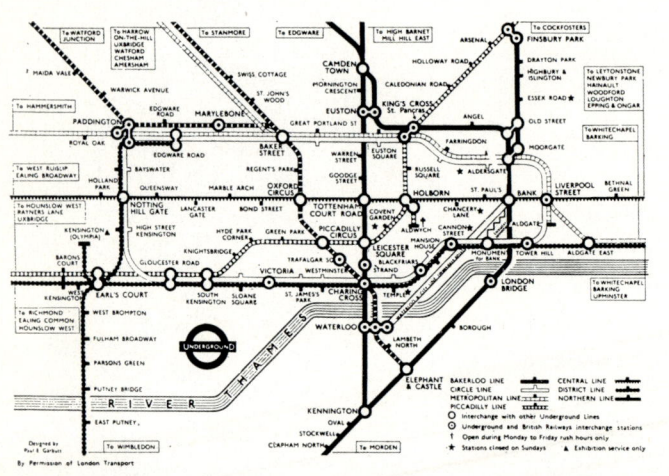

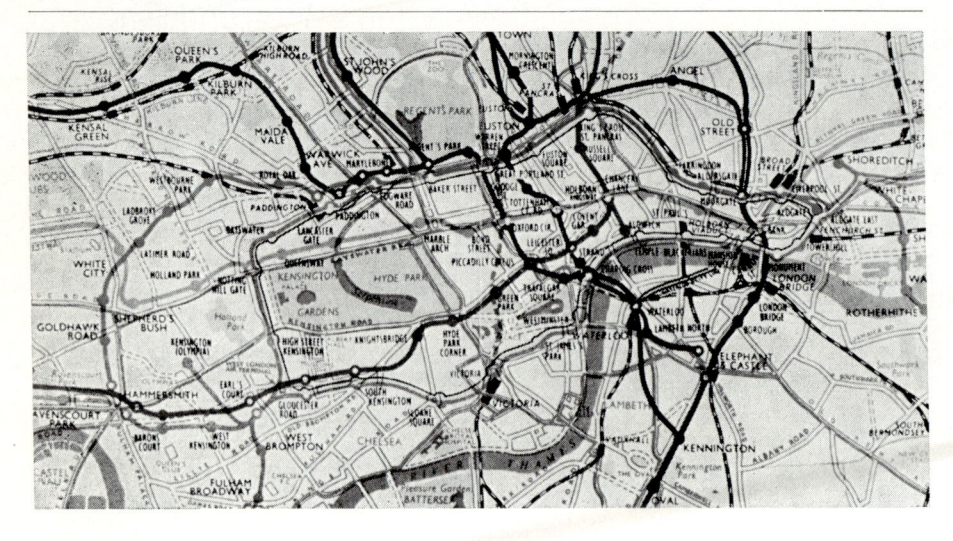

18 Schematized plans of a section of the London Underground and street-map of the area in question.

19   Wilfredo Lam (Cuba), The jungle.

20 Dance during initiation rite (of girls) in Africa.

21 Female dancer with two faces (Mexico). →

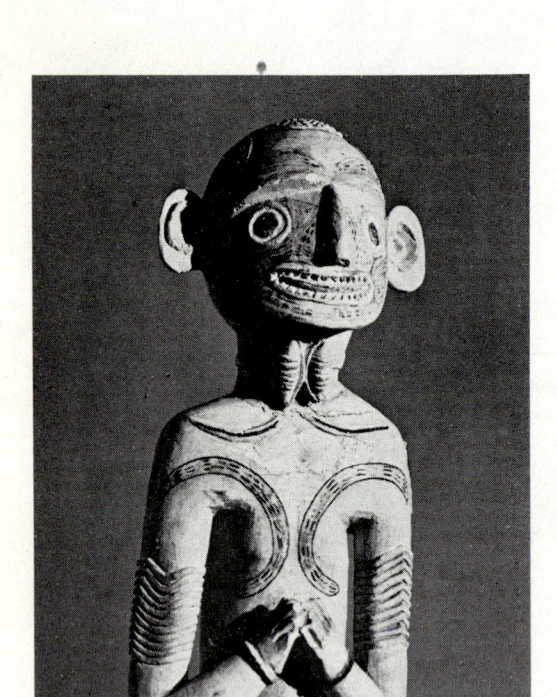

← 22 Ancestral image from Melanesia.

23 Structures on a door from Mali.

distancing is more a way of finding the right relationship to all that encompasses man and restricts him. Ontological thinking therefore has a broader basis than purely rational or even rationalistic thinking. Man realizes here one possibility of successfully determining a position that he can justify; and in this sense we may regard the studied separation of this reflective reasoning about all that is as expressing the same sort of relation we see in mythical and functional thinking too. We now present in outline some typical features of ontological thinking, set alongside those of the mythical and functional standpoints, so as to clarify the central characteristic mentioned earlier on. These features may be summed up in a simple diagram (ill. 24), showing how the subject (S) – that is, man or his thinking – achieves self-containment by assuming a disjunctive relation to the surrounding world, the object (O).

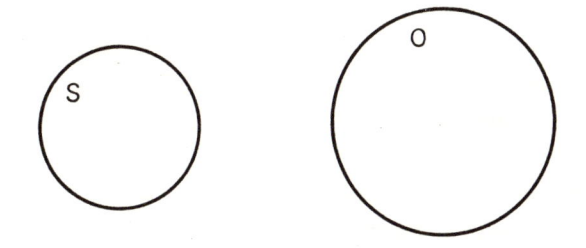

24

A main function of the ontological consciousness is to manifest in the fullest way possible that which is above and beyond man: in other words, the Transcendent in its overwhelming power. The 'ontophany' which Eliade mentions à propos of mythical thinking has close links with ontology. Writers like W. F. Otto and K. Kerényi have pointed out how the Ideas which for Plato constitute a transcendent reality have evolved out of the lustrous and overpowering figures of the early gods. With Aristotle supreme Being is also the godhead, even though as his thinking develops the religious definition of the divine tends to recede, making room for what are more purely ontological terms of reference. And then at the final stage of Greek philosophy Plotinus depicts the ontological point of culmination as the One, encountered beyond the distinction between being and not-being – the One with which the soul of man can achieve union by way of religious rapture or ecstasy. In later European thought the question of being remains so closely attached to the god-question that the 'proof of a god' argument comes to be one of the settled topics of traditional ontology. This 'ontophany' also found its expression in the temples. The Greeks would mark off a fixed space within which the power of the divine was represented not just in images but also in the aesthetic effect of the temple area and in the ascending lines of the columns (ill. 28, p. 76). The what is for us classical Greek temple evolved from more mythical cultic sites in sacred groves and the like, perhaps with the columns representing the original trees. This kind of development from mythical forms is even more plainly recognizable in the case of African Islamic architecture, especially where it falls within the sphere of negro art. The religion here is one without figures or images, in which any theory of being is overarched by the demonstration of God, and consequently the mosques – for instance, the mosque at Mopti in Mali (ill. 29, p. 76) – impress us most with their stark, vertical alignment.

However, there is a shift of emphasis. Greek philosophers such as Anaxagoras, Socrates and Aristotle were actually accused of 'irreligion' *(asebeia)*. They came in conflict with the duty owed to the city gods – which did not mean that they were not religious; for there are obvious religious features in their ontological systems. Where popular religion was concerned, however, their philosophy took an independent line. The division between the sacral and the profane was drawn much more sharply than in the mythical world view. Allowing that by this time temple and market-place *(agora)* might well be standing cheek by jowl, the gap between them was very striking. Life in the market-place was coming to be less and less governed by sacral tradition; but it was in the market-place that Socrates elected to force men to reflect and reason independently, by posing over and over again the question of the motivation, the reason (logos) for man's religious, moral and political behaviour. This way of insight, of perception, then led in Plato's case to profound contemplation of the peculiar and transcendent quality of the Norms, as that which governs and regulates not only action but all being.

Thus the mythical narratives assume more and more the character of profane tales. The primordial symbols of life and death, captivity and freedom, war and peace, are portrayed in vivid scenes and pictures which may indeed still have a moralizing purpose, but where the norms tend to form a backcloth to the passing cavalcade of human beings: the latter come to occupy the front of the stage. One can point to this kind of development in various cultures. A long period of time separates two illustrations which both tell us of human occurrences. Illustration 31 (p. 85) shows a mosaic with, among other things, some inlaid fragments of shell and coloured stone of the 25th century B.C., which comprises a scene of peace (from the so called mosaic standard of Ur). Illustration 32 (p. 85) belongs to the much later period of Persian art at the end of the 16th century A.D. and depicts Bihzan being rescued from the pit.

What all this implies is that nature ceases to be identical with the supernatural. The enigma of transitoriness, of the round of coming into being and of ceasing to be, is explained within the enveloping context of 'nature' as a process of growth, as the unfolding of potentialities (physis). From that starting-point one can acquire insight into the higher forces and laws which regulate that growth: the metaphysical. In later Antiquity 'metaphysics' denotes those of Aristotle's books which in the general sequence of his *oeuvre* came after the books on 'physics' (a broader concept than what is nowadays described as physical science). The experts are not agreed as to whether the term 'metaphysics' here initially referred just to the arrangement of the books, as is usually postulated, or whether it also signifies that metaphysics contains the ontological conclusions to be drawn from an analysis of the surrounding world in process of formation. This last is at all events what Aristotle was in essence aiming at. Much later on, the term 'nature' acquires a narrower meaning as the object of science, delimited by measurement and experiment. Then space, for example, becomes an absolute yardstick for changes in the world. Newton formulates a general mechanics in which space figures as such along with time. But he also speaks of this space as the 'sensorium of God', the field of perception of the divine omnipresence.

We should now be able to see where all this tallies with mythical thinking and where it differs from it. The natural is not totally isolated from the supernatural; but their interrelation is given in the context of an ontological or metaphysical theory and not in that of the extraordinary forces associated with cultic high places and the high seasons of ritual. If in mythical thinking nature first becomes really visible within a supernatural perspective, in ontological thinking it is more the other way round: metaphysics, proofs of God, eternal values, laws of logic – they are all consequences of the analysis of an encircling nature and of some given knowledge or other (e.g., the knowledge of good and evil, or that of mathematical forms). To represent knowledge, therefore, the Stoics are able to employ the image of a tree, on which 'god-theory' or theology is an offshoot of physics or the theory of being. The Transcendent or supernatural, for that matter, is itself described in a context of metaphysics as *'prima filosofia'*, as the basic philosophical discipline, where is propounded the unity of knowing and being, of human reason (logos) and cosmic ground (Logos).

It is again no part of our intention in this case to sketch in any detail the origin and development of ontology (the theory of what is) and of metaphysics (the theory of higher being). It should therefore suffice for us to round off this characterization of ontology as offering to elucidate the Transcendent to the fullest degree possible, with two observations refining to some extent on what has already been said. The first is that ontology does not lead to a static system but to an extremely dynamic analysis of all being; so that man's thought persists in aiming beyond the results already attained: the highest being is vested in nature, is concealed behind nature, is transcendently elevated above perishable nature (for instance, Plato's Ideas), lies beyond being and not-being (Plotinus), is to be named in both positive and negative terms (Thomas). Thévenaz shows how this urge to transcend leads in the end to a sort of inversion: it is in the knowing subject himself that one looks for the postulates of such an analysis of being, so that Kant can describe his theory of knowledge as a "metaphysics of metaphysics". On the other hand – and this is the second observation – this radicalizing of ontology goes along with an ever sharper and more exact demarcating of nature: as they develop, the sciences move from ontological speculation to giving a mathematical expression to phenomena, a process that Dijksterhuis calls the mechanizing of the world view.

A second function is allied to the foregoing and can therefore be put briefly enough: ontology likewise affords a foundation for the present. This is no longer done by re-presenting the primaeval age of myth. Rather, the guarantee of the present is provided as and when what is going on all around is made intelligible; and again this happens when we are able to explain the processes within time on the basis of operative but timeless laws. Very much to the point is the role fulfilled in all this by myth, allegory and image. Thus Plato employs 'myths', that is, stories which he has either thought up himself or has borrowed from mythical tradition. But ultimately these stories are to point us to the timeless reality of the Ideas, and not to render a primaeval age present once again. Allegory is to be used by later thinkers – for example, the Stoics, but also such a Christian thinker as Augustine – to turn stories based on popular belief into symbolic accounts of a philosophically and religiously grounded theory. In different forms we come across this even later still. Thus Descartes talks about the *'fabula mundi'*, which we may perhaps take to be a kind of didactic myth, because in it he expounds how we might picture to ourselves that, for example, man has emerged in a way amenable to scientific explanation. It is not too far-fetched, perhaps, to see in this development a line issuing in the 'as-though' philosophy of H. Vaihinger, in which the concepts themselves become mythical notations of what can no longer be expressed in ontological discourse. But by then we have already left the age of ontology behind us.

A third function of ontology is in line of extension with what has just been said: it is first and foremost a question of knowledge. To some extent, of course, even myth offered to explain the world; but thinking in its ontological phase sets much greater store by knowledge. Men try to trace the causes of what goes on and refer them to a supreme Cause. The ideal then, in Eastern as in Western thought, is the logical derivation of the many from the One. Even when some kind of pluralism (multiplicity of final causes) is adopted, there is still a formal or logical attribute that makes it possible to aggregate them (e.g., as 'elements', 'atoms', 'monads'). Indeed, all physical occurrences are seen in the last analysis as the unfolding in time of a timeless, logical process. Spinoza speaks of a logical *'consequi'* (ensuing) of everything from the divine Substance; and Leibniz maintains that accidental truths – that is to say, those which can also be denied without contradiction or which might have been otherwise (as: 'Caesar crossed the Rubicon') – are rooted ultimately in logical truths present in the mind of God.

This knowledge invariably relates to content of one kind or another: it is always, in other words, a view of something that is given. This is just as true where there is no longer any question of sensory perception, but where it is a matter of seeing "with the eyes of the mind" (Plato).

Descartes stresses the point that metaphysics and science cannot reach any further development unless there is an element of surveyal. Kant declares that even mathematics relates back to observation in the sense that pure space (in geometry) and time (in arithmetic) are conceived of. The Greeks employed the term 'theory', which actually means 'spectacle', to denote the knowledge of being at its highest. From ancient times right up to the 17th and 18th centuries mathematical axioms have been interpreted as fundamental insights which cannot be gainsaid: they are a matter of such direct insight that we may take them to be evident without more ado. Only when functional thinking starts to come to the fore does this also begin to change.

Several aspects of ontological thinking have now been briefly delineated here, which should make it possible to sum up this way of looking at things in a single term: it is all the time concerned with understanding *what* something is. Societies and world outlooks that are ontologically structured are focussed in the 'what'. Man's search is for the perfect and the ideal. But this is given only in the knowledge which reaches above and beyond the course of transient events to the perception and contemplation of the timeless, logically unimpeachable essence (fundamental being, the 'what') of all that exists, physically and metaphysically. Such insight is itself a liberation, signifying good; so much so, in fact, that mysticism actually speaks of a blissful contemplation of the essential being of things as unveiled in the being of God. Timeless perception is envisaged as a Light dispelling the darkness of falsehood, error and transitoriness (Aristotle, Augustine, Bonaventura). Truth resides not in the naming of mysteries at which the blood runs cold, as in myth; but it appears only as and when "by the combination of names with verbs man brings this or that to pass" (Plato) – a notion which in this modern age has fresh light cast upon it when the terms 'true' and 'false' are applied not to words but to propositions. Thus truth is the congruity of the representation with the thing itself *(adaequatio rei et intellectus)*; and Thomas speaks of a knowledge that penetrates to the essence *(penetrat usque ad essentiam rei)*, to the eternal ground of things. Thus we begin to comprehend the 'what' of things only when on the one hand we learn to distance ourselves from the world around, and on the other penetrate by that very means to the eternal essence of everything, which would seem to be vested in this 'what'.

Man and world

Within the context of ontological thinking a clear distinction emerges between man and world, subject and object. Whereas in the mythical world the human person hardly possessed, as yet, a self-contained existence and a distinct identity, ontological thinking enabled him to acquire a private domain, even an inner world of his own. There is a celebrated saying of Heraclitus, dating from the 6th century B.C., to the effect that for man 'ethos' is a 'daimon'. The precise import of this is disputed; but if with B. Snell, for example, we understand by 'ethos' a personal disposition and posture and by 'daimon' a divine power, then the saying implies that now the inner life of man is no longer a result or product of the effect of divine powers, but his own disposition has become for him a divine power. Later on, Socrates also is to speak of the 'daimonion' as a divine voice which is nonetheless the most distinctive thing about man himself. What is happening here is the transition from a view of man as an open field for divine, numinous influences to that of the spiritual life of the person as a private and secluded domain. Plato even compares the soul to an oyster imprisoned within its shell (the body), whilst in his later work (the *Laws*) he provides clear ontological demarcations, namely, of gods, of souls and of bodies. The soul belongs essentially to the supra-spatial, supra-temporal order. These threads run right through the course of history. They culminate in Leibniz's monadology, that is, in his theory of self-enclosed units (monads), knowing only interiority and at the deepest level unfolding their processes of consciousness purely in accordance with logical laws: "*le monade n'a pas de fenêtres*" – the monad has no windows. The soul is an isolated substance and knows the external world simply and solely by drawing upon its own internal one.

Analogous developments are to be found in Indian philosophy as well. In the Upanishads (800 B.C. and later) the atman (soul, essence, originally 'breath') has at first an entirely mythical function. Later on the atman comes to be conceived of as personal soul and as such is held, speculatively, to be in essence identical with the universal atman, which in its turn is regarded as brahman (the ground of reality). These brief illustrations are enough to indicate that the self-containment man achieves through ontological reflection may result in the delimiting of a thoroughly individual substance, as well as the insertion of the personal soul into an all-embracing world ground. The latter will usually be envisaged pantheistically, as divine Reality. Such a demarcation is often accompanied by a dualism in which the interior soul is sharply distinguished from the outward body. In the history of the sciences this ontological dualism has actually played a role in establishing the contrast between the mental and physical sciences. For that matter, various other ontological interpretations are also possible, such as immaterialism and materialism, both of which appear in the East as in the West.

However various the forms of self-identification may be, in each case the subject achieves some kind of self-containment by setting himself over against the object. Even if, subsequently, man and the 'world ground', subject and object, come to be identified as one, this happens thanks to a prior, intermediary stage of disjunction. Personal existence is much more than a role played out within a socio-mythical ambit. It turns out to be more a point of departure from which man is at last able to discover how things cohere in the spatial configuration of cosmos and society. In art we find the perspective element appearing in the draughtsmanship of a Bellini or da Vinci. As they do not in the socio-mythical context, the lines of perspective here unfold from their starting-point in the person who is looking at the landscape. The story goes that when a Japanese went to see an exhibition that included several of da Vinci's studies in perspective, he was moved to observe that anyone who drew the world around him like that must have had an especially powerful sense of his own irreducible person. If we look at illustration 34 (p. 87), which shows us a detail from the work of the Chinese artist Chen-Chu-Chung, we no longer have the kind of two-dimensional picture that we find, for instance, in Egyptian art (see ill. 37, p. 88). Yet even here there is no question of a perspective determined by the subject's position as observer. Notice, for example, the untapered lines of the roofs and courtyards, the human figures drawn just as big when at a distance as when close by. Utterly different – because orientated on the viewer – is the perspective employed by Bellini's fellow-townsman, Vittore Carpaccio. His narrative painting, representing the arrival of St. Ursula at Cologne, is striking for its stark, bold contours and convergent perspective (ill. 35, p. 87). One makes a jump, or even a breakneck leap, when one discovers contemporary man in the mirror of one's perspective, which is a theory of relativity in picture and so may be said to relativize one's own standpoint as a point of departure: etching by M. C. Escher, entitled 'Relativity' (ill. 33, p. 86).

It is not just the image of man that changes; the form and aspect of the gods develop along with it. From being indeterminate forces of nature (fertility, sexuality, energy, destructiveness), in the East and in the West they turn into clearly defined figures. The vital energy which as an animal power – that of the cow, for example, in India, Egypt and primitive Greece – at the same time determined the essential nature of a divine power is still there; but it persists as at the most a concomitant symbol or traditional appendage *(epitheton ornans)*. In Greek literature at this stage we encounter such phrases as "the owl-eyed Athene", "the cow-eyed Hera" (later understood in a purely metaphorical sense, as meaning: 'with large eyes'). It is perhaps in the bizarre figures of the Egyptian gods, mostly in the form of animals, that this provenance is most clearly detectable, while at the same time it is here that the decisive step is taken toward a more ontological cosmology (ill. 37, p. 88: a representation of the night sky with stellar divinities on the ceiling of Sethos I's tomb, about 1300 B.C.).

This trend advances still further as man ceases to be swayed above all else by the vital or numinous 'that' of the gods and in learning to stand apart proceeds to ask about the 'what'. In ancient Roman times we come across various writings with the title *'de natura deorum'*, concerning the nature of the gods: people begin to reason about and discuss the essential character of Deity; theology starts to emerge. This is something which the Christian tradition continues. The personal relationship to God is as it were condensed in reflection upon the person of Christ and its significance; but this does not deter theologians and philosophers from posing in precisely that context questions as to the 'what'. Complex dogmatic theories arise out of this ontological questioning, bringing into the foreground such typical 'what'-terms as 'nature' (the doctrine of the two natures of Christ) and 'being' or 'essence' (the doctrine of the Trinity). In philosophy tendencies of this sort culminate in speculations concerning the Godhead as supreme Being and Cosmic Ground.

All this should not be understood as a negative conclusion. Of course, the more negative component, which we shall be referring to later on as 'substantialism', is already becoming apparent. But in the first instance man's very independence is owing to the fact that he continues to stand in a relation to what environs him (the cosmos) and what governs him (the divine). These two, precisely because of their ontological delimitation – and remember that the term 'definition' refers to the delimitation of a concept – are themselves enabled to become clear focal points for reasoning and reflection on man's behaviour. This is the moment for us to mention the place of instruction regarding values and norms, which is closely connected with the view taken about a god and can sometimes be the source of a very highminded ethical system, free from the bonds of time and place. Whereas in the mythical world it was still a difficult business to make values at all explicit, in the ontological realm of thought they are consciously and knowingly defined. From Socrates to Kant, a growing sense of personal responsibility goes hand in hand with this ontological, but at the same time ethical, positioning of values and norms. The Ideas (Plato), natural morality (the Stoics and mediaevals), the 'moral sense' (D. Hume), the moral law within us (Kant) are but a few elements in a long and many-sided history in which moral norms have been located and assigned a name, with a view to ordering and guiding human society, whether that of the Greek city-state (polis) or of all mankind (Kant).

Changes in this society come about more quickly than is usual in a more primitive one; but it is of course ontologically structured, mostly in a carefully constructed hierarchy. In India we get the caste system developing. Parts of the history of Antiquity and the Middle Ages in Europe are characterized by feudal rule. Class and rank become prominent features. At times lord and serf find themselves opposed to each other and in conflict, only to make way, from time to time, for different but equally substantial distinctions, for instance, as feudal society passes over into one where the possession of capital becomes the norm for differentiating in practice both the distribution of goods and a man's social position. All this comes even more to the forefront as the ontological frame of mind gives occasion to the natural sciences to expand, and these in turn give rise to technology and trade. The relations demanded by production come to play a crucial role in the structuring of society, but likewise in the nature of historical progress.

History is one distinctive mark of non-mythical thinking. The sense of history is much more pronounced in the West than in the East; and still more again in the Christian consciousness than in that of the ancient world. In Antiquity the question is asked frequently enough how this or that has come to be as it is (Polybius, Tacitus), but as yet hardly at all what the end result of something will be. Christian-Jewish thinking is focussed much more upon a future, charged with a religious expectancy and hope (the Kingdom of God). This is known as the 'eschatological' tendency: that is, it is focussed upon the End of the ages. Thus Augustine's philosophy of history and his theology too puts heavy emphasis on the concept of time as unfolding itself from the standpoint of the personal human being (that is, from the here and now) toward past and future. Later still we find this more linear, future-orientated way of seeing history in non-Christian thought as well, for instance, in Voltaire and Marx. Quite often this conscious attention to history is regulated by a final ideal: the City of God (Augustine), Utopia (Bacon, More). Invariably, it implies an insight into the 'what' of history; and so for many thinkers it is signalized by a model outside of time or a divine plan or eternal ideas, prevailing over every age. To use a term of Spinoza's, we might speak of a history *"sub specie aeternitatis"*, seen in the light of eternity.

Substantialism

Ontological thinking helps to realize man's potential for achieving a proper relation with what surrounds him and governs him. It is not so much being obsessed by the 'that', but the analysis of the 'what' which gives its centre and its strength to the ontological standpoint. Subject and object discover the relation between them thanks to their reciprocal disjunction. Even this ontological thinking, however, exhibits a more negative component: an expression of man's endeavour to appropriate power to himself. This tendency within ontological thinking is denoted here by the term 'substantialism'.

The term 'substance' really signifies that which has within itself the capacity to subsist, to last. 'Substance', according to Descartes and Spinoza, for instance, is what has no need of anything else for its own existence. When we say 'substantialism', we are pushing this term to its extreme limit; so that man, the world and God, even values, are envisaged as entities existing wholly in isolation. Of course, it will hardly ever appear in this extreme form; but one can recognize it as a definite leaning in many varieties of ontological reflection. Fundamentally, substantialism isolates things; and so it entails a rupturing of the relation, the meaningful cohesion of man and powers (nature, society, norms). The vantage-point of the spectator, the thinking individual, becomes paramount; and the whole perspective representation of reality becomes a mirror of his own position. So great in fact is the degree of power exercised by the subject that the object vanishes from the field of vision as a result.

It would take us too far afield to trace this substantialist tendency in this, that and the other school of thought. We must, however, provide at least one illustration in order to show that this substantialism can turn up in mutually conflicting schools and can lead to a monism (doctrine of oneness) or to a pluralism (doctrine of multiplicity) or to a strict individualism. In Hindu thinking one comes across substantialist tendencies of a monistic turn in the later Vedanta philosophy. To some extent one can already notice such a tendency in, for example, the commentaries on the older writings supplied by Sankara (about 800), who taught a strict form of monism and reduced everything to the basic substance of the primordial Ground, Brahman. Contrasting with that there is, for instance, the doctrine of Hindu sects such as the devotees of Vishnu and of Siva, who saw their respective deities as real, personal Beings, not as a way of grasping Brahman – via intellectual delusion (maya) at that! In the West one could think of, among others, Spinoza, who regarded all that happens and all that exists as the logical result of the one Substance, the Deity. Or there is Hegel, who sees in the history of thought and of society the single process of the self-realization of the Idea, of absolute Reason.

One can also think of various forms of pluralism which as a consequence entail a multiplicity of substances that are self-enclosed and in no sort of communication with one another. In the later, systematized thought of the Nyaya Vaisesika (about 1600) we have the doctrine that knowledge is centred upon externally located objects: innumerable substances, radically distinct the one from the other. In the West, as we mentioned before, it is Leibniz who talks about the countless monads as substantial entities having no communication with one another at all.

We find a lingering effect of this idea in the logical atomism of the early Russell and Wittgenstein, where it is argued that the world comes apart into mutually disconnected facts.

This atomism, regarded as a substantialist tendency, is more prominent still in individualism; for the question here has to do with human society, described as the sum total of separate human atoms. That is not to say that no organization or planning can possibly be effected; but it is rather like covering things over with a net. The logical atomists of the beginning of this century, whom we mentioned earlier on, used to speak of disjointed facts that could be marshalled within the logical network of language and brought into relation with one another. Does this then mean that the cohesive relation between the facts is present just in that network and not in the facts themselves? So much prominence is given to the disjointed, individual facts that it seems perhaps a hopeless task to discover any degree of cohesion in them at all. The same point strikes one even more powerfully where people are involved, and one asks whether it is possible to find in them any sort of cohesion or social bond. To pinpoint the issue one might raise the question of what provides a basis for the state. Does the framework of the state rest on something which all the individuals concerned have in common: for instance, a social consciousness, as is argued by many of the champions of natural law (e.g., H. de Groot: man has an *"appetitus societatis"*; also Pufendorf)? Or must we assume as our starting-point an extreme individualism, according to which every human being is an egoist in his behaviour and out to resist everybody else: *"homo homini lupus"* (Hobbes), meaning that each man is like a wolf for the other; in which case the state comes about purely in virtue of an arrangement designed to ensure the safety of each and all.

The ancient Greeks had already pointed to the urge, so characteristic of man, which impels him to form communities and states. Even so, in that period and within that social philosophy the several divisions and segments comprising human individuals are already much to the fore. In his essay on the peculiar genius of the Greeks R. Harder says that their plastic art pictures man without the surrounding world and makes him into an isolated type: "Admittedly, these persons are not individualists but individuals. *'Individuum'* is the Latin translation of a Greek word; put back into its original Greek form it is: atom. Atomizing means suppressing the world of continuity between. The organic effluvium, the opaque, atmospherical factor, that warm glow which passes from man to man – all that is extinguished. These individuals are bathed in an air that is crystal clear and icy cold." Characteristic of the post-classical cultures of Mexico are the pillars belonging to the palace of the divinized priest-king Quetzalcoatl (ill. 36, p. 88) in Tula (Mexico). Each of the pillars, which formerly supported the roof, represents the princely ruler, who lived during the 10th century. Bathed as they are nowadays in the rarified atmosphere, they stress by the very fact of repetition the isolated individuality of man, which even at that time had begun to manifest itself.

The most extreme outcome of a substantialist mode of thought which altogether isolates the individual is solipsism. This we understand to be the doctrine that only the individual subject really exists. That is the subject, in fact, as the speaker or writer, who maintains that he alone *(solus ipse)* exists and explains the surrounding world, including his fellow men, as the product of his own imagination. This is a highly improbable notion; which is why Schopenhauer remarked that the champions of such a farfetched philosophy were to be found only in lunatic asylums. Yet in countless philosophical works one can find a discussion of solipsism, followed by a refutation. Is that a propitious sign? Or perhaps a realization that solipsism, after all, is a way of thinking that must be fought against, not in others but in oneself. And might not this perhaps be something not restricted to philosophy, but the expression of a general tendency of substantialist thinking, whether it happens to come out in science, technology, the organization of society or in art and in a particular outlook on the world?

No more than the mythical or functional attitude of mind is the ontological one just a particular theory or manner of knowing. Ontological thinking is more a way of acting, cogitating, willing, feeling, making, organizing; and so it lays a distinctive mark on the total structure of a given culture. Ontology is that way of acting and reasoning which attempts to find the right relation between man and powers through distance or disjunction. In this sense man and society fit into rules that may lead to a meaningful relationship. Yet even here the endeavour to seize power for oneself turns out to be inherent in ontological thinking. As soon as that thinking arrives at a closed system or at a rigidly ordered society, feudal or capitalist, or run in accordance with unassailable party discipline, then distance threatens to become rupture. Values and concepts, individuals and even parts of the person like body and soul come to be envisaged as self-enclosed substances with an autonomous existence. Man, thinker and agent, tries to isolate and to demarcate, intending in that way to exert power over his environment.

Substantialism also leaves its traces in art. Of course, the transitional stages between purely ontological art and its more substantialist tendency are fluid. Even so, it is possible to exemplify the distinction with a number of illustrations, using once again the mode of portraying woman and architectural style. The manuals on the subject present Greek sculpture as a prototype for the portrayal of classical beauty; and indeed Greek plastic art does offer an often sublime interpretation of the 'what', it does outline very clearly the essential character of the human figure. But one can cite other examples too, such as the splendid wood-carving of Kitagawa Utamaro (second half of the 18th century), which depicts Japanese women (ill. 41, p. 106). When the correct relations are disturbed, however, so that the resultant shape, stance and gesture come to assume an autonomous existence, it is as though a dimension drops out; and then we get a more substantialist version. One can detect this in, for instance, François Boucher's Venus (1751; ill. 42, p. 106). This has little that is godlike about it; and therefore, although the traditional attributes (shell and doves) are reproduced, it cannot stand comparison with, say, Botticelli's Venus (ill. 43, p. 106). The whole scene suggests a confined field of vision, presents a rather self-sufficient, dreamy young woman and emits an atmosphere of coiffured sensuality which, although not unrelated to it, is yet at infinite remove from the magical eroticism of the Venus of Willendorf (ill. 26, p. 75). An example of a fine, hierarchically structured building with a style and a spiritual background in perfect conformity with the ontological frame of mind is provided by the temple of Vishnu at Sriranganthaswani in southern India (about the 15th century; ill. 45, p. 107). A more ontological structuring of this sort does not begin to be substantialist until the building draws its exalted character, its grandeur, entirely from within itself, until, in other words, it becomes an expression of its own intrinsic mightiness. The castle of Neuschwannstein, built as a piece of neo-Baroque, may be taken to illustrate this point (ill. 44, p. 107).

Under the influence of substantialism everything tends to become rigidified. In religion and philosophy dogmas become fixed, the structure of the state and moral actions are determined on the basis of eternal laws, man and the world are tied to formulas deriving from the state of this or that branch of knowledge at a given period. All this serves to blot out alternative possibilities. Any sort of creative advance, not in conformity with fixed, pre-established solutions, is out of the question. Moral decisions are all deducible from the system and cease to call for any new or hazardous commitment on the part of persons continually renewing an awareness of their responsibility. Thus genuine transcendence disappears, no longer can anyone alter course for the future; for all are hemmed in and held within the confines of the immanent.

As man determines to control, determines to bring phenomena within the range of his own immanence, his own power, so do they become isolated one from another as a result. They then assume an unreal character. The inner world, the psychic realm, is sharply differentiated from the outer world, the realm of the physical. But the result of that is that as soon as one settles into one of these two areas, one loses sight of the other and treats it as unreal. Starting from the physical, objectively determinable mechanisms in man leads to the notion of *"l'homme machine"* (Lamettrie), whereas if one takes subjective experiences, direct apprehensions of the surrounding world and the like as one's point of departure, the whole physical world becomes something unreal.

Again, nature and the supernatural are substantialized to such an extent that the relation between them is destroyed. Men advance certain 'values', that is, timeless norms, which must be taken as a guide in matters ethical, poliltical and aesthetic. They also speak of 'God' as the supreme Substance out of whom the unending programme of the world process logically flows *(consequi)* and unrolls itself in time. No sooner is the supernatural thoroughly systematized, rationally demonstrated and brought within the rules of reason in this way than it completely disappears; for after all, communication is severed, if what is most exalted is at the same time that which is wholly contained within itself. It is but a single step from the sublime to the unreal.

That step has been taken. If the power of human thought, science and technological activity to dominate and control is complete, then what is other is no longer of another order, what was once horrifically strange

25 African cultic image of a mother and child.

26 The Venus of Willendorf (prehistoric).

27 Temple of a Bandu sect in Africa.

75

28 Temple of Athènè Nikè.

29 Mosque of Mopti in Mali (photo: Michel Huet, *Afrique Africaine*).

has become so familiar and so calculable that it has vanished in the process. Even a child can see that the emperor's clothes exist only in imagination. F. Nietzsche gives utterance to this when he hails the collapse of the world of values and describes this whole vision of a higher, self-sufficient reality as *"Hinterweltlerei"*, which is to say: so much delusory nonsense regarding a phantom world behind the scenes. Is there not still something that lies hidden beyond immanence, beyond the power of human thought? An unknowable Substance? The Unknowable (H. Spencer)? The *"Ding an sich"*, the 'thing in itself' (Kant)? But even this dissolves; and neo-Kantians point to the virtue of scientific thinking, which converts every self-subsistent reality *(Ding an sich)* into the formulas of a universally human reason.

Thus the world becomes unreal. Substantialism heralds the transition to present-day culture, the transition to a new form of liberation, not this time from the demonic world of magic but from the meaninglessness of substantialism.

IV

Functional thinking

The transition to functional thinking

Functional aspects human thinking has always had, especially when it has been closely tied to action and to man's pattern of living. Yet there is good reason for using the term 'functional' to describe our modern culture, because the functional aspect is much more salient now than it was in mythical and ontological thinking. Here again, of course, such a characterization cannot claim to provide an exhaustive account of a period but only to offer us a simple model that makes it possible to structure various phenomena. Our primary concern here will be with the shifts and changes occurring in widely separated areas of culture. To ensure that they be handled in such a way as not to elude every attempt on man's part to intervene and to exercise his social responsibility, we shall try to map out this functional thinking. Our account of the preceding phases of mythical and ontological thinking was not intended to provide some kind of historiography but simply to form a background against which the structure of functional thinking might emerge more clearly.

Just as one may regard ontology as a liberation from the magical tendency in mythical thinking, so one can see the functional mode of thought as liberating men from substantialism. Because contemporary culture is in many respects still in a transitional phase between ontological and functional thinking, the functional approach to things will not be felt by everybody to be a liberating experience. Above all in the field of religion, of art, ethics and politics many people are deeply sensitive to the loss of familiar certainties. Others, however, are just as fiercely critical of the traditional standards and verities, which no longer mean anything to them and which they can only regard as so many means of coercion, imposed by authoritarian or metaphysical *force majeure*. If we can analyse the liberating character of functional thinking, this may in fact help us to achieve a reorientation which will break through all these tensions and open up the way to the future.

The kind of ontological thinking that degenerates into substantialism is marked by alienation: that toward which it assumes a disjunctive posture in order to reach a right relationship – a relationship, that is, to the divine, the norms, the truth, other people, an instrument, the social structures – gets separated and becomes something alien to man's thinking. To begin with, his purpose was to find his proper relation to the powers all around him; but because he then fixed them in definitions and pinned them down in isolated ontological positions, they seemed to become fundamentally alien, incredible and unreal. We hear tell, and rightly, of the 'crisis of certainties'; and this expression is apt in so far as the whole business of substantializing, of providing a metaphysical safeguard for values, norms, the Deity, the human soul, reason, humanity and a great many things besides has resulted in the crisis we now associate with precisely those lofty ideals which man had thought to save by bringing them under his control.

It is over against all this that we are able to see functional thinking as a kind of liberation. It comprises that way of reasoning, theorizing, proceeding, deciding, working, which above all else seeks to bring about actual cohesion, a real relation to the powers and forces of our environment. As we shall see, this means that a lot of things, sublime as well as commonplace, have to be completely re-defined. This further implies that within ever widening areas of reference structural interconnections and affinity are being exposed to view. Whereas substantialist thinking isolated everything – so that, for instance, values denoted by such terms as 'truth', 'goodness', 'beauty', became further and further removed from one another – now the same terms almost coalesce, for example, when functional thinking re-defines them as 'authenticity'. This re-defining process, of course, is itself no longer an isolated intellectual pursuit but the expression of a total life-pattern in which theory and practice bear closely upon each other. So a lot of ontological divisions disappear: art, decoration, architecture, urbanism, habitat, planology, socio-psychological structures, work, recreation, technology (to name only this particular string of words) are mingled together in countless ways and between them form a whole network of connections.

Mythical thinking, then, effected the relation of man and world, the relation also of man and powers, more especially by enabling him to participate in, and feel himself obsessed by, the powers in question. In ontological thinking this was achieved by means of disjunction or distancing. In functional thinking, however, the relation itself moves into the foreground. If we may propose this in a simple diagram: the subject (S) still appears standing over against its surrounding world (O), but this time no longer as a self-contained entity (datum) but prised open and addressed to the object, which in turn is addressed to the subject. There is a cross-reference here:

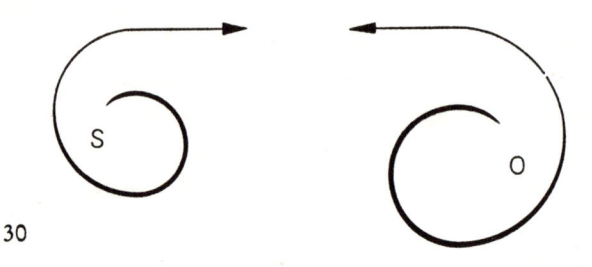

30

This can happen, however, in a number of markedly different ways. Modern modes of thinking and experiencing are extremely variegated and full of contrasts. Two divergences of this kind, which nevertheless display the same basic pattern of functional relations, are the following: one tendency is to recognize and accept as real only that which speaks directly to man, which directly affects him. This we may call the more existentialist form of functional thinking and living, because here personal involvement becomes the criterion. What is extolled as an eternal norm or as self-subsistent Substance or as absolute truth has no part in this direct involvement in existence as a mode of private experience and is therefore meaningless; it no longer signifies anything. What may well be grasped by the intellect and yet remains inaccessible on a personal and emotional basis falls outside the range of what is held to be authentic – that is, genuine, true, real. This way of thinking is not confined to the various *Existenz*-philosophies, so called, but is everywhere in vogue as an attitude to life; nor has it to do with a movement of thought aimed at repudiating a systematic body of knowledge (even though one does sometimes encounter such a tendency) for this sort of existential involvement also figures prominently in various forms of pragmatism and of modern epistemology. There is a refusal, for example, to take the abstract as a starting-point. Instead, the aim is to start from the concrete datum and on that basis to arrive at more abstract rules; or else one begins with a specific instance from which one attempts to infer a general principle, and not the other way round, as in ontological thinking. Thus one works through 'close-ups', as it were, using the particular and personally recognizable as a means of access in one's approach to the whole.

A second tendency is to restrict attention to what can be perceived and substantiated by the senses. Whatever falls outside this is unreal or meaningless. We may call this the more positivist form of functional thinking, because here direct verification and such data as can be positively registered become the criterion. What had been extolled as sublime Reality or as absolute norm cannot any more be brought within the range of man's observational and testing procedures. Even when it is still possible to follow a thing intellectually – traditional arguments, for example, or speculative metaphysical systems – or even when something may still make an appeal to man's emotions, it will be judged to be meaningless discourse all the same, if no methods can be devised of deriving verifiable assertions from such traditional, speculative pronouncements or expressions of feeling. This attitude is not confined to the adherents of this or that school of philosophy or to those whose business is with the physical sciences. In many quarters people simply sweep aside abstruse utterances on absolute norms, being no longer able to see how they could have concrete consequences for day-to-day, practical life. Unverifiable assertions of this sort no longer work in modern society; and so people insist on having hard information and on procedures of various kinds that will put beliefs and opinions to the test. The role of the mass media should be mentioned here, but also that of applied psychology in various forms, of opinion polls and of statistical research.

However much, therefore, the linear pattern presented by modern culture may shift and change, it is still possible to find a measure of convergence in it. What used to be metaphysics now becomes more an analysis of the value-content of terms that were used in that metaphysics; and so linguistic analysis soon becomes a practical habit. Ontology, which had tried to point to laws and structures in reality, crosses over into phenomenology, that is to say, the study of phenomena whereby everything that occurs is analysed in its relatedness to the observer. The old dualism between an underlying reality and a transient world of phenomena which some Eastern thinkers have actually referred to as 'illusion' disappears. It is now some long time ago that the philosopher and psychologist, Herbart, came up with the slogan "whatever appears to be points to being"; and in a more recent period the phenomenologist, Husserl, adopted the same catchphrase. But the 'being' in question is no longer some self-subsistent entity, hidden behind an outer veil of transience; it is what stares one in the face and can be taken in hand: whatever is concrete, is accessible to empirical observation and functions within the life-pattern of man. Ethics too is no longer the supernal realm of eternally valid rules which it may be open to us to discover through the intellectual process of reasoning. On the contrary, ethics now is an ethics in the making, an ethics continually being re-formed and re-formulated within concrete and often tense situations. Ethics turns into the justification put forward for this or that specific choice which modern man arrives at in, say, an industrial or political context and which frequently bears the character of a compromise. Problems of justice too are set in a different context. There is no idea of justice in an abstract sense; it is more a question of social and political actions and the extent to which these amount to a meaningful programme calculated to bring about practical ends, like peace, radical social change and welfare.

Another thing that is often very concrete and at the same time charged with an ethical content is the artistic representation of love. Where the beauty of the human form is concerned, the ideal conception of this accordingly becomes more intent, more stark and lies more in the functional reference than in any naturalistic interpretation. We offer two illustrations for comparison here, the first of which can still be counted as belonging to the ontological stage and the second to the functional, although both evince some connection with the other phase and therefore show us something of the transitional forms as well. Illustration 46 (p. 108) is of a work by the baroque painter, Guido Reni, of Bologna (about 1600). It depicts the race between Atalanta and Hippomenes, with Atalanta picking up the golden apple which Hippomenes has deliberately dropped. The beauty of the human figure is here given expression; and the view of man is an ontological one, even if the rendering is much starker than in the Renaissance and the dynamics of their movement and billowing mantles establishes a relation of both personages to the race in which they are engaged. But the modern sculpture by the Italian, Marcello Mascherini, entitled 'Song of Songs', is more functional still. The lines are quite taut, the tension and the tenderness are present together and stress the mutual involvement, so that the ethical dimension of this Song of Songs becomes functionally perceptible. For the very reason that Mascherini still has recourse to classical forms – and in certain respects even to more primitive Etruscan art – his work signalizes the rise of a more functional outlook (ill. 47, p. 108).

Aspects of functional thinking

In the earlier chapters we remarked on various functions of mythical and ontological thinking. After all, even these mental attitudes have a job to do within a society in that they are meant to put on a proper footing the relationship between men and powers. It speaks for itself that in functional thinking and living it is the functions rather than any features of a self-subsistent kind which have to be made the object of analysis. Since the whole life-pattern has become preponderantly functional, in this case we need only elucidate certain aspects of functional thinking. Thus the present chapter, against the background of the earlier ones, does no more than prepare us for subsequent chapters in which a more vivid picture of the pattern of modern culture can be presented.

A primary aspect even of functional thinking is that it is meant to ensure the full manifestation of the reality around and about us. Yet the differences with ontological thinking in this respect are indeed striking – so much so, in fact, that one almost has to snatch at new forms of language in order to put them into words. The truth is, we are no longer dealing here with a reality which man can locate over against himself and then describe on that disjunctive basis; nor is it a question of contact with supernatural powers, as in mythical thinking. What man is looking for now is a *direct* relation to what surrounds and governs him. The central question, therefore, is no longer that of being but of purpose. It is not what things, events and human society are that is disclosed in functional thinking, but to what extent they make sense and can be meaningfully described or handled. In rational argument, social consciousness, art and theology man tries to give form to meaningfulness or the absence of it. And this question as to the purpose or meaning of things relates both to the reality being assessed and to one's own existence.

When we declare the meaning of a thing or process, a direct relation is formed between such a phenomenon and the ways in which man deals with it. The meaning of a thing is the manner in which it is worked into the human pattern of actions and ways of thinking. Human society appropriates the surrounding world in science, art and technology and so unveils reality. Only when a thing can be lived out and thought through on a basis of meaning, is there any question of something authentic, something real. One may think in this connection of some of the things said by, for instance, pragmatist philosophers and analytical thinkers: "what a thing means is simply what habits it involves" (C. S. Peirce): thus the pattern of habits is also the significance of something. Or again: "that which guides us truly is true" (J. Dewey), and: "the meaning of a word: its use" (L. Wittgenstein) – which is to say that what a word signifies comes to light in the use made of it, in the manner in which the word functions. But existentialist thinkers too have described the reality around us in terms of the meaning of things and processes, a meaning which appears only within the frame of reference provided by human existence. It is not things in themselves, things which are just there, that are primary, but what is taken up by caring and attentive existence (M. Heidegger); it is not fixed truths and essences that take precedence, but existence which exercises choice and realizes itself in a meaningful way: *"L'existence précède l'essence"* (J.-P. Sartre).

Here again the professional thinkers are only voicing what is common matter for discussion in a much broader context. The whole of a man's education (and of mankind's) is geared to learning how to distinguish the natural environment, society and history. But modern education does not stop short at inculcating or recommending the imitation of timeless rules, or the acquiring of some absolute understanding. Instead, human experience provides a starting-point, with a view to making it more meaningful and richer in significance by continually reorganizing such experience so as to be able to regulate future experience as well. Or in the words of the philosopher and pedagogue, J. Dewey, whom we were quoting earlier on: education is "that reconstruction or reorganization of experience which increases ability to direct the course of subsequent experience". We shall be analysing the functional character of modern education and social learning-processes more closely in later chapters. All

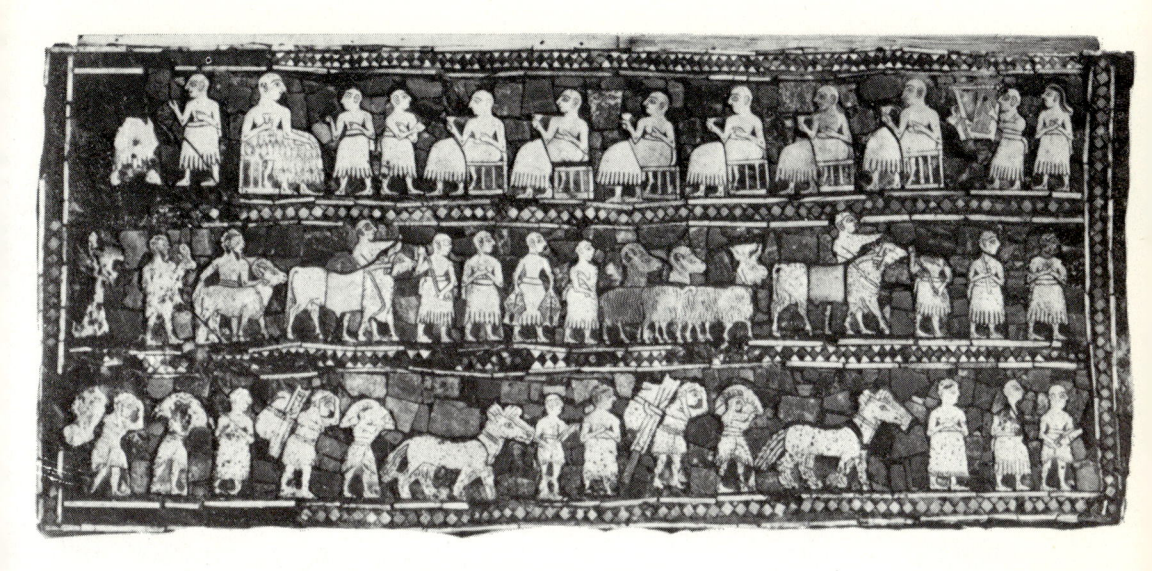

31 Sumerian mosaic:
peace scene
(25th century B.C.).

32 Persian miniature:
story of the release of
Bihzan (16th century
A.D.).

33 The observer's position is relativized: M. Escher, Relativity.

34 Perspective not related to the individual observer: drawing by Chen-Chu-Chung.

35 Perspective related to the individual observer: V. Carpaccio, St. Ursula enters Cologne.

36 Divine individualism: the pillars of Quetzalcoatl in Tula (Mexico).

37 Gods depicted in the guise of animals in the tomb of Sethos I (ca. 1300 B.C.).

that we want to point out here is that within functional thinking the full manifestation of the reality surrounding us assumes a different, a more practical and active character.

That applies not just in the sphere of education but to the whole of social life. To recognize or identify something is to see the significance, the meaning of the thing; and this in turn results in the realization of that significance in practice. Rightly enough, it is one of the most frequently quoted utterances of Karl Marx that whereas philosophers have always interpreted the world in different ways, the point now is to change it. The reality, including the social reality, that manifests itself within the functional pattern is invariably also the activity of enriching the meaning and significance of nature and history by reorganizing human experience. In the social activity of modern man this comes out even more strongly, as will appear in the chapters that follow. Ethics is no longer a matter of administering eternal norms, but the step by step transformation of conflict situations; political and social activities are no longer a matter of steeping mundane events in the light of a supra-mundane ideal, but of incessantly testing ideals against the possible realization of practical ends, and of re-structuring a particular society. Art too acquires a more immediate, less august character by putting surfaces and colours to work in such a way that they gain in expressiveness. Even things which society has discarded, such as rusty metal, old food-tins, rags, may be redeemed, as it were, because in a functional context they acquire an unexpected justification. Thus in his *'Hommage à Brassaï'* (ill. 50, p. 117) Jaap Wagemaker has brought together different sorts of materials such as wood, bits of metal, nails, paint and succeeded in using them as an expression of spatial structures. At another level the same thing happens in architecture, where the building is no longer seen as an end in itself – as it is in the substantialist tendency (cf. ill. 44, p. 107) – but is "a spatial composition" (M. Breuer), intended to give expression to man's life and work. Architecture and town-building manifest the meaning of man's world, the whole theatre of human life, and in this functional context fulfil their proper role. In the first instance and in ordinary usage the term 'functional' applies to architecture and furniture-design. The photo by the well known photographer, Versnel (ill. 51, p. 117), not only shows pieces of furniture that are typically functional (that is, having their shape determined by the purpose for which they are intended) but is itself, qua photograph, an artistic-cum-functional way of approach to the object. Thanks to its functional character, the chimney-stack on the building which houses the heating system at the new university of York (Great Britain) has a powerful aesthetic effect (ill. 52, p. 118).

'Warranty', 'justification', is a term that looms very large in the functional approach to things. How can man ever find his justification? It is a question often asked by modern thinkers. For an answer they look to the socially meaningful way in which man is able to function. No longer is work regarded as a thing, a kind of substance, which one can negociate and trade in. Working is a way of realizing our distinctive being as men. The financial results of our labour, taken together with very many other aspects such as work-satisfaction and working conditions, motivation, the inventive drive, recreation, living conditions and so forth, constitute a sort of mosaic in which each constituent part is functionally arranged to subserve the meaning of man's functioning as a whole. All this may even adumbrate a shift in the goals envisaged by a large business or even by the whole of industrial society, because the profit motive can come to be less isolated from a more functional way of vindicating the welfare of man in society.

With all this, the sharp distinction of the natural from the supernatural, so typical of ontological thinking, disappears: not in the sense that the natural merges into the supernatural, as proved to be the case in the mythical life-pattern, wherever the two were conjoined, but rather that the supernatural is absorbed into the natural. As we were saying at the beginning of this chapter, the crisis of certainties implies, in fact, that the sublime, self-subsistent Ideas and Powers have become unacceptable and meaningless. Only if and when words like 'God', 'norm', 'creative inspiration', 'truth', are enabled to function within the natural proportions afforded by human activity and experience do they recover significance. Logical analysis, psychological research, phenomenological description, the study of social consequences, in short a whole arsenal of functional methods of verification is employed to ascertain in what way terms which were once used to denote the supernatural can still be linked up with the natural conduct of affairs in a given society.

We may mention as a second aspect, in direct association with all that, the provision of a basis for the present. This specification, appropriate enough to the role that myth had fulfilled in the life of primitive man, may seem somewhat strange within a more functional idiom. There is, after all, no longer any question of seeking to base a contemporary situation on a supernatural constellation, as in the earlier stages of thinking; but neither is it the case that the world is now closed and is exhausted in purely natural data. It is precisely a more functional account of human nature and society that introduces a major dynamic factor: the natural situation is never fully secured but has to be captured or overcome; and the question as to the justification of human existence and social structures, as they have arisen in history, remains a pressing one. In this respect a grounding, a justification for the prevailing situation is called for over and over again.

Such a justification is not forthcoming on a mythical or ontological basis. Indeed, nothing is more striking than the difference from this latter kind of thinking; for it is impossible to vindicate a current situation by deriving it rationally from eternal ideas, a timeless plan in the mind of God or a latently rational human nature. No; a meaningful ground begins to exist only as and when we succeed in making a situation viable. Technology and recreation, psychotherapy and art, theology and urbanism – from a functional viewpoint they are all closely bound up together, provided only they can be successfully integrated within the rationale assigned to concrete situations. The motives that operate and the meanings assigned may well extend far above and beyond a particular situation, the immanence of the situation may be enlarged (may acquire transcendence); but if that does happen, it must be bound up directly in some way with the here and now.

A third aspect is the part played by knowledge in functional thinking. As soon as we compare this with the more ontological ideal concept of knowledge, it becomes clear that an important change has occurred. This change, which also has a significant bearing on the whole field of didactics and education, might be typified as in the first instance a shift from theory to practice. That means in this context that understanding is no longer tied to certain substantial truths which are in themselves open to scrutiny or rational disquisition. No; understanding is a product of the correct way of working with things and symbols. This, of course, is the most striking aspect of the formal sciences like mathematics, sciences that are quickly gaining in influence, and as the scope of their application increases are setting their stamp on modern teaching methods. In the preceding chapter we pointed out how an ontological interpretation derived mathematics from fundamental propositions, axioms, enshrining evident and recognizable truths. One proceeded from basic data or entities, the nature of which was equally substantial: for example, 'point' and, as the outcome of a point in motion, 'line'. Nowadays we no longer start, in the case of a formal system (e.g., mathematics or logic), from any substantially definable data. On the contrary we speak of 'primitive terms', that is, of elements, usually denoted by algebraic symbols, which in themselves have no significance at all. Likewise axioms are not immediately recognizable truths, as in an ontologically interpreted geometry: for example, that the shortest link between two points is a straight line. Axioms become relatively arbitrary conventions, that is to say, rules showing how we must operate with the primitive terms. Thus among other things they indicate what we are to understand by such terms as 'line' and 'straight'. Conjoin this with a limited number of deductive rules, which show how from one term one can legitimately infer another (for instance, from 'a' we may derive 'ab', not 'ac'), and one gets a purely formal system of symbols plus rules with which one can operate without needing to represent anything. Thus it ceases to be a matter of elaborating upon already well established, evident percepts or eternal truths (for example, that the three angles of a triangle are equal to the sum of two right-angles), and becomes an affair of arbitrary symbols which acquire their meaning only when one applies to them the operations (possibilities of combination, inferences) established by convention or consent in the axioms or implicit definitions. Their meaning therefore derives from the functions allocated to them via the rules.

Although there would appear to be a considerable gap between formal systems and art, in modern art too it is possible to discover a tendency which ascribes significance to colours and forms, not because of a visual and recognizable content already present in them but by virtue of the more formal function which the various elements have.

Of course there are also trends in art – just as there are non-formal sciences, for that matter – which do take as their starting-point elements with an already visible and substantive significance. Yet even in those cases there is a shift from content to function, because, for instance, forms, landscape, ways of portraying people, are conditioned by some function or other: perhaps an unusual way of looking at familiar objects, or in 'purposive' art a particular message which somebody wants to bring before the public.

Perhaps this is most clear in the case of modern physical science, which is certainly conditioned in part by formal systems (e.g. mathematics) but is itself centred substantively upon a given reality or world of phenomena. In the very early part of this century the philosopher, Ernst Cassirer, brought out a study on the changes in the physical sciences, under the title *Substanzbegriff und Funktionsbegriff*. He argues there that the physical sciences are making less and less use of a substance-language and more and more of a language of function. As opposed to the concept of 'kind', deriving from Aristotle's logic, in which the particular exemplar was defined partly by means of the general concept, modern physical science employs the concept of function. This concept is not meant to provide a substantive definition of a phenomenon, but to present the necessary relations which determine it. The particular is therefore not reduced to an abstract concept; but it is a matter of being able to define *this* specific phenomenon within the network of functional relations in a scientifically adequate fashion. The philosophical notion of substance gave rise to the question of what might be supposed to lie concealed behind the apparent datum. That question has lost all meaning. The aim now is not to give us the picture of a nature which is self-subsistent, but schemata in which the various interrelations are reproduced as exhaustively as possible. 'Mass', 'force', and so on are not new entities, but instruments of thinking. What is now understood in the physical sciences by 'matter', Cassirer concludes, is not a perception but a conception.

Similar ideas turn up in other philosophical and scientific traditions. Cassirer is himself a neo-Kantian. He recast and extended Kant's methods and subsequently applied them, with the same functional approach, to the mental sciences. Some twenty years later we find a more positivist thinker, R. Carnap, interpreting the general structure of scientific knowledge in terms pointing in more or less the same direction. For instance, he too refers to the changes in logical reasoning that have the effect of transforming the 'graphic' content of concepts – what one might perhaps envisage, let us say, in connection with the concept 'mammal' – into logically manipulable functions: for example, a set of rules expressing the interrelations of a number of characteristics (the manner of feeding the young, hairiness, and so on, to be listed as: p, q, etc.). After another twenty years or so we have the physicist, W. Heisenberg, saying that modern physical science is no longer concerned with imaging a nature which is there, ready to hand (the ontological view, one might say) but with the scientific investigator's relations to natural phenomena.

This trend, which we have exemplified by referring to just a few of the ideas and interpretations current today, extends well beyond the physical sciences – further indeed than cognitive activity in science as such. A. Rapoport, J. Piaget and others have pointed to the part played by the operations of the human cognitive process in such elementary matters as affirming that something or other is constant: for example, when one recognizes a durable object or a fixed attribute or an invariant relation. In this case it is not, not even in day-to-day experience, a question of things which are simply given and constant. In fact we should not conceive of such a condition of constancy as being 'thing-like'; we should think of it more functionally or as Rapoport will have it, operationally (the term 'operationalist', used here later on, has as we shall see a different meaning). The truth is, it is all a question of the degree of stability with which experiences can be communicated. 'Ghost' and 'atom' denote phenomena of which various groups of persons claim to have had experience. But whereas we assign a definite reality-value to the latter term, to the former, normally speaking, we ascribe none. The term 'atom', after all, occurs within a network of statements which exhibits much more coherence and offers room for explanation over a broader field of events than does the term 'ghost'. By using an example of this sort Rapoport shows how terms have meaning by virtue of the manner in which they function.

We can now typify the functional approach to things by a single word. Just as the mythical mode of experience was concerned with the 'that', and ontological thinking with the 'what', so the functional approach relates to the 'how'. Questions about existence (the 'that') and about essence (the 'what') are not thrust aside; but they only present themselves within the context of the way in which a phenomenon functions (the 'how'). One cannot simply ask about the essential nature of matter, life, man, values, without first discovering which mathematical equations control the relationship between physical phenomena or what processes are characteristic of a living organism or of human behaviour and the assignment of norms to that behaviour, via symbols. How something happens and is completed does in fact determine the relation to the individual experiencing, perceiving or identifying it in that particular way. It is quite possible, for instance, to assert that certain norms exist, or even to utter profundities about their import; but modern man feels no involvement in any of this. It is not real to him unless it can be shown how such norms may function concretely in the life of the individual and of society.

Illustration 38 exemplifies beautifully the two worlds described by the terms 'ontological' and 'functional'. The car driver is obviously wondering which direction the pushcart will take, since the man behind the cart and the figure on top of it are pointing in two different directions anyway. But if we look carefully we see that the cart is carrying a Greek statue. It represents an orator clutching a scroll and underlining his words by gesticulating with an arm. He is speaking of deep things, budges

38 Left or right? A functional and an ontological indication (cartoon by Plose).

neither from his point nor his pedestal, without indicating concretely what it is all about. His gesture is not in the least functional, but only rhetorical. The state of mind he represents is the ontological, perhaps even the substantialist one. The man behind the cart belongs to the modern world. His gesture is functional, because it shows which street he wants to turn into. The artist has captured most skilfully the practical and referential character of the functional attitude. There is also a big difference between this rhetorician and the famous composition by Ossip Zadkine, 'The ravaged city', which stands in Rotterdam, where it goes by the nickname of 'Jan Gat' – i.e. Johnny Hole (ill. 58, p. 127). Here again we have the functional approach; and one cannot understand the figure, with its hole, unless one takes not the 'what' but the 'how' as one's starting-point. Quite wrong, of course, is the ontological interpretation of this work, which takes it to mean that as a result of the bombing in 1940 the centre of Rotterdam was completely destroyed (the hole) and the outskirts remained standing (the rest of the figure). No; the figure does not reflect or interpret any factual event, but it embodies the stress, the tension of a city full of people, threatened and at the same time struggling to rise up out of that threatening circumstance. Functionally speaking, therefore, the hole indicates what is quintessential, the tension, or if you will, the soul of the composition. That hole is not something to be localized; its effect is felt right through the taut and rugged curve of the large figure. If the hole is not there (in ill. 59 the opening has been filled in) the figure becomes ponderous suddenly and more substantialist, so that the functional force, the 'how' of it disappears.

It is not only in everyday experience but in the sciences and philosophy, in religion and art as well that so many changes can be understood better if one uses as a key-word the therm 'how'. In all these spheres people used to think that whatever the term used or the form given, they could grasp and assimilate everything, if only they had some understanding of what the word or the form, taken at its face value, was claiming to denote. Words like 'God', 'faith', as well as norms in ethics and forms in art, carried their own intrinsic meaning within themselves. Nowadays, however, all such certainties are evaporating. Not because modern man is nihilistic and living in a void, but for the very reason that what they entail has to substantiate itself and become authentic: from now on the 'what' becomes apparent only within the 'how'. Many inherited terms are therefore coming up for an overhaul; but this is a constructive factor in the development of functional thinking. In physics as it was at the turn of the century a term such as 'simultaneity' presented no problem; for, as in everyday life, its meaning was reckoned to be self-evident. But in Einstein's special theory of relativity all this is changed. According to Einstein we cannot know what the term 'simultaneity' signifies unless and until we are able to specify the method required for establishing a simultaneity of events: the 'how' becomes an explicit question; and this entails a renovation of science. Analogous examples can be taken from the sphere of philosophy as well. As early as 1920, or thereabouts, L. Wittgenstein was writing that a logical proposition can only say "how a thing is, not what it is". And not long before that, a philosopher of a wholly different complexion, E. Husserl, described his phenomenological method as an analysis of the "*Gegenstand im Wie*", the object of enquiry, considered from the standpoint of its 'how'. This 'how' then builds a direct relation to the person carrying out the investigation, or at any rate to the function of the investigator. 'How' implies, in fact, a particular angle of vision and thus the standpoint of the observer. This comes very much to the fore in modern physical science too.

Man and world

In the context provided by mythical thinking man had not so far acquired a full identity, and as a subject not yet self-contained, he was in a sense captured by the object, the socio-mythical orbit. Ontological thinking succeeded in distinguishing as opposites man and world, man and powers. In the functional approach, however, relation is more prominent than distance; and so here self-contained entities are opened up once again. This does not mean that the hard-won private identity of the human being is lost, but that it can no longer be regarded as an isolated datum. Personal identity, like that of powers and norms, is a functional affair, constituted in relations.

The effect of the ontological attitude in art was, as we have seen, to ensure that what were often rigid lines of perspective regulated every detail of the landscape, the point of reference being the position of the subject or observer. One consequence is a curious distancing of the spectator. In functional thinking this alters completely. No longer is it the self-sufficient subject that forms the already given point of departure for the proper ordering of landscapes, objects and surfaces. No; there are queer lines of perspective, sometimes even giving the impression at first that they are not there at all – and this in such a way that the spectator gets his position assigned to him from the coercive structure of the painting itself. The spectator is no longer a factor given in advance, but emerges, as it were, only through what is happening before his eyes; whilst on the other hand his participation in the work of art is necessary in order to create structures in what is initially the bewildering confusion of the work. Then at last the 'how' may lead us to a 'what'; and the interaction or reciprocal relation proves to be indispensable. Georges Braque has expressed in a painting the view he had from his studio of the Sacré Coeur in Paris (ill. 53, p. 118); but it is only when in one's capacity as spectator one leans out of the window oneself, so to speak, that in this very movement the spatial construction of that perspective begins to emerge. Compare with it the perspectival drawing by Escher (ill. 33, p. 86): this is modern, in so far as it gives expression to the relativity of the observer's position; but on the other hand it still belongs to the ontological sphere, because it is not until we get to a work like Braque's that the spectator is obliged to construct the perspective for himself.

We were saying at the start of this chapter that the functional approach breaks through a good many fixed lines of demarcation and specialized areas so that, for instance, the sharp, classical-cum-ontological distinction between truth, goodness and beauty recedes. This classification often went hand in hand with the recognition by anthropology of three faculties in man: namely, of knowing (truth), of willing (goodness) and of feeling (beauty). The example we have just given of the interaction between spectator and work of art is a very good illustration of something that is a commonplace in modern psychology: that dividing things up in this way is extremely artificial. In fact, all three of the aforementioned faculties have a part to play in this. As a matter of fact, what is entailed here is the close correlation between man's perceiving and his motor system. The spectator's involvement with the work of art has a motory character; and various psychologists and physiologists have been able to establish experimentally that even in the ordinary processes of observation the motor system is involved: thus whenever we perceive an object, there are concomitant muscular enervations which anticipate our approach to the object in question or our handling of it (E. Straus, F. J. J. Buytendijk).

It is precisely by a functional approach to man that we bring out the unity of man in his various relations. Here again the consequences are far-reaching; and so far we have taken only the first steps along an exceptionally constructive road that may lead to many kinds of new scientific and practical initiatives. This might be illustrated by a later pattern in which previous lines have been further extended. Various investigators have concluded that the correlation between perception (and knowing) and motor system (and willing) is also a crucial, determining factor in any analysis of scientific methodology. This is not maintained on the basis of the argument that one could explain scientific methods and logic purely in psychological or even neurophysiological terms. Framing rules which will enable one to reach correct conclusions in a particular science is not at all the same thing, of course, as describing how someone actually thinks when he is dealing with a scientific problem: the former is methodological, the latter psychological. No; it is precisely when we take a methodological standpoint in examining the functional or operational character of scientific knowledge that it turns out to be a question not just of describing pure facts or giving a purely theoretical account, but equally of constructive interference with phenomena. Pure theory and logical rules, it would appear, are not to be detached from technical procedure and practical understanding. M. Polanyi speaks in this connection of the "tacit dimension of knowledge"; whilst in a different context similar ideas have been given some prominence by J. Piaget, when he puts the emphasis on how knowledge comes about and in so doing assigns an organizing function even to mathematics and logic. If we extend such lines still further in yet a different way, we get to some of the immense problems to do with the relation between science and technology on the one hand and social responsibility on the other: questions that we shall be going into in later chapters.

The whole image presented by man undergoes a profound change. Man ceases to be either an isolated individual or for that matter an amalgam of two substances: mind and body. Man's spiritual or mental character cannot be looked at as something detached from his bodily and social conduct. It is the very way in which man, as distinct from the animal, behaves – not governed purely by instinct, able to handle and devise symbols – which determines his mental character. Mind is therefore no longer a substance, a higher level in the life of the soul or of the 'inner man'; it is rather the total orientation of man. That is why the sharp division between inner and outer worlds disappears. There is no strictly private and isolated inner life, because the most inward experiences are partly conditioned, after all, by language, by habits, upbringing and relationship to other people. Indeed, the advent of the term 'the subconscious' is bound up with the functional idea that in the human being there may be interior aims and impulses which remain hidden from the individual himself but can be rendered visible in relation to somebody else (doctor, therapeutist, psychiatrist). Conversely, the outer world turns out to be less purely exterior, because every human being experiences and perceives his world from within a projection of his own: the disturbed person shows us as in a mirror how much a particular sort of world is connected with his peculiar way of orientating existence. Collectively too man describes and explains the world about him through his own pattern of culture and world view. The very nature of science itself in any given historical period carries the mark impressed upon it by the cultural pattern; one has only to think of the distinction made here between ontological and functional thinking.

If we are to examine the real nature of man, we must stop regarding him as an isolated being and begin to analyse how man functions in his world: namely, his culture. It is on this that many different kinds of enquiry – social and cultural anthropology, the phenomenology of religion, the study of symbols, information theory and praxology – converge. Culture is then thought of not so much as substantive or as substance, but as a verb, as the manner in which man expresses himself. In every phase, and in all the forms, of his history man tries to find the right relationship to the powers and forces that surround him. Here his relation to the divine becomes a special point at issue. At the very beginning of this chapter the point was made that in and by itself the question of the supernatural is meaningless and can only be handled properly when set within the question of the natural. This implies, not that the divine is eliminated but that the God-question be raised in a functional context: how can the term 'God' be given a concrete setting in the routine relationship which the person and the community adopt vis-à-vis their history. There is no longer any place either for theism or for atheism in the

39 The ontological view of God (cartoon by Cork).

traditional sense, because both the affirmation and the denial of God's existence were here rooted in a pre-determined interpretation of the term 'God'. From a functional viewpoint, meaning is precisely what the term still has to acquire. Both rejection and acceptance of the divine call for substantiation. What 'God' is we do not as yet know, because it is no longer a question of defining something ontologically given, as, for example, 'supreme Being'. The functional approach to the question of God requires openness: the key words to our existence can only become charged with meaning as we proceed. Cork's cartoon pokes fun at the ontological conception of God as a supreme Being located beyond man and above him (ill. 39, above), whilst the poster (ill. 54, p. 118) is trying more to express a functional view of God as a transcendent dimension of the world and life of man. These two pictures, both of groups of people walking, make a fascinating contrast: only in the second one is there any possibility of a meaning that really will emerge 'step by step'.

All this one can trace in the development of more recent religious and theological ideas. One is faced with new insights which are surprising and, for the religious person, extremely disconcerting as well. Phrases like 'the death of God' and assertions that as a 'he' (in the third person, that is) God does not exist, but proves to be a significant reality only as a 'thou' (that is, the person addressed), both occur in the initially bewildering picture presented by modern religious thinking. But if one stops asking in the first instance the question about the 'essential being', about the 'what', and attends first and foremost to the 'how', then very different trends are seen to converge in the God-question, once it is framed in a functional context, however much the subsequent answers may diverge. The questions are posed by Christians and atheists – in the most recent Marxist thinking, which has a less ontological, more functional focus, even the God-question plays a major role – just as much as by the devotees of Eastern religions. In various movements of renewal within Buddhism and Islam people are trying to make the question of the divine more real by involving it more closely with the practical conduct of modern society. The 'new religions' of Japan are inclined to take developments in the psychological and social fields as their starting-point in order to arrive at a modern form of religion. In Christian thinking the centre of gravity is shifting away from a systematic theology, with its more dogmatic and ontological stamp, and toward a structuring or exegesis of how the name 'God' has been operative in history and how it ought to function now. In this context the figure of Christ is no longer envisaged as a lofty idea, as was often the case in the last century, but as a historical, concrete person who made the divine something intelligible by 'enacting' it as an indispensable criterion for the great issues of hope, guilt and the humanity that men share together.

The same kind of developments in man's relationship to the surrounding powers are taking place where values are concerned. The latter have ceased to be sublime and timeless entities and have tended to become structures that envelop man and exceed his own control. A new sense of responsibility arises from the need to keep redirecting, and perhaps in some cases breaking through, these structures so as to realize values that will no longer be foreign to what is happening in the contemporary world. All these tendencies entail 'secularization'; which is to say that what used to be the sacral now comes to be located within the natural world, so that the world at the back of it, the metaphysical controlling factor, disappears. This gives a new élan to the sense of history which, more than in mythical and ontological thinking, plays a positive role in the functional life-pattern. The question of the future to which present-day developments are likely to lead is really one about a new functional responsibility. Radical alterations in the structure of society, so very much dominated up to present by relations based on productivity, are part and parcel of all this. In the chapters that follow we shall be examining various aspects of it in more detail.

Operationalism

Although we are still very largely in process of moving from an ontological to a functional pattern of culture, even in the dawn of this new phase it is possible to single out the negative component. Just as within myth it was magic, and in ontology substantialism that expressed man's ambition to take complete control, in the functional approach this appears as operationalism. The term 'how', central as it is to the functional position, suggests the referential and open character of phenomena. Operationalism, however, reduces them to the operations by means of which they are brought into being; and this has the effect of aborting their referential aspect. Admittedly, the end result here is not a collection of isolated, self-subsistent entities, as with substantialism; but there is a correspondence all the same, because, albeit in more dynamic fashion, references and relations are held back within a more manageable set of data.

This needs to be clarified by a number of examples. First, however, on a point of terminology, it should be pointed out that 'operationalist' is not the same as 'operational'. The latter term is not used here in a pejorative sense: it denotes the possibility of characterizing a given phenomenon in terms of certain operations. Sometimes, of course, the two terms may merge into each other; and that can supply us with our first illustration. In modern psychology the term 'intelligence' is usually given an operational definition; which means that 'intelligence' is not taken to be a particular quality or substance located somewhere in the mind of the subject of the experiment. 'Intelligence' indicates the result one obtains by applying a given test; and what the term signifies is thus wholly determined by the method of gauging employed. But such an operational method of defining phenomena becomes operationalist only when the method itself is made into a general theory to the effect that one can obtain an exhaustive definition of the phenomena in operational terms. Thus there is a test for ascertaining and measuring colour blindness by the use of a particular method; yet the assertion that colour blindness is nothing other than the results obtained with that test is operationalist.

The obvious objection is that whilst such a test can of course furnish a scientific criterion for ascertaining colour blindness, we must not proceed to equate the criterion with the phenomenon under review. Ultimately, for the person concerned, colour blindness is still something like, let us say, an inability to distinguish certain colours, even prior to and apart from the fact that in a qualified way, as it were, this particular faculty is brought out in the test. Illustration 40 shows us how various functions of a living creature, in this case actually a snake, may be 'operationalized'. Organs are represented in two-dimensional panels, activities in three-dimensional ones; the functional interconnections form a complex network that is both an organizational scheme and an example of a scientific model.

In philosophy and the theory of science at the present time a considerable discussion is going on about the feasibility and limitations of operational definitions. 'The meaning of a word is the method of its verification', to quote a celebrated dictum, which however is no longer accorded general validity nowadays, because methods of establishing or verifying something are never settled once and for all. They develop along with the sciences and the scientific equipment; and that process is stimulated precisely by paying continuous, nay, methodical attention to the inadequacy of the operational criterion (the verification-method) in respect of the phenomenon to be described. If one really insists on taking the narrower operational meaning of a word as determining its whole meaning, then one is cutting oneself off from the possibility of discovering further alternatives in the approach to this or that phenomenon. For an operationalism of that sort the meaning of phenomena (such as colour blindness, mind, work-satisfaction, time) is vested entirely in the operations carried out by man as the controller of such phenomena. In that way transcendence – or to put it more simply, man's scope for action – is forfeit.

All this calls for some further comment. In physical science P. W. Bridgman has pointed out the usefulness of operational definitions, for example, of the term 'time'; and in psychology B. F. Skinner has done the same. In later work, however, both men have also pointed to the limitations inherent in operational definitions. To assess 'work satisfaction' exclusively with the aid of insufficient test criteria may have disastrous consequences in practice, should the discrepancy between the offi-

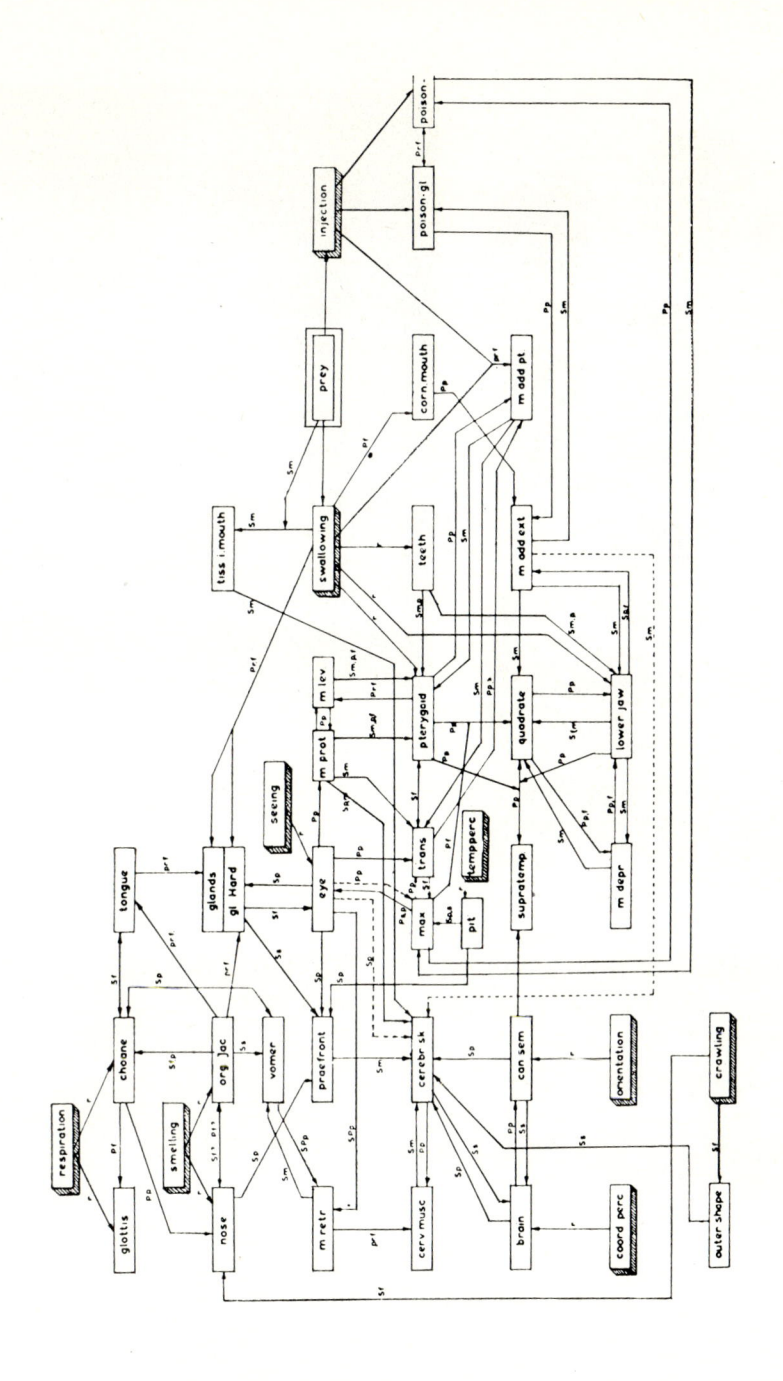

40 Operational diagram of a snake.

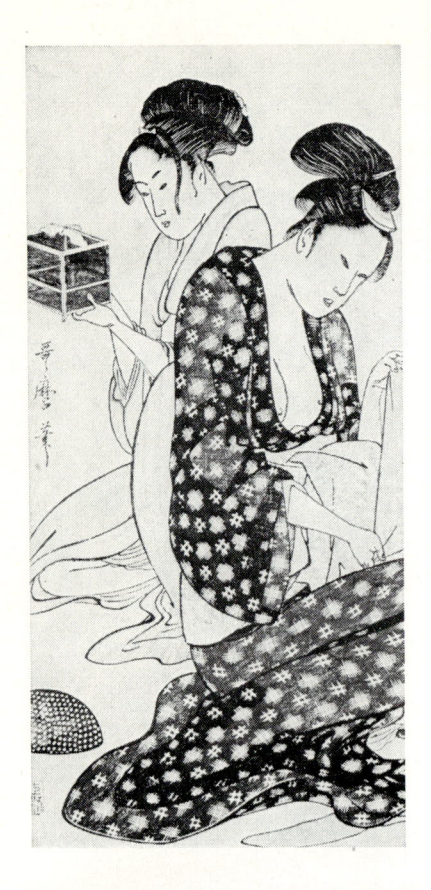

42 Substantialist representation:
F. Boucher, Venus.

← 41 Ontologically based notion of form:
Kitagawa Utamaro, Japanese women.

43 Ontological representation: Botticelli,
Birth of Venus.

44 Substantialist architecture: castle at Neuschwanstein.

45 Ontological architecture: the temple of Vishnu in Sriranganthaswani (India).

46 Ontological with functional emphasis: G. Reni, Atalanta and Hippomenes.

47 Functional representation: M. Mascherini, The Song of Songs.

cial operational investigation and their own experiences be detected by the workers. In the context of this chapter, however, we need not go into any more detailed examples. It is better to point out what is the general tendency: for an operationalist reduction of phenomena to result in a one-sided exercise of control on man's part. The functional reference is lost; and the very nature of the phenomena is constituted by their operations.

This trend becomes ominous when it begins to affect the whole existence of man and society. Is it on occasion possible to operationalize man himself? Take as a simple illustration of this the card index kept by a super-specialist in some branch of medicine. Information about patients is obtained through the work of nurses, psychologists, doctors and so forth, and is then entered on a card. The super-specialist does not himself visit the patient but issues his instructions, basing them on the up-to-date information entered on the relevant card. It has happened, of course, that owing to a misunderstanding a daily entry of information has been made on a card and the specialist has issued his instructions on the strength of it, when the patient was already dead. From an operationalist viewpoint the patient had continued to exist!

The same issues arise if we envisage the divine and, for instance, norms in purely operationalist terms. The surplus value – that which remains above and beyond each momentary experience, operation or definition – disappears. The powers with which man is always being confronted are displanted by their own operational imitations; so that the divine, for example, is nothing but the projection-mechanism of man's feelings, values nothing but guidelines or directions laid down for the better governance of society. But along with all this man's own identity disappears as well. Just as substantialism reduces man to a solipsism, so does operationalism reduce him to a mere cipher or role. Man is then swallowed up in the rules of a comprehensive, bureaucratic apparatus; or else he is totally exteriorized in the many roles he finds allotted to him. He is then simply the role that is expected of him, and ceases to be himself. The door is wide open to such expressions as 'other-directedness' and 'self-alienation'.

The contrast between the functional and the operational is again illustrated by the modes of portraying woman in modern art (ill. 60 and 62, p. 128) and from architecture (ill. 65 and 66, p. 130). An illustration of the structures of the three stages (mythical, ontological, functional) and of their negative components (magical, substantialist, operationalist) may be had by comparing illustrations 15 and 25 respectively with 41 and 43 and with 47 and 60 (representations of woman), 45 with 63 (architecture) and by comparing the illustration of negative components 26 with 42 and 62 and illustration 27 with 44 and 66. So far as the illustrations we are presently discussing are concerned, Giacometti's interpretation puts an even heavier emphasis on the 'how', so that the effect is to imbue the material with a more unyielding, intractable aspect, even, than is the case with the already functional version offered by Mascherini (ill. 47, p. 108). It is hardly surprising – illustration 15 (p. 46) and 16 (p. 47) having already served to show this – that Giacometti's work likewise has some affinity with mythical art, as witness the figurine of an Etruscan goddess (ill. 61, p. 128). In its surrealistic fashion Dali's 'Burning Giraffe' reflects an operationalist view: the opened drawers and the whole rigid and gadgety manner of treating the female figures point to a prosaic manipulability and perhaps to the techniques of depth-psychological analysis as well (ill. 62). The functional architecture of Frank Lloyd Wright, whose now famous 'house over a waterfall' is reproduced here (ill. 63, p. 129) shows us culture and nature in a harmonious interaction. In an austere form functional architecture is anticipated in the Japanese farmstead reproduced here (on the campus of the International Christian University in Tokio; ill. 64, p. 129, and 65). Contrasting with this unpretentiousness and openness is the more self-sufficient, operational interior, designed for maximum effect (ill. 66).

The effect that operationalism has on everyday life and society is one of the central questions confronting us today. To what extent is an open and referential-cum-functional approach in danger of being battened upon by scarcely noticeable manipulations which are all the more difficult to pin down because they come not from any specific person but rather from a particular way of thinking and acting? From school textbooks right through to a range of familiar household gadgets there are certain technological artifices, patterns of persuasion, ways of setting about things and categories of thought that influence our behaviour. To distinguish here between a functional and an operationalist position is of major importance. One has only to think of the technical and organizational means available for increasing the efficiency of education and production, or of the exaggerated attention paid to sexual matters. On the one hand this brings out the liberating insight that the individual discovers himself, nay, even finds his identity in the opposite sex, in the unrestrained exercise of his sexually functioning love. On the other hand there are operationalist components too, especially when love is allowed to merge without remainder into eroticizing behaviour-patterns and feats of sexuality. Then the referential character of sexuality disappears; and functional emancipation turns into a loss of personal identity.

Functional thinking does not imply, therefore, that any change will happen automatically and as a matter of course. Operationalism is a fundamental component of the functional position, because it serves to express the tendency toward an arbitrary, high-handed attitude present in every form of human thinking. This taking over of control, as we have observed a number of times already, is at the same time a loss of identity. Man and society dissolve in the subtle web of operations in which nobody is really anybody any more. This is so because operationalism reduces all meanings into the immanence of the operations themselves; and in so doing it blocks all access to alternative ways of escape from the impasse of this loss of identity. That is why functional thinking is always more a pointer to a kind of responsibility than to a state of affairs.

V

From technology to organization

Technology as a function of the body

On the importance of technology to present-day culture hardly anything more need be said. But when it comes to the function which that technology ought to fulfil there is no agreement at all. Even so, there are developments pointing toward a more functional approach. At first the rapid development of technology was something that got out of hand, because although people recognized the usefulness of technology, they hardly knew how to incorporate this into their everyday experience and cultural creativity. This is beautifully illustrated by some of the writings left by the French flier and author, Saint Exupéry. To begin with, he observes, the machine stood for something strange, something that did not really belong. The aeroplane's engines were fixed on to the outside; and they caught the eye because of their outsize proportions and the rattling, erratic noise they made. As planes developed, however, the engines became more and more an integral part of the aircraft as a whole. The noise too became smoother and smoother, as the component parts of the mechanism became more perfect. Eventually, with the increase in speed the aerodynamic lines became important, because as little resistance as possible had to be offered to the atmosphere. This meant that the machines were assimilated to the flowing lines of our modern aircraft, lines which have even had an aesthetic fascination, so that the machine came to be part and parcel of the aeroplane's aesthetic form. The same thing happened with the sound of the engines: it became more and more regular – to such an extent, in fact, that the aviator can hardly distinguish any more between the smooth, quiet throbbing of the engines and his own heart-beat. Having come to the end of its development, says Saint Exupéry, the engine shows an inclination to conceal and thus to efface itself. Two types of aircraft, the one following not fifty years after the other and both being intended to transport a relatively large number of people, may serve to illustrate this flowing together of the lines (ill. 71 and 72, p. 139).

We were arguing in one of the previous chapters that a more functional approach will often eliminate the sharp divisions between such ontological areas as are denoted by the terms 'truth', 'goodness' and 'beauty'. This is also evident in the growth of technology. Writers like Spengler and Klages, who regarded the development of technology in a negative light, could see in its products only what was anti-aesthetic and anti-human. Nowadays people are much more alive to the possibilities of integrating technology, even aesthetically, into our culture. A traffic flyover may disrupt the landscape; but it can also be so adapted stylistically that a harmony with the surroundings is achieved. For a considerable time now 'industrial design' has been an accomplished fact, marrying industrial production with concern for aesthetic form. Conversely, a positive appreciation of technology is making its way into art; so that technical procedures in working with metal, welding techniques, the use of cement and plastic may be essential elements in a work of art.

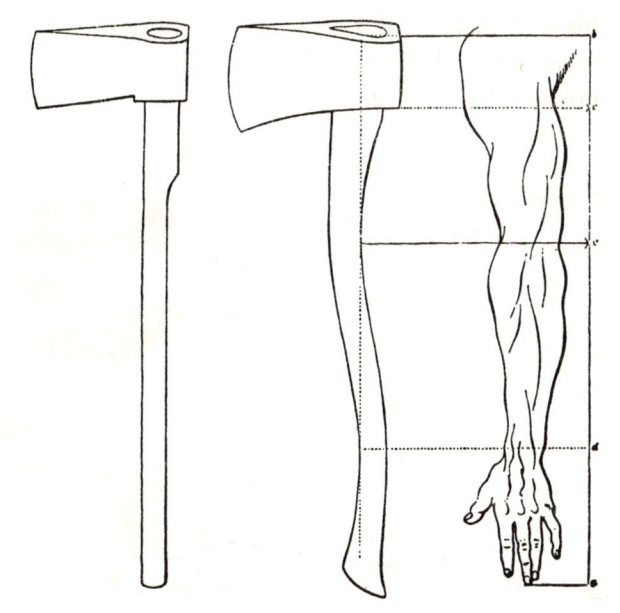

48 German and American axes; the latter compared with the human arm (as by E. Kapp).

113

All this acquires more of a background as we begin to attend to the kind of functional views of technology advanced by a number of philosophers and several biologists. They can be summed up in the proposition that technology is really an extension of the human body. These ideas are already to be found in the last century, when under the influence of the philosopher, C. G. Carus, E. Kapp framed his remarkable theory of 'organ projection'. This German emigrated to America. There he noticed that the German axe he was accustomed to using was not so efficient as the American forester's axe, which because of its curves closely resembled the human arm. Illustration 48 is taken from Kapp's book and shows both axes, the German and the American, the latter compared with the human arm.

Might one say that the human arm has to be projected onto the material so as to turn it into an efficient implement? Kapp subsequently develops this idea into a philosophical observation. Like Carus he points out that his own eye was bound to work in the very same way. Nowadays one can find this parallel between camera obscura and human eye illustrated in books dealing with physiology as well as with physics (ill. 49).

In a roundabout way, therefore, man learned from the instrument something about his own body. Had he not in fact, albeit unconsciously, already been projecting his body into this or that instrument? Kapp goes further and predicts that using this method, we shall be able to explain

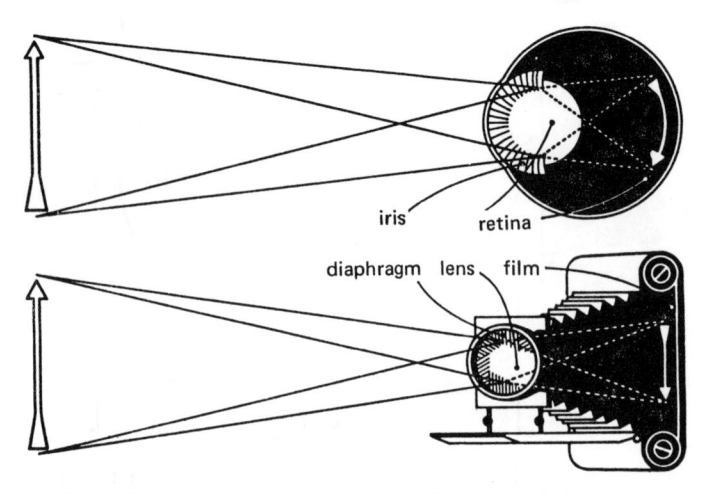

49 Resemblance between the camera obscura and the human eye.

man's nervous system in terms of telephone and telegraph wires, because man is actually projecting in them something of his own bodily processes.

Ideas of this sort are being borne out in a number of respects. Modern technology – cybernetics, let us say – has produced models that can not only help to account for human muscular action but can explain the central nervous system. Moreover, recent biological concepts support the idea that technology is an extension of organic life, more especially of the human body. If, functionally speaking, we define a biological species in terms of those vital functions which transform the environment, then we must likewise define man biologically by means of his technological functions. After all, from a biological viewpoint it is technology that makes possible the conquest of the environment and thus the further progress of life. With the animal the instrumental use of the body takes place via its bodily organs, which serve it as a weapon of attack, means of locomotion and of defence and of obtaining food, a protection against cold, and so forth. Among animals the use of implements is a sporadic business and does not lead to systematic fabrication and improvement. With man the case is different. Thus it was a feature of his human nature that Neanderthal man, who lived from one to two hundred thousand years ago, made use of a diversity of implements (visible, for instance, in the left foreground of the reconstruction depicted in ill. 73, p. 140).

Just because he extends his body in his instruments, man enjoys an enormous range: he can supplement feeble bodily organs with instruments, he can observe and measure (space and time) by means of instruments, he can put them to work while he himself relaxes and can make machines or appliances observe while he is asleep, and above all he can so change, replace and improve the instruments that the extension of his body in this way would seem likely to go on evolving for ever. A biologist has said that man really ought not to be classified as a single biological species, but he constitutes as many species as he employs types of instrument.

It is precisely this use of instruments that helps bring out a feature typical of all life: adaptation *and* resistance to the environment. In this connection L. Mumford brackets technology and art together, because they both form a culmination of the creature-creator unity that is man. Mumford argues for a synthesis of technology and art on more or less the same grounds on which in the same period H. Bergson held out a prospect of complementarity between technology and mysticism: the extension of the body and the extension of the mind constitute a single whole. Thus technology typifies man, not as someone alienated from life but as someone capable of incorporating technology into his own existence, since adaptation and organization are the two aspects of the progressive integration of non-living nature within the horizon of man's life.

The instruments are many and are always changing, a fact closely tied up with man's capacity for establishing new forms and achieving an ever evolving process of adaptation and organization. This marvellous potential for coordinating and creating instruments is intimately connected with the organ of organs, the instrument of all instruments: man's central nervous system. This capacity man has for coordination and organization will come up again in a later chapter. In the present context it needs to be pointed out to what extent man is able to express the coordinating function of his own bodily organs, to set it outside of himself, as it were, in technology. Even his own central nervous system it to a certain extent projected in modern technology.

If we are to work all this out in more detail, we must first make a point about the relief afforded to man's mental faculties by technology. One is sometimes given the impression that man is losing some of his mental powers because he is putting too much confidence in technology. Thus Coomeraswamy bemoans the fact that the introduction of printing techniques and of alphabetism in general has very much undermined the Indian's capacity to memorize things. Whereas he used to be able to rely entirely on his memory and recite great chunks of the Vedic writings by heart, he now has to pore over the written word. Yet it is highly questionable whether we should in fact regard this as an entirely bad thing. As over against considerations of that sort one might point to the relief afforded to memory and to the mind in general, thanks precisely to written words. Language and writing, L. Lavelle declares, constitute the memory of mankind. Such an unburdening, such an emptying, may well be a good thing, if it sets the mind free for new enterprises – even if that process does involve the loss of certain natural gifts. Primitive peoples, for instance, would sometimes appear to be gifted with a natural telepathic faculty. Communication between members of the tribe happens spontaneously and sometimes without any words being exchanged, messages

50 Functional release of material: J. Wagemaker, Hommage à Brassai.

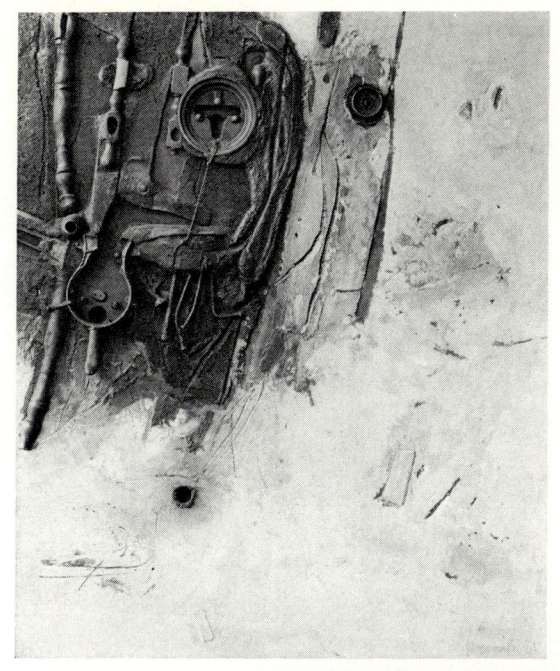

51 Functional: J. Versnel, photo of furniture.

53 The observer constructs his own perspective:
G. Braque, View of the Sacré Coeur.

52 Functional: chimney-stack,
University of York.

54 The functional notion of
God: a Kirchentag poster.

and thoughts seem to get across over great distances without the interposition of mechanical means such as drum-signals; there is often a presentiment of important events, and so on. But as civilisation and technology increase, so do these gifts disappear. The more telephones, the less telepathy. Is this a major loss? Telephony and telegraphy make some natural gifts superfluous; and yet they involve a broadening and even an extensive democratizing of natural endowments, because it is no longer the medicine-man or a favoured few who enjoy the privilege but anybody who has the apparatus necessary for communication ready to hand. The question that might well be asked, however – a question that we shall have to put with ever greater insistence in the coming chapters – is whether man does in fact utilize the forces thus released for new tasks suited to a growing, worldwide culture, equipped with every technical and organizational resource.

Technology is more than just an artificial and unnatural fact. Technology is not so much a substantive, a sum total of complicated instruments; it is more a verb, at any rate the deposit of man's technical activity. The most far-reaching, long hidden potentialities of the human body are brought out in technology. That is why, as we were describing earlier on, man often gets to learn about his own bodily functions indirectly, by way of his own technological inventions; and it is also why some natural gifts of human nature perish, or rather, are taken over by technology. But in a sense they are then not destroyed, at least as long as the technology does not turn into an alien obstacle but remains linked to the proper bodily existence of men as an extension and manifestation of it. This is how the difference between the body of the animal and that of man comes to light, because the latter is bringing out new possibilities all the time, so opening up a history without end. Various authors, including F. Meyer, have therefore concluded that biological evolution continues in man in the form of technological evolution. Evolution is purely biological when it is just the distinctive bodily form that is changed, as well as the behaviour patterns associated with it, as we can see in the slow evolution from unicellular creatures to pluricellular marine animals to vertebrates, and when these in turn acquire a yet more highly organized form in the primates. But among these primates it is man in whom evolution spills over, as it were, into the external world: matter is transformed into an extension of the organic bodily form; and so evolution finds itself allotted boundless scope for movement and change.

Technology as an extension of the body also implies that man will proceed to transform and control his environment. Whereas the animal is still more or less totally imprisoned within its world, man proceeds gradually to span the world itself. The human arm and hand are extended in the ritual implements with which man compasses the world in the mythical phase; they are portrayed, as being almost of a piece with the human limbs, in the rock drawing shown as illustration 55 (below). In modern technological society it is the artificial arms and hands used in modern industry for seizing hold of dangerous material which illustrate the enlarged outreach of man in this respect (ill. 75, p. 140).

Man's long technological tentacles embrace the landscape, lines of communication span the world, electronic brains circle around neighbouring planets. Thus technology turns out to be a great deal more than the purely material phenomenon it is often, and wrongly, taken to be. Technology is above all a way of evolving, of acting, of making history. The field of technology marks the range of man's responsibility.

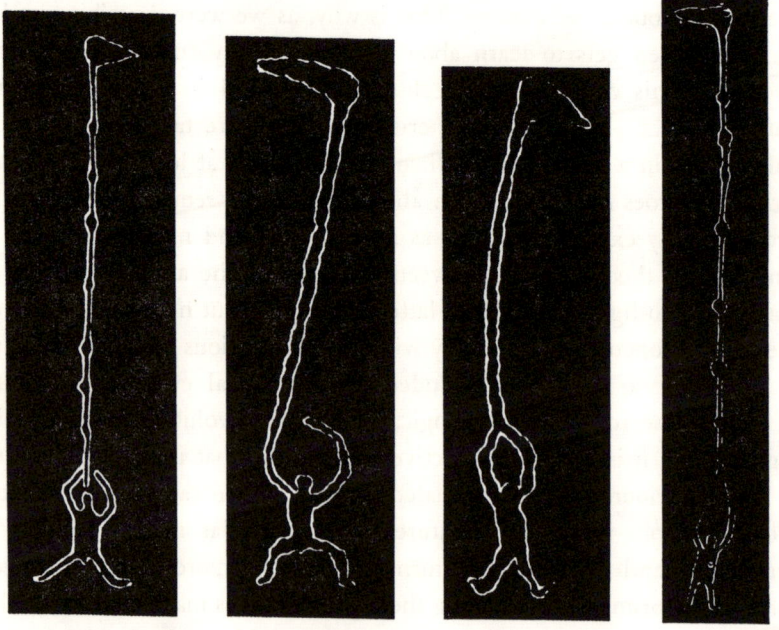

55 Extensions to the human hand: ritual implements in a prehistoric rock-drawing.

Technology as a function of mind

It really is impossible to see technology as simply and solely a manifestation of the human body. The fact is that if we give a primarily functional account of the human body in its open potentialities for transforming the world around, and therefore in its not purely natural but more historical role, this in itself entails a consideration of what manifests itself as the mind of man. This comes out in the evolution of technology, which one can regard as an increasing exteriorization of various human functions. To begin with, technology consists in a process of adaptation to the forces of nature, a utilizing of man (as slave) and beast, of wind, fire and water. The tool is one of man's first creative achievements, which he has to deploy in using natural forces, because of his need for the lever, pole, shoulder-harness, windsail and the like. Technology in this preliminary phase Mumford describes as 'eotechnology'. A subsequent phase in which the machine plays a primary role he calls 'paleotechnology'; and the most recent phase of technological evolution (characterized by the use of electricity, for instance) he calls 'neotechnology'.

In this chapter we too shall be working with the threefold division to some extent analogous to Mumford's but with the stress more on the process of advancing exteriorization that accompanies technological evolution. With Steinbuch and others we would distinguish: machine technology, energy technology and information technology. These three constitute phases in the development of technology. Its roots are to be found, prior to the machine period, in the eotechnology to which we referred a moment ago and which had at first a highly mythical orientation. Machine technology comes into being largely within an ontological outlook. In energy technology, and especially in information technology, there is the fulfilment of a more functional approach. All three forms of technology come about through an increasing exteriorization of man's faculties. We shall describe this in greater detail below, when it will become clear that technology is more and more assuming the character of an exteriorization of the functions of the human mind ('memory', 'associating', 'learning').

Machine technology exteriorizes mainly the muscular functions of man. From the lever to the modern fleet of machines we can see how man's energy has been enormously enhanced and how at the same time various kinds of operations can be greatly accelerated. Obviously, a machine is not to be regarded as simply an extension of man's muscular movements. A machine usually combines a whole range of tools, which is why it also incorporates various rules of coordination. Human muscles do not in point of fact work as independent implements, but in the context of man's total behaviour in a physical sense, which in turn is itself orientated on concrete situations that have to be recognized and controlled. Attempts have often enough been made to explain man in terms of his own product, the machine or implement; but the result of this was on the one hand to reduce him to an isolated and in that sense 'abstract' mechanism, and on the other to ensure that he barred his own way to any amplification of what is to be understood by 'machine'. We should therefore not seek to explain man in terms of the machine but vice versa: the machine by reference to man, in order to explore possibilities of progressively subtilizing the machine, refining it and involving it in tasks properly attuned to human situations. Thus in an endless process the machine can be 'concretized', that is, taken up into man's evolution in culture and history. The machine is not a thing in its own right, but through the lines of projection supplied by the distinctive bodily character of man is bound up with man's entire social and cultural context. Thus a society where slavery exists, as it did in the ancient world, is not going to arrive very quickly at a machine industry, even if scientifically speaking – one thinks, for example, of mechanics, which already existed in ancient times – the conditions for it are present. A mythical world view must also make impossible the objectivizing processes necessary for a machine technology. In contemporary studies concerned with cooperation for development research into the context of technology is once more becoming urgent.

From all this two main points emerge. One is that machine technology can be seen as primarily an exteriorization and enlargement of man's muscular strength. The second is that these technological machines must never be envisaged simply as things-in-themselves, since they are always tied to the total context of human culture. Both points serve to remind us that technology can never be a cut-and-dried affair; for it is an open process, embodying on an increasing scale the potentialities that are within man. Technological development is something that never ceases to engage his concern. Forms of society, methods of organization, the training of technicians, projecting technical modes of discourse, development of the applied sciences: it is all part and parcel of technological evolution. A detailed study would have to give all this much more minute consideration; and that would reveal the many phases and innumerable shades of difference through which technological evolution advances. This will not be necessary, however, for the more general observations we wish to make here, the purpose of which is to emphasize, from the standpoint of technological development, man's organizational responsibility. That is why we are able to restrict ourselves to an outline of the three phases of technological evolution.

As man's faculties are continually being exteriorized in technology, scientific and social factors come into play. An energy technology is possible only as and when science makes some headway in the field of mechanics and the analysis of different forms of energy. In a social context working conditions are progressively lightened, and habits and customs refined, concomitantly with the shift of the technical instrument over to the force impelling that instrument, as happens with an energy technology. That technology does after all produce the power that must drive the machine. Of course, even in the eotechnology use was made of natural sources of energy such as running water and wind. But that man would himself be in a position to produce these forces – that came about only after thousands of years. The petrol-horse, patented in France at the end of the last century, still conforms entirely to the natural shape of a provider of energy, but has already made the crucial step from a source of energy deriving from nature to one constructed by man (ill. 56).

We can say that the steam-engine (1850), the electrical hydraulic

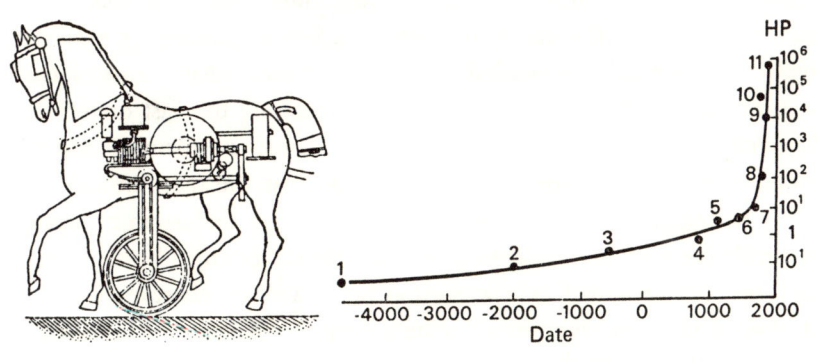

56 Petrol-horse (patented in the 19the century).

57 Graph of increasing energy production.

generating plant (1930) and rocket propulsion (1955) are landmarks (see F. Meyer's chart, ill. 57) in the development of an energy technology.

In this particular technology man as it were externalizes potentialities that lie deeper below the surface of his bodiliness than did the projection of his muscular strength in machine technology. Our energy technology reflects and so makes clearer the fact that we must not interpret man himself just by reference to the models provided by his own technological production. Muscles are not machines that can be isolated. Muscular contraction requires a specific supply of energy, which in a very refined way is provided within the human body by chemical substances (such as ATP) containing a lot of latent energy. Thus an energy technology integrates the machine into a broader, more dynamic context, standing closer to the archetypal instance of technology: man himself. The more technology approximates to man – or to put it another way, the more man exteriorizes his own capacities in technology – the better will technology function and the more will it relieve man, enabling him to shoulder other tasks. In the case of the classical machine man still has to supply the energy himself or get it from the forces of nature. In an energy technology man couples together mechanisms, some of which carry out the mechanical operations whilst others furnish the energy needed for the purpose.

This development is continued into the third phase: that of information technology. When the energy for powering mechanisms is itself supplied by machines, then the only job left for man to do is to superintend those mechanisms. Now information technology provides mechanisms that take over even this regulatory function. For controlling or regulating machines information is needed. We have to know what norms to assign to a mechanism; for instance, whether it is running too fast or too slow. We must also observe how the machine is in fact performing and then compare our observations with the norm, so that the machine can eventually be regulated in such a way as to obviate any undesirable variation. A regulative machine must therefore possess something like a 'memory', with the norm retained in it, as well as being able to 'observe' deviations. By means of a reactive process (the cybernetic principle) the deviation can then be eliminated.

Contributory to this information technology, therefore, are a number of important new inventions in the field of mechanics, for each one of which, taken severally, there have been precedents. For a start, just think of servomechanisms. This is a combination of mechanisms on two sorts of level. The first one supplies the 'brute force' and requires a great deal of energy: this does duty as a slave or 'servus'. The sole purpose of the second one is to guide or control the first and, just as the lame leads the blind man on whose shoulders he is seated, is as it were grafted onto it. For this master or managing agent only a little energy is needed: a slight pressure of the knee or a weak electric current can be enough to control a large machine. The steering control of a car is a familiar example of this. Then we might mention cybernetics or the study of regulative control, which analyses and programmes the reactions, that is, the possibilities of feeding back from a given output a signal that will regulate the input. Both these factors have a role to play in the thermostat of a central heating system. The third thing of some importance is the technical possibility of coding and storing information. Punch-cards are a splendid example of that and can be used as a 'memory' for cybernetic mechanisms. A fourth mechanism is that of information recovery: machines that make observations for the purposes of a regulative system, in a simple form by means of a photographic cell, for instance, and in much more complicated forms where a whole succession of instruments and calculating equipment comes serially into operation. This last brings us finally to a fifth possibility: that of combining and processing data logically, an example of which is provided by the calculating machine.

The combination of all these possibilities has resulted in computer technology, which makes it feasible to collect, store and process information to logical conclusions, to establish norms and control them, in short to put into practice information-processes that can effectively regulate machines and sometimes directly assist man in taking action and making decisions. In this connection such terms as 'observing', 'memory', 'thinking' have been used, terms indicating the extent to which man has indeed exteriorized here many more intrinsic capabilities of his own in the machine. Information technology, therefore, is an extremely subtle interplay of electronic apparatus, networks, rheostats, linking mechanisms – and all this in association with artificial languages for 'feeding' such mechanisms and with programming that will settle and record the overall impact of their action. In comparison with machine- and energy-technology, information technology presents an extremely refined, flexible and indeed cunning aspect. The hand of man wields the axe-blade to be seen in the foreground of illustration 73 (p. 140); but the selfsame hand may also clasp the punch-cards belonging to this information-epoch: cards which really relate now not to the human hand but to the human brain (ill. 74, p. 140). Man has taken several hundred thousand years to perfect the dressing of stone, but only a few thousand years to move over from the Stone Age to the Atomic Age. It is 50,000 years since the human skull showed any obvious sign of further anatomic evolution: the evolution of culture has taken over from genetic evolution.

In the course of development from machine- to information-technology the focal point shifts from the 'what' to the 'how'. Of course the functional aspect is not absent in the case of the classical machine, because the coordination of component parts and rules of procedure are factors even there. Energy-technology, however, is more refined in any case, because at the centre here is the generation and input of the energizing impulse. But what is paramount in information technology is the variety of ways in which machines can be regulated. Then too information technology has come to play an independent role, simply by functioning as a processer and gatherer of data. No longer does the computer serve merely to regulate large machines or industries. It has become an end in itself: man can not only get information technology, in conjunction with other technologies, to carry out his work (including his managerial functions) for him, but he can also put his questions directly to the computer in order to obtain a solution to problems with which his thinking and decision-making confront him. Although the computer takes neither the decision nor the responsibility out of his hands completely, information technology can unquestionably perform a great deal of preliminary work and by operating more swiftly and more logically can even obviate a lot of mistakes and purely emotional decisions. It is precisely in cases of this sort that the functional aspect of information technology comes to the fore: the relations between various factors are determined, the relevance of information vis-à-vis a set of given criteria is registered, disparate data are processed to yield a coherent result, in short, guidelines emerge as to how one should proceed to use the data in question, marshal chaotic data in a logical fashion and take them as a basis for making decisions.

The outcome of technology in this case is an exteriorization of the

58 O. Zadkine, The ravaged city.

59 Without the aperture the same sculpture looks cumbersomely substantialist.

61 Mythical representation of goddess (Etruscan).

60 Functional delineation of woman by Giacometti.

62 Operational version of woman: S. Dali, Burning giraffe.

128

63 Functional architecture: Frank Lloyd Wright, House over a waterfall.

64 Functional architecture: Japanese farmhouse.

65 Functional architecture: interior of the house in ill. 64.

66 Operational: architecture dominated by a pretentiously technological style.

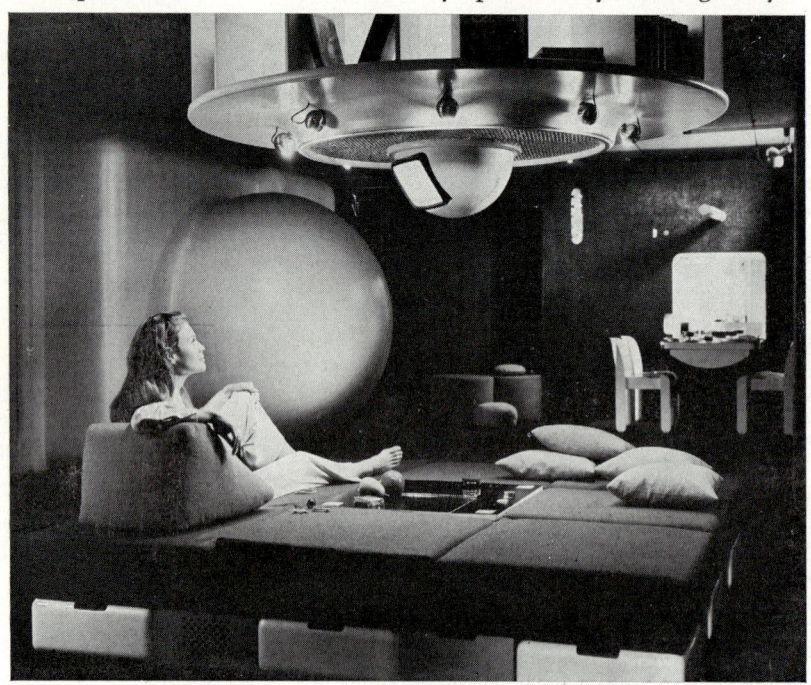

human brain; and so it assumes more of a mental character than a material one. Again, we are helped the better to distinguish that brain in its functional aspect, thanks to a study of the logical, conjunctive processes which qua exteriorization actually furnish a model of the human brain. The point is frequently made that 'information' constitutes a quite distinct category alongside matter and energy, because while matter (e.g., printer's ink, flags) or energy (e.g., electric impulses) are as substrata admittedly indispensable to information, the latter is not itself a derivative of them. The same information may be conveyed by letter, radio, flag-signals and the like, where the quality of information is more directly linked to the ordering of the material (that is, to the 'how') than to the material itself (the 'what'). All this may serve on the one hand to show that the human mind is not just an isolated, immaterial substance, but is very much of a piece with the whole organizational scheme of the human body and brain, and on the other hand that technology – certainly information technology – is not simply and solely a material phenomenon but is intimately bound up with various regulative processes exteriorized by the mind of man.

Man's activity as organizer

We have said on more than one occasion already that by reducing man without remainder to the models of man that he produces in his technology we do him an injustice. Technology constitutes an aspect of man's evolution, an unfinished process; and in the forward movement of his technology man is continually externalizing, as it were, new potentialities that lie deeper below the surface. We have also pointed out the interconnection between technology and human culture as a whole, social constellations and that sort of thing. Technology resembles art, for example, in its capacity to expose new forces and new powers latent in man; and thereby man discloses in some measure how he tries to find his proper relation to the powers that affect the individual and society.

Information technology uncovers precisely this kind of new horizon: man's capacity for organization. In itself that capacity is nothing new. In inflexible and hereditary forms an ability to organize is present even in the animal kingdom. The society of primitive cultures is characterized by what are sometimes very stringent, equilibrated forms of organization. The expressions of human culture in ritual, art, decoration, the dispensing of justice, fabrication of tools: all this calls for the organization of labour and of behaviour. Thus one of the oldest of human activities, hunting, demands a carefully considered form of organization; which is why the hunt presents a consistent pattern over the centuries, whether as related to the mythical phase (rock-drawing, ill. 76, p. 149) or the ontological (hunting scene by Paolo Uccello, ill. 77, p. 149).

In a more primitive society, however, this organizing activity is still very largely subordinated to the myths which form the supreme regulative system and, because they refer back to a primeval age, lie beyond the immediate outreach of any structuring on the part of man. Within a more ontological thought-pattern organization tends to be an activity based on a given substantial factor, be it princely ruler, or church, timeless ideas, or an arcane, immutable 'human nature'. The functional approach, on the other hand, puts man's organizing activity more at the centre. It is from the 'how' that we learn to recognize the 'what', not vice versa. The modern questions of chaos or order, senselessness or meaning, are issues that relate to the way in which personal existence and society are organized. And if forms of organization become rigid, thing-like structures, that does not put an end to opposition or protest, because renewal is of the essence of each and every organizational process.

Information technology is not, of course, identical with the whole capacity for organization, but forms a distinctive component feature of it. Information is never a matter of disjointed data; but information technology processes the data into an organizational whole. Generally speaking, therefore, modern methods of organization make use of information technology. Organizing is in fact a business of gathering information and processing it so as to produce an effect on the milieu. E. Schrödinger says, à propos of living organisms, that they can only keep themselves going by incorporating material from their environment and assimilating it to the highly organized structures of their cells and of their whole dynamic economy. This leads him to declare that living creatures nourish themselves not so much on foodstuff as on order. This displacement of the 'what' (foodstuff) by the 'how' (order) we can express even more vividly by saying that man and his communities are nurtured on information. Information (and with it the sciences, for example) then ceases to

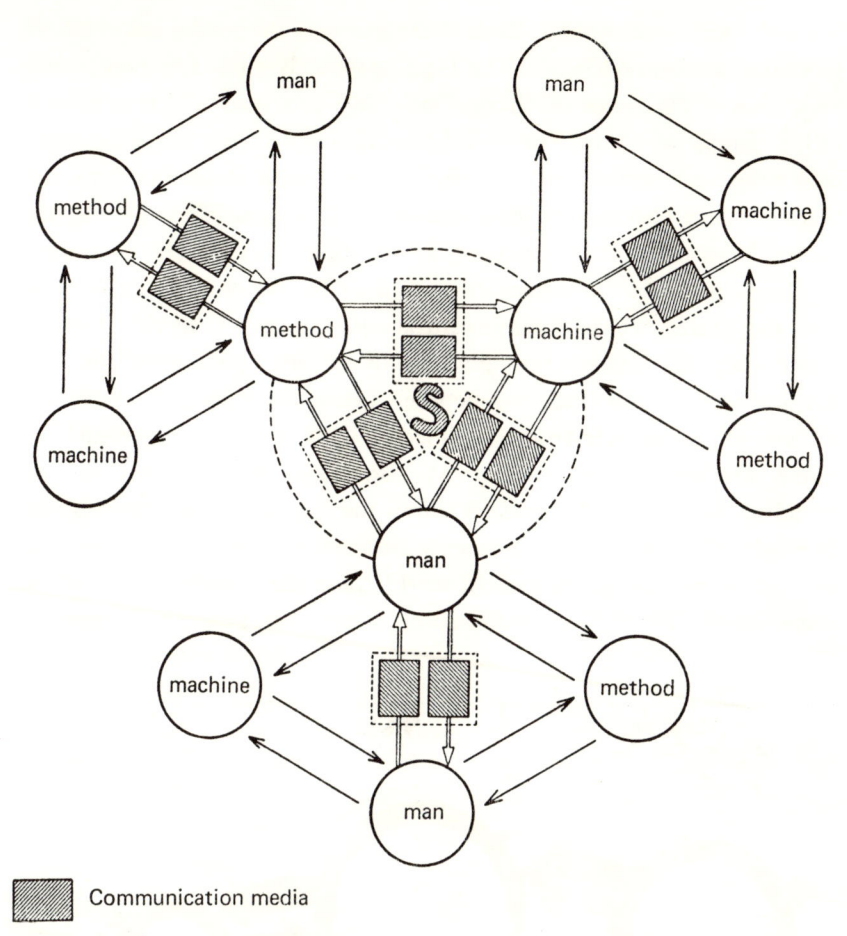

67 Organizational diagram (from: H. Thierry, *Organisatie en leiding*.

be a substantial end in itself; instead, it serves to reinforce man's potential, the opportunities at his disposal for finding the right relationship to the world around him.

Organization is a characteristic feature of open systems. By 'system' we mean a composition of elements of which one can say that they constitute a unity by virtue of the circumstances in which that system exists. In this sense the term 'system' is used in biology, physics, psychology, organization-theory and so forth. Such totalities used to be described more as a kind of things; and the unity of such a totality was formulated on a basis of common attributes. Thus there emerged the model based on the substance/attributes scheme. The term 'system' is more functional: even very diverse categories of things, including processes which cannot be called 'things' at all, may be pulled together as a system by virtue of the conditions and methods of procedure which, being invariants, turn such heterogeneous elements as these into a single system. Thus people, machines, rules of conduct, precepts, information-processes and so on may together constitute one system, because their totality consists in the function they fulfil within their organizational context. One can therefore create diagrams designed to give an operational picture of the communication-processes occurring between persons, methods and machines. Scheme 67, taken over from H. Thierry, helps us to see very clearly the interaction between the system (S), formed in this way, and the surrounding subsystems. Scheme 68 shows the import and export processes in world trade, where the continents are envisaged as systems. These are only crude models, of course. In world trade the European Market, the countries of Eastern Europe and so on form more genuine systems; and

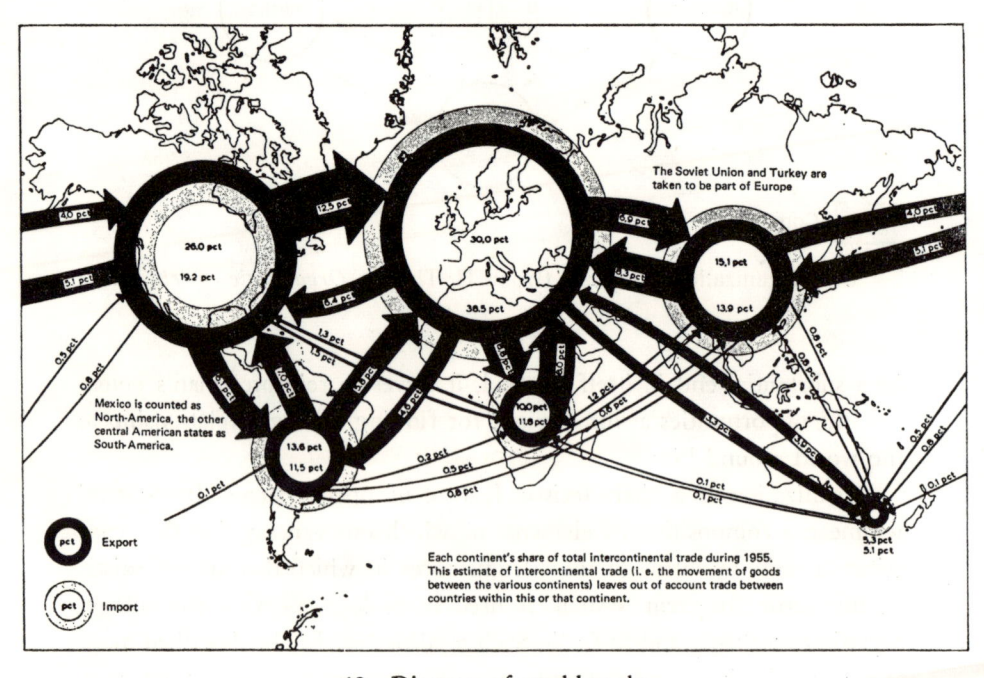

68 Diagram of world trade.

then the association of partners outside the central system – say, of African countries with the European Market – inevitably makes it a more complicated affair. It requires little enough imagination to form a mental picture, in the vein of illustrations 76 and 77 (p. 149), of the unutterably complicated, colourful and frequently dramatic scenes that make up the real processes and events behind such operational schemes.

It must already have become clear to some extent that a system is much less self-evident and immediately accessible than a thing. One has to be able to delimit a system. Thus it will not be all that easy for the non-expert to recognize a system in a group of animals plus a certain territory, including possibilities of feeding, rules of behaviour and so forth; a great many things in the immediate environment of such animals fall outside the system; things that it would not occur to him to consider, such as distant noises made by other animals, belong to the system. Now we can view a system entirely by itself or in association with the milieu, with its surroundings. In the former case we speak of a closed, and in the latter case of an open, system. An open system is harder to fence off than a closed one, as a process of interaction is going on all the time: an open system keeps itself going by extracting all sorts of things (matter, energy, information) from the environment and using them to build itself up. In respect of such open systems we speak of the organizational activity. It is an activity; for an open system is never rounded off, never over and done with: that would spell death to the system. An open system is properly described as 'meta-stable', in that it continues in being through all the changes and chances of growth and decay, even though all its elements (e.g., constituent cells, or personnel) may be replaced in the process. That is why in the case of an open system a dynamic and functional definition in terms of its organizational pattern is better than a static one, in terms of its constitutive elements.

For the reasons we have just explained we can define 'organization' here as a typical feature of open systems, in that their tendency is to maintain themselves in an incessant process of interaction with their environment. More relevant, therefore, than the noun 'organization' is the verb 'to organize'. The organization is a structure which is secondary, however, to the function. The most important question is not what an organization consists of, but what its purpose is meant to be. This makes sufficiently clear the connection with information-processes, because information comes about through the arranging of elements in a specific order; but as to what those elements consist of (smoke-signals, electric impulses), that is a more or less haphazard business. As a process organization is something wider than an interchange of information, because it engenders the whole internal arrangement of elements and subsystems, as well as governing whatever interaction takes place with the environment.

What end is served by organization? In the case of biology it is perhaps enough to answer: the maintenance of life. In the case of human culture, however, such a reply is inadequate and would indeed reduce that culture to a purely biological function. In its turn, life itself is evaluated in a particular way, on the basis of an organization: namely, that of our view, our understanding of life. Is it meaningful or meaningless? Are there cases where to prolong life just becomes pointless? Such questions are being raised nowadays in, for instance, the medical sciences. Later on we shall be going into this in order to show that the question of what is socially and morally meaningful cannot be resolved out of hand, on purely biological or even sociological grounds. As we shall see, an entirely new learning process, embracing the whole of mankind, is needed to give fresh answers to the question of what end is to be served by the organization of modern culture. At all events it is essential for every human organization to indicate repeatedly – and that will mean, as often as not, creatively – what are the ends, the objectives, of the organizational process.

All this goes to show that such a process must never lead to a state of fixity. An organization which is not on the move will fall into a state of disorganization and is in danger of perishing altogether. Of course, one can often establish an organizational scheme or 'blueprint' which goes on functioning well for a considerable time. But then there comes a critical moment at which some transformation is necessary. It is important to recognize such critical moments; and we shall be helped to do so if we never cease to regard the organization, even though it remains apparently stable for quite a time, as a process of continuous interaction.

This interaction has two aspects: adaptation and transformation. If one is determined simply to change the world around, without oneself trying to achieve a proper degree of adaptation, the organization spins out of control and ceases to make any point. If one is bent simply on adaptation, then the organization becomes unduly passive and with some change in the situation it can no longer muster the energy and imagination to cast itself in new moulds.

There is a marked difference between human organizations and those of the animal kingdom. We were describing earlier on how technology is a form of evolution in which, instead of the body itself being transformed (as in the case of the animals), the material environment is put to use. That gives to human evolution a much broader range, so that evolution proceeds to work itself out not just in nature any more, but in history. It remains to be pointed out in that connection that this has also made possible a tremendous acceleration of evolution. The transformation in the nature of living forms, for instance, the development of the five toes possessed by the earliest horse (eohippus) into the modern horse's hoof has taken millions of years. The transformation within human history of one kind of implements into another and better kind can happen within a century. Hence the charts (taken from F. Meyer: 69, graph of increasing speeds, with the several peaking curves taking over the one from the other; 70, increase in the number of inventions within a given period of time) not only indicate an increase in energy-potentials and speeds achieved by various means of conveyance, but also give some idea of the shortening of the timescale on which such changes have come about. It is as though human history were flowing by the faster, precisely as we come to be conscious of technological evolution.

This business of the rate of acceleration is raised here, because yet another new factor would seem to be relevant at this point: in nature the

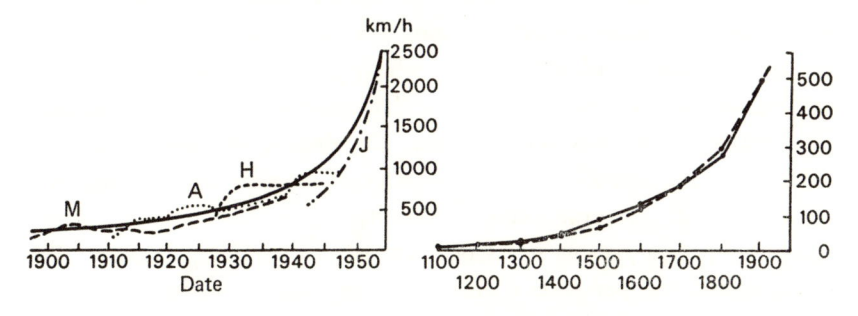

69, 70 Graphs showing the increase in speeds and the number of inventions. M: motor-car; A: aeroplane; H: hydroplane; J: jetplane.

137

forms of organization happen, without the living creatures concerned being able to exert any direct influence on them. In the history of human culture it is quite another matter. Man acquires ever greater opportunities to influence and control his evolution himself. To begin with, his technology only enables him to interfere with the world of nature that surrounds him; but eventually he proceeds to condition his own nature as well, through the medical and social sciences. The more man encroaches upon the course of evolution, the faster it is able to move. His very nature becomes increasingly amenable to modelling and variation within history – which is a sharp blow to the old idea of an unchanging and unchangeable 'human nature'. What sort of creature man actually is becomes more and more a matter of how he acts upon himself and his society.

We were saying earlier on that in the technological phases of processing matter, then energy, then information man brings out and subjects to his control ever deeper and deeper potentialities from within himself. The result has been to set nature increasingly, if gradually, within the range and encompassing power of man, instead of the other way round. What has been said about man's capacity for organization makes this even more conclusive. Modifying his own nature and piloting evolution, these things would seem to be the very stuff of organizing. The alien powers of nature, encountered in fear and trembling within a mythical world and in an ontological world described from a distance, now at last lie within the functional orbit of man. Organization is the system of rules, the totality of dynamic guidelines, which one pursues in order to exert an influence on widely separated things and processes. The element of control plays some part in every organization. When a bicycle is steered by its rider in a sudden gust of wind, this in itself evinces to some extent an organization of movements, which goes along with the cyclist's learning to control his motor (muscular movements) and informatory (observations) faculties. Furthermore, the degree of control can only be known in relation to the ends and purposes we mentioned before: ends characteristic of any organizational activity.

All this puts a greater stress on man as an organizing creature. First of all, within the perspective created by technology the world came to be located within the body of man, now extended and enlarged. In the second place it appeared that in consequence of this technological evolu-

71 An aeroplane of 1920: with a few well wrapped up passengers a DH9 leaves Schiphol for London.

72 An aeroplane of 1969 the Concorde, capable of carrying 132 passengers, and built jointly by Sud-Aviation and the U.K.

73 Neanderthal men with implements.

74 Human hand with punch-cards.

75 Extensions of the human hand: 'grabbers' in modern industry.

tion it is the *mind* of man that encompasses the world. All that is intensified by organization on man's part, which through technology, various means of information and rules of conduct proceeds to control the surrounding world. The world of nature is brought more and more within the orbit of human history. As he learns to organize, man no longer perceives outside himself an alien and threatening nature but the illimitable sphere of his own responsibilities. He is bound to keep on raising the question of the meaning of man and society in order to arrive at those provisional aims which give direction to his organizational programme. Man qua organizer breaks open the world as a natural and closed system, turning it into a structure that points beyond itself. The world, within the history of man's organizing activities, itself becomes 'word', that is, becomes part of a considered and formulated programme. The thing, itself static, comes within the motive action. Culture, it would seem, is the precipitate of a strategy.

VI

Culture as a programme

Culture as a learning process

All living creatures affect their environment and in one way or another make their mark upon it. From tracks, nests, burrows, gnawed trees and the like one can often recognize which sort of animal lives in this or that territory. Man, however, has a much more radical and varied way of affecting his environment. Whereas an animal will, generally speaking, adapt itself to the world around it, man adapts his surrounding world to himself; and whereas an animal displays only a modest degree of variation and development in its behaviour, man shows evidence of a very dynamic history, so that man is continually producing new forms which he has an ever increasing ability to control. The development of technology and of his capacity for organization, as outlined in the previous chapter, is evidence enough for this.

Most animals not only possess inherited patterns of behaviour, but in the course of their lives are also able to acquire new patterns or to modify existing ones. This is known as 'learning'. Yet this learning would seem to have only to a very limited extent a lasting effect on animal behaviour. There may perhaps in the long term be some deposit in the form of hereditary changes – the question is matter for dispute – and if so, this would mean that not everything thus acquired is lost again at death. But in general hereditary transfer of what has been learned is not possible for animals. How should it, after all, apart from the carriers of hereditary characteristics contained within its own body, package what had been acquired so as to bequeath it to the following generations?

But what man has acquired by learning – and with him this is a great deal more than with the animals – he can of course transfer apart from his own body, apart, that is, from the route provided by biological heredity. As to packaging, he has the possibility at his command of using language. A subsequent generation can get to know, and commit to memory, by the use of language whatever previous generations have achieved, so that nothing is wasted. What each generation learns is then piled on top of what has already been acquired by earlier generations; and so there is an enormous accumulation of knowledge and understanding. There is no need for men to suffer all over again the trials through which former generations had to live and learn. Obviously, as soon as it becomes possible to commit language to writing, then to code it in abstract symbols and store such data mechanically (information technology), there then emerge even wider opportunities for the accumulation of learning processes.

Thus what is really involved in this transference is a type of heredity which by-passes the body, a socio-cultural heredity, as various biologists (Dobzhansky, Waddington) have called it. Here again we see how man is able to exteriorize, to bring out bodily potentialities, and so to achieve much broader, much more rapid transformations. This field of transformations is human culture. Whilst the animal continues to live and act within nature, man develops himself in culture. Culture is a persistent transforming of nature; and to that culture belong man's technology and organizational skills, which we were discussing earlier on. Just because culture covers such a wide area of human activity, from agriculture, the manufacture of implements and so forth to social norms, art and religion, we should really take the medium of cultural transference and development on a broader basis than just language by itself. Certainly, language is specially characteristic of man's potentialities for learning, but can itself be seen as a component part of symbols. Man has symbols at his disposal, indeed, constructs them. As "animal symbolicum" (E. Cassirer), he is the 'culture-being' which far transcends the more stereotyped mode of existence that binds the animal to nature.

Before we go on to explain in more detail what precisely we are to understand by these symbols, and how they function, we must first reach a sharper definition of the human learning process. Learning is the acquisition of new skills, insights, rules of conduct and possibilities of expression. Properly speaking, therefore, we mean by learning a kind of acquiring which calls for something more than just natural adaptation or development. The purely natural functions, such as breathing and digesting, have come about through a long process of natural evolution.

Implicitly, that is to say, not yet as separate functions with their own specialized bodily organs, processes of this sort occur in unicellular creatures. Through differentiation and specialization there emerge in living creatures respiratory organs, a central nervous system and so on. It is difficult to describe this evolutionary process as 'learning', even though the term is so used, from time to time, in a figurative sense. 'Learning' should be called a cultural rather than a natural process, not because it is unnatural or contrary to nature, but because in the learning process nature as something given is more object than subject: in the learning process nature is transformed, whether it be nature outside of man or his own nature.

Seen from this standpoint, the whole of culture is one great learning process. In his art man is always searching for new forms of expression. In religion too he is not concerned with static entities or purely timeless truths; but in the symbols of language, signs and actions, and in relation to each new situation, he seeks to respond to the divine Power which he experiences again and again in new ways. His technology and his capacity for organization lead him to cast the means of production, the possibilities of communication and his accustomed ways of working and living into a variety of ever changing moulds. An ostensibly unalterable nature, once set within the dynamic, active context of human culture, is all the time presenting a new face, as it is drawn into the accumulative power of human history.

You live and learn; experience teaches fools, as the old saying goes. Yet it can happen that in the teeth of the harshest experience we become more foolish than ever. Indeed, prosperity and success may simply facilitate the process. Learning does of course imply an accumulation of information and experiences; but that is not to say that learning always leads to positive results. No more is culture as a learning process any guarantee of real progress and improvement. Precisely because culture is a learning process, one is bound to ask: what about criteria, and what about the ends proposed? We shall focus more on this as the central question in the next chapter.

An essential part of learning is the framing of questions. Such questions, which cannot ultimately be separated from socio-political, religious and ethical issues, indicate what is perhaps the most obvious difference from the animal's natural behaviour-pattern – although, as we have said, learning does take place there as well, but then without any recourse to symbols and therefore in more constricted forms (that of conditioning, for example). An animal may experience hesitation, confusion, possibilities of choice, even perhaps a certain amount of wonder or astonishment, but not the *question,* which quite consciously has ceased to take the natural course of events for granted. When a teacher simply pumps answers into his pupils, so that they are learnt by heart, he is pushing the pupils back onto the automatic and natural level where they will deteriorate into automata or conditioned animals. Learning is not authentic unless one has found for oneself the way out of an impasse, or how to transform an unsatisfactory situation. To do this one has to have ceased to regard such a situation as acceptable and to have set a question-mark against whatever is given in the natural course of things, so that in one's question the situation is no longer regarded as self-evident, and in that sense one has already moved above and beyond it. To put such a question is to open up other possibilities than those already given. One may envisage general concepts in language, for example, as replies to questions that reach out beyond concrete things and occurrences. Is the tree as concretely perceived something totally self-evident? Or may we perhaps wonder whether there do not exist other, and quite differently shaped, trees? The term 'tree' is a general concept, an open pattern of expectation, as it were, to be filled by innumerable objects that the future will reveal, all of which may be classified as 'tree' and recognized as 'tree'. A learning process is necessary so that starting from things as concretely and vitally encountered, one can arrive at the schematized structure of human language, which puts out feelers, so to speak, with a view to future control of as yet unfamiliar phenomena. Learning something, hence also the acquisition of knowledge, goes hand in hand with acquiring possibilities of action and experience. Culture as a learning process is tied up with the whole of man as a knowing, acting, experiencing and self-expressive being.

All this could be put in another way by using data from information theory. Human beings and animals are continually acquiring information; but in order to be 'information', it has to be recognized as such. Signals that provide one species of animal with very important information – the colour of a petal, say, for a bee, or the scent of a predator for a deer – another kind of animal will simply fail to notice, because they fall outside its vital sphere of interests and the organic equipment corresponding to that. To a limited extent animals are able to substitute for familiar, stereotyped signals new ones which simply take their place (substitution of signals in the conditioning process: the dog which learns to interpret the sound of a bell as signalizing food). Man on the other hand has an immensely large area of opportunities for learning here. He not only needs to learn how to identify certain tokens as a substitute for naturally given signals; but he has at his disposal symbols which he can design and develop for himself. The token or sign still has a natural link with the original signal, either because the token has been handed down with the behaviour-pattern (an instinctive token such as the bees' dance, indicating direction and distance of the spot where honey has been found), or because in a particular situation (and not by hereditary transmission, therefore) the token is communicated, being thrust upon the animal by the environment (as with the conditioning of an animal; only here is there a question of 'learning'). The symbol, on the other hand, is described as 'conventional' (Dewey, Whitehead, Cassirer, Langer) because it does not have this direct and natural, or extorted, relation to vital data. Sometimes the symbol is even conventional in the narrow sense of being established by agreement. Sometimes it is bound up with the whole history of the process by which the mind of man and human culture have come into being, as with the primal symbols ('archetypes') of religion and myth. That smoke is the sign of fire is true for man and for very many species of animal. That news of an outbreak of fire can also be conveyed by less natural symbols such as flag signals, morse code, newspaper reports, is true for human culture alone.

Basic symbols like 'sun', 'water', 'fish' have a function in human culture that is qualified sometimes by a religious, sometimes an artistic, sometimes a technological context as a means of communication. In fact, we can never keep these aspects entirely separate: in the life of man his instinctive existence is assimilated to a never-ending learning process in which man is always giving new meanings, new facets of significance, to the world around him. The hieroglyphics of ancient Egypt provide a beautiful example of such a process, whereby the primal symbols become a means of technological communication (ill. 78, p. 150). But this picture-writing also retains an element of aesthetic transcendence, an artistic perspective. After his visit to Egypt, Paul Klee used a six-line arrangement of colour-writing to paint a similar kind of communicative symbol-language in his 'Legende vom Nil' (ill. 79, p. 150).

It is clear from all this that learning is more than a process of gathering information. More specifically, it is a way of obtaining information which in the long term makes it possible to incorporate initially unfamiliar phenomena into patterns which are familiar. It must be obvious by now that this is especially true in man's case, because he can go on enlarging his field of information and because for him this field is much less closely tied to nature and is much more conditioned by culture. Information which one receives but which is already known to the recipient in advance we call 'redundant information'. The hairdresser who on a glorious day observes to his customer how fine the weather is is supplying redundant information. What takes place in the learning process is a conversion of information in the narrower sense (surprising or bewildering information) into redundant information. Two preconditions are involved here. First that the recipients are not so much constrained either by nature (as animals are) or by tradition (as is sometimes the case with human beings) that they are unable to stand back from the available patterns of information; in other words, that they are unable to raise any question, for to ask a question is the way to open up every given pattern of information. Secondly, that there exists some distance or discrepancy between the recipient's redundancy (subjective redundancy) and that of the learning situation (objective redundancy). This objective redundancy is what we encounter in the facts which any instructor has at his disposal, in the syllabus offered by an educational institution, in the situation of science and of practical knowledge, in acquired wisdom, in the possibilities of expression in contemporary art, and so forth. In the broadest sense objective redundancy is embodied in the entire cultural pattern of a historical period.

Culture may therefore be envisaged as an open system of rules. Open, because all the time there are flowing into it new interests, new influences, which function as 'information': for instance, the discovery of other cultures, of one's own past, of new parts of the world or natural forces; attending to economic crises or changes in society; new aspects of material, technical proficiency and of the possibilities of perception disclosed in art, and so on. Thus there is a continuous reaction (a cybernetic process): man's cultural activity is tested against its end results, its congruity or incongruity with new potentialities and aims is declared, hence there is a retroactive effect on the cultural activity itself, so that it can be controlled and even sometimes restructured. Thus an approach which takes information theory as its starting-point leads once more to the same view of culture as the great, dynamic learning-process of mankind.

Inventiveness

We must now turn our attention to a single issue. Symbols afford a greater distance to what is given in nature; and on that distance there rests the possibility of human learning, individual as well as cultural. Then the superiority lies no longer with nature or with the outward situation, as it does for the animals; but in the learning-process of culture nature and situations are drawn into the orbit of man's ability to regulate them. This can sometimes mean that a whole situation may be not simply extended but even restructured. A simple example taken from language may serve to illustrate that. The term 'tree' makes it possible for us to experience and deal with surprising and bewildering forms, which so far are unfamiliar, as familiar after all ('But that thing is a tree!'), so that what was unknown can be reduced to redundancy. Anyone standing by a river, however, may point to the tree and say that it would be a good 'boat'. In knowledge as well as in action what is taking place here is a restructuring of the thing given, which encroaches upon a situation in a creative way. If a human being who has always been called 'slave' is all of a sudden referred to as 'free', then this is an even more creative encroachment on the whole social world.

This point makes it clear that objective redundancy is itself not static and is not comparable with the much more stereotyped, instinctive patterns of animal, natural society. The symbols are themselves 'conventional' in the sense that they belong to human culture and fall within a field of responsible action. And here it is often the turn of individuals to bring about a new outlook and so to form a starting-point for the cultural learning-process. This is not to say that without any relation to the history of his culture and the rules of symbolic interpretation belonging to his own time an individual can bring about a new way of

76 Prehistoric rock-drawing: hunting scene.

77 P. Uccello, Hunting scene.

149

78 From basic symbol to communication: journey in the hereafter (Egyptian tomb-drawing).

79 From basic symbol to communication: P. Klee, Legende vom Nil.

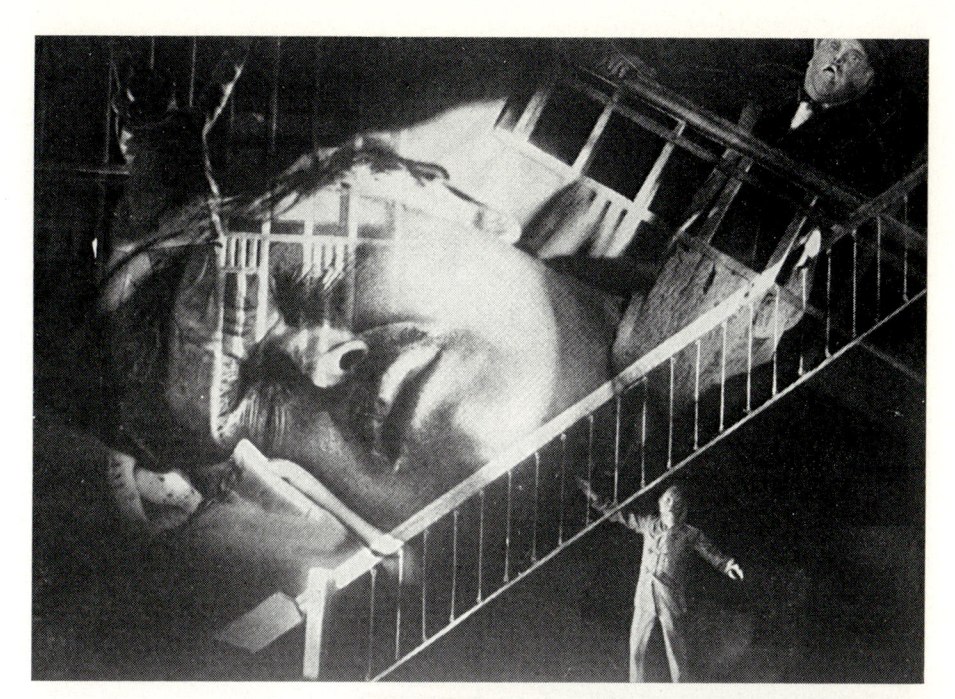

80 Depth symbols: a shot from the surrealistic film by G. W. Pabst, *Geheimnisse einer Seele* (1926).

81 Restructuring: the 'mystical mill' on a capital in the church at Vézelay.

82, 83, 84 Restructuring: a work by Klee turns into a plan for a town centre.

acting and knowing. It is more as if a force of renewal, already detectable beneath the surface of a particular period or group, breaks through in a single person. Great renovators of religion and society, inventors and creative scientists, prophets and artists, demonstrate by their personal action that the symbols belonging to a group and a culture are not timeless but can be transformed in a learning-process. Even the primal symbols or archetypes which are salient and recognizable features in the history of primitive and modern peoples and individuals are still not purely natural data – that would imply a kind of fatalism and a refusal to accept the possibilities of historical renewal. They can only continue to be of some psychical or cultural value (for instance, in psychotherapy or in art) so long as they undergo a succession of crucial reinterpretations. They can only go on being 'the same' symbols, as it were, if they are continually being transformed into 'different' rules. Thus depth-symbols may come to speak a new language under the surrealist eye of the camera which tries to visualize in film the hidden world of the psyche (ill. 80, p. 151; from 'Geheimnisse einer Seele', by G. W. Pabst, 1926).

Symbols are rules for understanding, action and expression. By means of symbols man does this, that and the other with his world. 'Learning', therefore, is not only an intellectual activity but a transformation of the life-pattern. Symbols are things for use, signposts for orientation, instruments for transformation. They are exponents of various styles of intercourse between men, the orientation of people's lives, the organization of society, the whole business of technological interference with nature. Thus man's task of transforming the world around him is accomplished through symbols, which are themselves the precipitate of rules. Technological procedures, political policy, social conduct, the achievement of form in art, systematic and logical reasoning, in short, all the activities of man exhibit certain rules that guarantee the cohesion of the individual symbolic actions. Earlier on, we defined learning as a process of incorporating unfamiliar phenomena within familiar patterns of expectation or rules. It turned out that in the course of the learning-process subjective redundancy approximated to objective redundancy, that is to say, the system of rules operative in a given culture. But even these objective rules were neither fixed nor timeless. And indeed the most radical form of learning is the one centred not on the transformation of particular symbols but on the transformation of an entire regulative system of symbols.

The question is something that opens up a confusing situation and can provide a perspective in a situation of impasse. The highest and most human form of learning is that which can set a fixed system in a problematic light. The question which presents not only individual symbols but overall rules as a problem makes inventiveness possible. The rules are sometimes written, like those of a legal code or a manual of scientific methodology, sometimes unwritten, like those of behaviour-patterns respected within a culture, or those of a particular form of art. Such rules vary a great deal; but they tally in this respect, that they embody a regulative action, a sort of equilibrium, holding a social constellation in a state of balance. That equilibrium is never static but is all the time subject to greater or lesser deviations and disturbances. The rules will intercept and correct breaches of this sort by characterizing them either as incorrect (e.g., in a scientific methodology) or as improper (e.g., in a code of social behaviour). Sometimes the rules will even admit of certain exceptions. Then again, alterations in component parts may be admissible, as generally in the rules of language. Yet there may be situations in which this dynamic balance is disturbed so much that a drastic restructuring of a system of rules becomes necessary. Then it becomes very evident indeed what had in fact been happening all along: namely, the historical changes that make it necessary to provide guidance and control by repeatedly revised systems of rules.

New rules call for inventiveness. Of course, they will never be totally new. There is the restructuring; but there is also the aspect of continuity, ensuring that whilst human history is ever new, it is also something we can recognize. All the same, it may sometimes require a social and political revolution, a religious reformation or a Copernican volte face in science to achieve an adequate restructuring. Old rules are often fixed, to the extent that the outlook of people and groups may be tightly fixed too. Inventiveness is not anarchy; nor is it a purely irrational impulse, because only a renewal that is effective and can achieve something in the social, artistic or scientific sphere can be described as 'inventive'. It is from the way in which renewal functions that we can tell whether or not it will result in a restructuring.

There are differing patterns of inventiveness; and à propos directly of the preceding paragraph we shall mention two of them here. First, a new system of rules may present the old system as a problem, may really move above and beyond it, and yet afterwards absorb it into itself as a simple marginal case. That is what happened, for example, in the case of the Copernican revolution. The Ptolemaic view of the world, with the earth as its centre, became a simple model incorporated into that of Copernicus, which offered new rules of computation for a universe with more bodies than just the earth, sun and moon. Again, the creation of non-Euclidean geometries, in which the new rules implied a definite curvature of space, went beyond the Euclidean variety, creatively speaking, and contained the possibility of framing such mathematical propositions as that the sum of the angles of a triangle may be less than 180 %: assertions which in the old system had been simply foolish. But on the other hand that old system could be subsumed as a simple, marginal case – namely, as the geometry of a space with zero degree of curvature – within the wider system of rules of the non-Euclidean geometries. In more recent politico-social thinking revolution has sometimes been examined and defended as a method of restructuring. The renewal of society via evolution then becomes a marginal case of wider rules according to which 'revolution' is no longer seen as due to social and political processes getting out of hand, as in the previous, more stringently demarcated system of rules appropriate to political evolution, but as a new form of the regulation of such processes. Here we can again distinguish non-violent and violent revolution, each of which has to be analysed on criteria of effectiveness and humanity.

A second pattern of inventiveness links together two already existing but not interrelated systems of rules. In this case a particular area or process under examination is seen as an element of both systems and so appears within a broader field of functional possibilities. A simple example may illustrate this, one taken from A. Koestler's study of creativity. Archimedes, vexed by the problem of how to calculate the specific gravity, and therefore the volume, of a handsome crown belonging to his master, steps into his bath and notices, just as usual, how the water rises as he submerges himself. The rest of the story is well known and is easy to guess, anyway. What is the creative element here? It is this, says Koestler: that two very different systems of rules (or 'matrices', as Koestler calls them) suddenly, at a certain point, coincide. It shows that the problem to be analysed can occur as an element in either matrix; and so it acquires a broader field of rules in which it applies. And that entails the solution of the problem in question, as well as the creation of new scientific rules.

Of the categories of inventiveness abovementioned we offer here two illustrations. On one of the capitals of the Romanesque abbey church at Vézelay (France), dating from the first half of the 12th century, there is a representation of the 'Mystical Mill'. This shows how the Old Testament rules are incorporated in, and assimilated to, the New Testament, but acquire a new meaning in the process: the grain of the Old Testament is ground in the mill of mysticism into the meal of the New Testament (ill. 81, p. 151). An illustration of inventiveness which brings two unconnected systems of rules within a single but broader context by establishing a particular element as coincident or common to both is to be found in the next three illustrations (82, 83, 84, p. 152). The architect F. van Klingeren, sees a canvas by Paul Klee and from it makes a photo (ill. 82) which he interprets as a basic structure for a town centre to be built in Lelystad (the urban centre of a newly reclaimed polder; ill. 83); and this then develops into a scaled model (ill. 84).

These two examples of patterns of inventiveness are enough to remind us of the prime importance attaching to this form of learning-process. The central feature is that one learns how to move out beyond an existing system and to operate outside the existing fixed patterns of rules and of settled outlooks. This 'transcendence' results in new and more ample rules. 'New' here refers not so much to the obtaining of additional or different data (information) but to the acquisition of a new viewpoint on the information already to hand. The elements may remain the same; but the total system of rules is changed; and that involves a more fundamental kind of renewal than the supplementing of an existing system with new data. All this has far-reaching consequences for teaching and for methods of research. Arousing curiosity, furnishing information, learning ways and means to expand an existing area of knowledge – all that is insufficient. Indeed, we might say that traditional education still operates far too much in this sphere, the sphere of the 'what': we learn what a thing is, we become proficient at establishing existing insights, and so run the risk of finding that the knowledge gained is soon out of date. This 'obsolescence of the intellect' has already been pointed out in many countries and has even been put at five years for some lines of study. If on the other hand we make use of methods centred more on the 'how', then we learn not so much given facts and insights as ways of applying rules in order to control new information that may arise in the future.

This aim is best pursued by adopting a new viewpoint with regard to existing facts and finding new rules that will introduce unexpected possibilities and groupings into the existing arsenal of knowledge.

This principal form of learning-process entails our becoming fully aware of the rules of organization already in use. These may sometimes be taken so much for granted, and often enough may operate so automatically through the tradition of education and upbringing, that we are hardly conscious of them any more. But as soon as they are made explicit, we are able to stand off from them and see them for what they are. The next step is to treat them as presenting problems and so to clear a way for the realization that quite different systems of rules may be possible. The two examples we gave before of patterns of inventiveness may serve to illustrate all this. One might sum up this form of learning by describing it as a 'sensitivity to problems'. The very process of questioning helps to demarcate the field of available knowledge, restricts that field and, in particular, reveals something of the structural confinement of such an area. In this way a restructuring is made possible. That 'sensitivity to problems' is a typically human potentiality for learning, which 'transcends' every existent programming, for instance, of an animal by its instincts or of a computer by the logical rules realized in it.

Bear in mind too, à propos of all this, that 'learning' is not confined to pure knowing, a solely cognitive process. When a solution is found to a difficult social situation because the existing rules are radically revised in a creative and inventive spirit, this does of course involve theoretical understanding; but it still has many other components such as emotional involvement in the whole area of the problem, practical intelligence, a feeling for the relative character of the current position, and so on. That is why, as we have said more than once already, the whole of culture should be thought of as one great learning-process. Learning has a practical character in the first instance, because a situation has actually to *be* transformed. Theoretical insights and the various sciences help in this respect in that they marshal, select and with the aid of symbols (e.g. mathematical, chemical) and technological operations (e.g., experiment, test) transform the available data. But then the outcome is bound to be an extension of man's control over the chances and changes of the world around him.

The brain and culture

In the preceding chapter we were saying that man progressively exteriorizes himself: various potentialities latent in man are brought out to an ever increasing extent in technological advances through which muscular strength, energy and information processes are realized. In this chapter we shall be looking at culture as a human learning process that transforms the world. Following up these two points, we must now move from the outside inwards, as it were, in order to show how this culture, still envisaged as a process and an activity, reveals something of what goes on in the individual human being. We shall be concerned, therefore, with those neurophysiological processes in particular which occur in man's central nervous system (CNS).

We shall mention only a few of the facts to be found in many manuals on this subject, just those data, in fact, which serve to throw some light on the learning-process associated with culture. Once the link has been established between the physical man (muscular strength, CNS and so forth) on the one hand and man's mental world (information technology, learning-processes, culture) on the other, we should be in a position by the end of this chapter to say how the material and economic changes in history can also be viewed as mental-cum-cultural phases within a historical learning-process.

That speech, thinking and memory are connected each with particular regions and functions of the brain has been known for a long time. Famous, of course, are the drawings of the human brain by the anatomist, A. Vesalius (1514–1564), included in his *De Humani Corporis Fabrica* (ill. 85 and 86), which marked the outset of several centuries of continuing research on the brain.

During the past few decades, however, a great deal more has been brought to light on the subject as a result of interdisciplinary research, to which animal psychology and physiology, the analysis and construction of electronic machines, cybernetics, symbolical or mathematical logic, biochemistry, electro-encephalography and similar disciplines have made

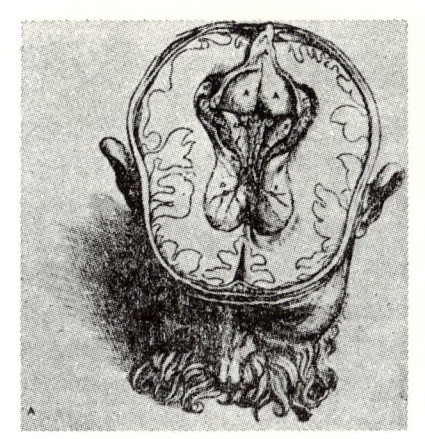

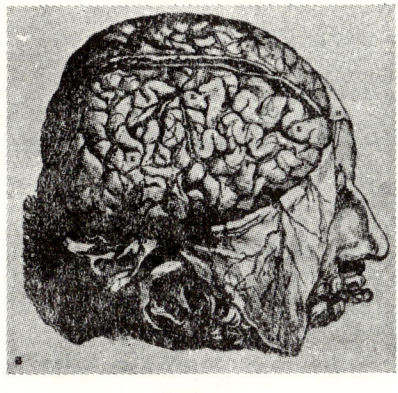

85, 86 Drawings of the human brain by A. Vesalius (16th century).

a major contribution. We shall consider a few examples here.

The nerve-cells or neurons in the brain-cortex which have to do with information processes are interconnected by a very fine ramificatory network. A highly simplified model like J. P. Schadé's sketch of linking elements in a part of the cortex of the cerebellum will suffice to give an impression of this (ill. 87).

Even in a condition of rest and sleep, for instance, it is the seat of continuous chemico-electrical processes. Within the area of a pinhead are located tens of thousands of neurons, many of which are in action alternately or else together, emitting a stream of pulsations (the neurons then 'fire off'). Each neuron has inputs and outputs. Using a very rough and simplified approximation, one can distinguish three types of event: (1) When one of the inputs registers an access of current, the nerve-cell discharges; this is known as 'facilitation'; (2) The cell discharges only when all lines of supply are 'live'; this is called 'summation'; (3) When a supply or feed-in is live, this acts as a break and the cell is unable to discharge; this is described as 'inhibition'. These three types of event can be illustrated by three linkage-models in which an access of current in p, q and so forth alters the position of the bridge so that the main current is able to flow through or, in the third case, is cut off. In the first instance a supply of current to one of the inputs is sufficient, in the second case all inputs have to be live, in the third case such a supply should not be present (diagram 88).

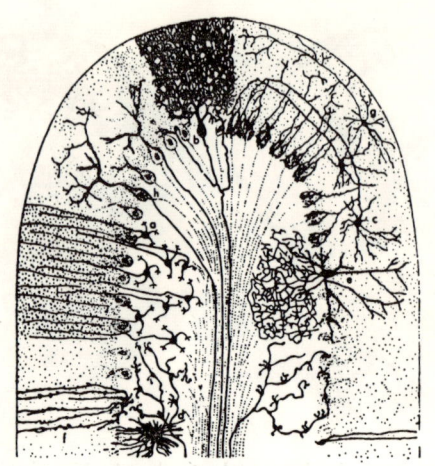

87 Linking elements in the cerebral cortex (from: J. P. Schadé, *De functie van het zenuwstelsel*).

In reality the situation is far more complicated, partly because the threshold-value of the neurons is often variable, so that for example the same neuron may discharge on one impulse, or on two or on three, and so forth. The immediately preceding stimulation of a cell will often have the effect of raising the threshold-value; and then more impulses will be needed for a subsequent discharge within an extremely short period of time. It is the combination of millions of simultaneously occurring processes of this kind that gives rise to a substantial part of man's behaviour: noticing, not noticing, seeking, shunning this, that or the other, taking a decision, postponing a decision, gathering, storing, divulging information, and so on.

In logic we distinguish, among others, the following operations. A total, composite assertion (proposition) is true as long as at any rate one of the statements comprising it is true. We call this operation 'disjunction' and denote it by the symbol 'V', which in the spoken language is repre-

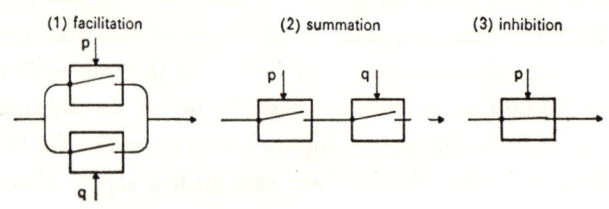

88 Models of elementary linkages.

89 Vegetating in a primitive stage: stilt-fishers in Ceylon.

90 Vegetating in a far advanced stage: planting rice (from a Chinese print).

161

91 Producing: contrast between industry and traditional modes of travelling in India.

92 Fish-eye photo of a supermarket.

sented by the word 'or' (e.g., 'it is raining or it is cold'). This disjunction has the same sort of structure as the 'facilitation' aforementioned. Another logical operation is that which is true only if all the constituent statements are true. This is known as 'conjunction'; the symbol for it is '$\wedge$', in speech 'and' (e.g., 'it is raining and it is cold'). This conjunction corresponds to 'summation'. The logical operation which has as its consequence that a true proposition becomes false and a false one true we call negation; the symbol here is '—', in speech 'not' (e.g., 'it is not raining'). This operation corresponds to 'inhibition'. Naturally, every existing logical system is much simpler than the linkage-system of the cerebral cortex; and yet there is a striking similarity between such logic and a simple model of linking-processes in the cortex. One conclusion, therefore, is that the rules of symbolic logic can have a relation to (or to put it more technically: may be interpreted as) rules in accordance with which processes of a neurophysiological character occur. There is a second conclusion possible: namely, that the basic forms of man's logical reasoning connect or cohere with the rules aforementioned, in accordance with which cerebral processes happen. The more far-reaching question then arises as to whether the whole regulative system, including the learning-processes (the finding of new rules), of human culture does not therefore cohere with the structure and development of the CNS.

A first step in the direction of a positive answer may be taken by posing a counter-question. Is not the question we have just raised fully consonant with a materialist reduction of mental thought-processes to physical processes in the brain? Indeed, any account of cerebral processes will involve a description of all sorts of physiological and biochemical reactions. But a physical account still turns out to be inadequate here, precisely because it is concerned with the analysis of rules in accordance with which such physical processes occur. This becomes evident in the first instance as soon as we contemplate the so called trigger-mechanisms. These are taken to signify a physical process with disproportionately large consequences. The fact that those consequences are so considerable is itself the outcome of certain rules by which they are gauged. A few examples will be needed in order to make this clear. First of all two instances which are not themselves in the category of trigger-mechanisms but do offer some resemblance. In the purely physical order we have the snowball effect – for example, of a stone which starts to roll in the snow the length of a mountain-side and gradually sets going a whole avalanche. The effect here is incommensurably great; but it can still be fully explained within the physical plane, so that no extra rules are required to enable us to assess the effect. A second instance is located entirely within the order of a symbolically – that is, non-physically – determined system of rules: by one move with a pawn the king is suddenly put in check. Here the disproportionately great effect is wholly accounted for on the basis of the rules of chess. Somewhere between these two types of case lie the real trigger-mechanisms; in the physical plane they have disproportionately large consequences (as in the first example), but that is by virtue of the fact that the physical process itself owes its importance or relevance to non-physical rules (as in the second example). The thing from which the term derives (the pulling of the trigger of, for instance, a revolver) provides a good illustration. The trigger is pulled through the centre of pressure so that it suddenly slams forward. But this abrupt, physical effect acquires its significance only from the system of rules which the technician has built into the weapon, as it were, and by means of which, via a series of processes such as the explosion of powder (processes in themselves fully explicable in physical terms), the effect of firing off the intended shot is accomplished.

The distinctive thing about a trigger-mechanism, therefore, is that one can describe the whole process in physical terms, but without having as yet understood what the real point of it is. Every mechanical product, the physical processes apart, is also governed in its structure by the rules which its constructer has incorporated into it; and this is the context within which alone each physical process gets its relevance. Now this also applies to the more figurative sense in which we employ the term 'trigger-mechanism'. The neurons in the cerebral cortex 'fire off' in response to a particular threshold-value and a specific combination of impulses, a combination which, as we showed before, is in fact logically analysable. It is understandable that here too we should speak of a trigger-mechanism. The sudden effect – something characteristic of all the examples we have given – has a genuine trigger-action in this case, because processes result from it that can be described in accordance with certain symbolic rules: for example, the operations we mentioned earlier on of disjunction, conjunction and negation. Within the broader pattern of the cerebral cortex these rules even cohere, as it turns out, with those of human behaviour, indeed, of human culture as a whole.

Thus we really have here two levels, which are closely interrelated: the physico-chemical processes and the rules within which those processes become relevant. That becomes clearer still when we consider the patterns that emerge in the CNS. The firing off of neurons is not an individual event but a constituent part of what amounts to programming of the cerebral cortex. This programming most likely depends on certain patterns in accordance with which the neuronal processes work in combination. There are specific routes which the impulses follow and which together form a network or blueprint. Two ways of demonstrating these patterns to some extent have been tried so far: first by experiments with animals who have undergone learning-processes, for example, by 'learning' the way through a maze. The animal's behaviour is such that after a time it knows directly what is its way through the complicated maze; indeed, it even succeeds in combining sections of the route, learned in different parts of a maze as though it had a map or plan at its disposal. We do then speak, in fact, of an 'inner map of the environment'; and this inwardly available map is, one supposes, a pattern of neural routes that has emerged during the learning-process. Another method is by brain operations performed on animals: certain activities acquired by learning do not in every case disappear as a result of this, even if the operation involves interference with parts of the brain having a direct connection with such activity. That again may point to the existence of more comprehensive networks to which various parts of the brain contribute.

Two relevant points arise here which are especially important to an understanding of man's cultural tradition and learning-activity. The first is that experiences are combined into patterns and are conserved as patterns. There are differing theories about the nature of this registering of experience. The physiologist, Eccles, concludes that it has to do with the synapses (the supply tentacles that affect a neuron) and an increased capacity in them to allow passage. The biochemist, Hydén, believes that changes occur in a certain chemical substance (RNA), in which experiences are chemically coded. At all events something like a blueprint emerges in the cerebral cortex, certain systems of rules which cohere, nay, which even form the 'inside' of the symbolic rules (of science, art, religion, ethics) in the outer world of man. McCulloch and Pitts have tried to analyse the logic of the cortex's linking processes in more detail and

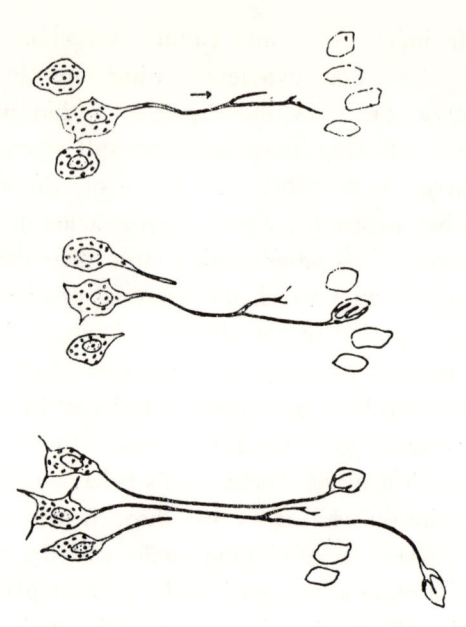

93 Growth of a pioneer neuron (from: J. P. Schadé, D. H. Ford, *Basic neurology*).

speak of neuronal impulses which form patterns having a relative constancy. They constitute the inner side of man's normative behaviour; and the abovementioned researchers even talk of universal norms held within the circuits of the brain: 'trapped universals'. F. C. S. Northrop has elaborated on this in his philosophy of culture, concluding that by way of such universal patterns in the brain mankind programmes itself, as it were, and may sometimes even arrive at new forms of programming. Thus an ideology is the exteriorization of such a programming.

A second point of major importance is that these patterns can be altered. 'Learning' is the augmentation of knowledge or, to put it more accurately, an enlargement of the possibilities of regulating the surrounding world in knowing and acting. After all, the 'how' may sometimes be more important than the 'what', as we showed earlier on in this chapter. In what way do we increase our grip on the world? What deviations and strange – surprising as well as dismaying – events is it possible nevertheless to integrate within an already available network? This network is the whole gamut of symbolic rules, as well as their interior, their inner side, namely, the patterns in the CNS which make up the 'inner map'

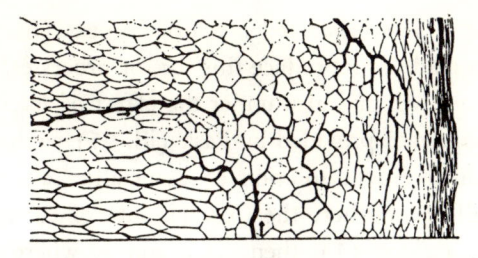

94 Growth of networks (from: J. P. Schadé, D. H. Ford, *Basic neurology*).

with a view to the orientation of life. 'Learning' then, to echo Steinbuch's definition, is the adaptation of the interior model of the outer world to the changed constellations of that outer world.

Such a learning-process probably entails new connections or combinations arising in the brain. The 'network' is for ever in motion, grows, at other points is broken down again and forms a fluctuating plan that anticipates possible events. Pavlov thought that in the case of animals' learning processes within the brain a kind of emanation took place from existing cerebral tracks to other parts of the brain, so that new combinations would come into being. In a revised form one can find similar notions in the latest theories current in neurophysiology. In the development of the very young brain of a child the neurons seek their goal, as it were, via their extremities (axon), in order to establish connections. In a very simplified form the accompanying illustration 93 represents such a 'pioneer neuron', the growth of which is copied by younger neurons, so that

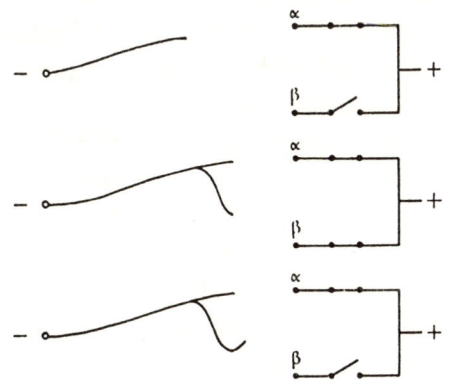

95 Growth of filaments for a network (from: G. Pask, *An approach to cybernetics*).

over a period more or less organized networks appear (ill. 94). An attempt has also been made to reproduce this sort of processes, which occur in connection with growth and also under the effect of learning, electrochemically. In the diagram provided by Pask (ill. 95) we have filaments growing in a conductive acid solution of a metallic salt. In the three phases of growth illustrated here the flow (input) of current occurs, in due succession, via *a* alone (1), then via *a* and *b*, where the growing filament proceeds to ramify (2), next the current is routed again via *b*, so that this branch begins to swerve toward *a*. This model shows how in the CNS too new combinations are able to grow. And as these combinations are part of a whole network that in its turn finds expression in a particular pattern of behaviour (myth, ethical norms, scientific methodology, etc.) in the outer world, it is obvious that in this way quite new rules of procedure, of policy, may come about in a learning-process. We also speak of 'strategies': a number of rules, taken together, can add up to a total way of approach to things. Sometimes the replacement of a single connection can offer entirely new logical possibilities, just as a single move on the chess-board may sometimes imply the changeover to a different strategy. These alterations in strategy are among the most characteristic differences between the human and animal brains (the animal usually commands innate strategies only, perhaps a very limited number that may be acquired). Such changes are also the most striking feature of the various restructurings of human society and the dynamic course taken by the history of human culture.

If finally we take the two aspects together – the evolving regulative system of the human CNS and that of man's cultural behaviour – it then appears that we are concerned with a strategy or programme vis-à-vis the world around. In this context knowing and acting are as one. In criticism of the term 'inner map' as applied to animal behaviour, it has quite rightly been pointed out that the animal does not just have an objective image or cognitive model of its world but is always in action: simply to know how the maze is put together is not enough: the animal must be able to walk through it. It is also evident, on the other hand, that the animal possesses more than just recollections of a succession of walking movements; put water in the maze, and the rat will find its way just as purposefully by swimming. Knowledge and action together constitute a programme for acquiring a more practised touch in dealing with the world. In man's case this is at the same time a radically symbolic transforming of that world, which may be more or less adequate and calls for perputual review and alteration. Questions arising from what are surely seen to be the most fundamental motivations of animal and human behaviour – the urge to exploration, the sexual urge and the impulse to preserve life (the avoidance of death and hunger) – have a part to play here and at any rate where they concern man, fall within the broad perspective of the question as to the meaning of the reality of life itself.

Vegetating, producing, consuming

In the foregoing sections we have been considering the cohesive relation of the 'mental' (symbol-cum-deportment, the question as to the meaning of existence, and so on) with the 'material' (CNS with neuronal linkage-system). That cohesion is also there in the development of man's learning-processes in the different phases of culture. Culture is man's way of getting the measure of his world, of running himself in, so to speak, so that the natural is always being transformed, via symbol-conduct, within the perspective of 'meaning', of the 'sense' in things. This meaning goes along with elementary needs, like the need to sustain life, sexuality, the sounding out of one's environment (the urge to explore, already present in animals). But in man these things are not constant and are never determined purely by instinct: he transforms them, suppresses or sublimates them, turns them into motives for his crimes and for his artistic creations, assesses and criticizes them within the perspectives of love for his neighbour and trust in God, lets them carry him on to revolutions, to discoveries in science and to the exercise of leisure: in short, man transforms them in the context of the question of a meaningful existence.

Culture as a whole is governed partly by material and economic factors, but also by the need for transforming things and extending the meaning assigned to them. For mankind, therefore, every material situation implies also the need for attaining a learning-process in which the economic-cum-material situation can become more meaningful and is drawn, via a selective procedure, into the sphere of man's decision-making. This basic notion is elucidated here with the aid of a highly simplified model. It is not our claim that this serves to typify the basic human passions and the chief phases of human development (that would be impossible) but only that it presents for discussion a particular approach which with some elaboration and exposure to criticism may perhaps gain in significance as a guide-line for today. Then again, the model has been smoothed out so as to fit in with the phases of culture as unfolded in the early chapters of this book: the mythical, ontological, functional positions. In the model developed here the learning-phases – vegetating, producing, consuming – tally with that earlier division.

The most primitive, that is to say, initial situation of man in his material setting is that of vegetating: i.e. searching for and picking up whatever is capable of sustaining life. In describing this primal situation some writers give us a picture of tiny clans, scattered over large areas, which as gatherers, hunters and so on succeeded in furnishing their elementary needs. Naturally, in all this the question as to the meaning of events as a whole is by no means absent; and so there is a subtly ramified, mythical encounter with the world, in which the problems of hunger and repletion, death and life, guilt, punishment and purification, sexuality and fertility find expression. Of course, these symbolic rules and the geographical environment are geared in with the hard struggle for existence. Myth, as Lévi-Strauss puts it, provides rules for the exchange of goods, women and information. The vegetating process cannot take place just at random. Relations between men – but also those which have reference to the powers of nature – have to be regulated. Alternatives need to be distinguished and resolved upon. And so one might speak of a first great learning-process: the learning how to vegetate. A characteristic image of this primary mode of subsistence is afforded by the stilt-walking fisherman on the southern coast of Ceylon (ill. 89, p. 161). A more advanced stage in this process of learning to vegetate is depicted in the engraving (ill. 90, p. 161) that shows the planting of the new rice. Rice-growing, which demands a great deal of organization, takes place in a number of different phases which a European artist in the 18th century copied from Chinese drawings.

If for the sake of convenience we reduce the elementary grounds of animal and human activity to three, we would then be in a position to speak of the major issues as being concerned with death (hunger-stimuli and so on), sexuality (rules of marriage, the mystery of fecundity) and

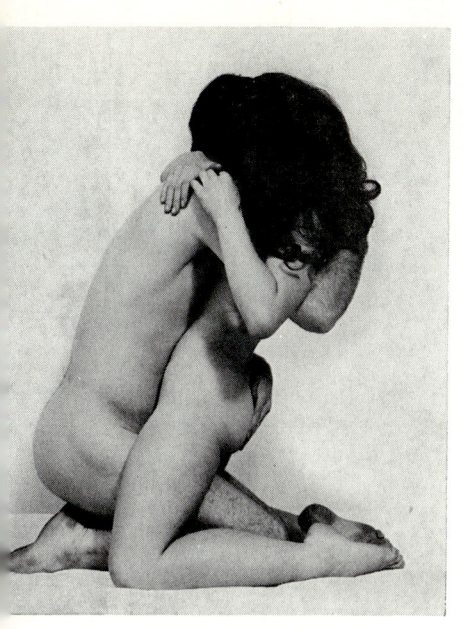

Sexuality: contemporary openness (cou-
from M. Toft and J. Fowlie, *Variations*).

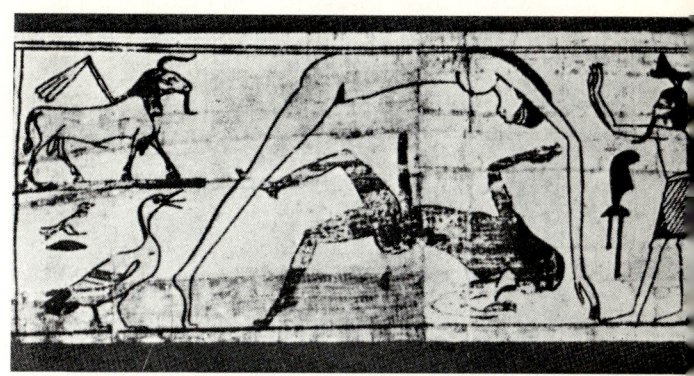

97   Sexuality, as cosmic event: the earth-god is desirous of union with the goddess of the vault of heaven (picture on an Egyptian papyrus).

98   Sexuality: Victorian bathing-costumes.

99   G. de Chirico, Mathematician.

100   Galileo's apartment (reconstruction) in Pisa; development of natural science.

101   Moral and social consequences of science: G. Doré, Slums in London.

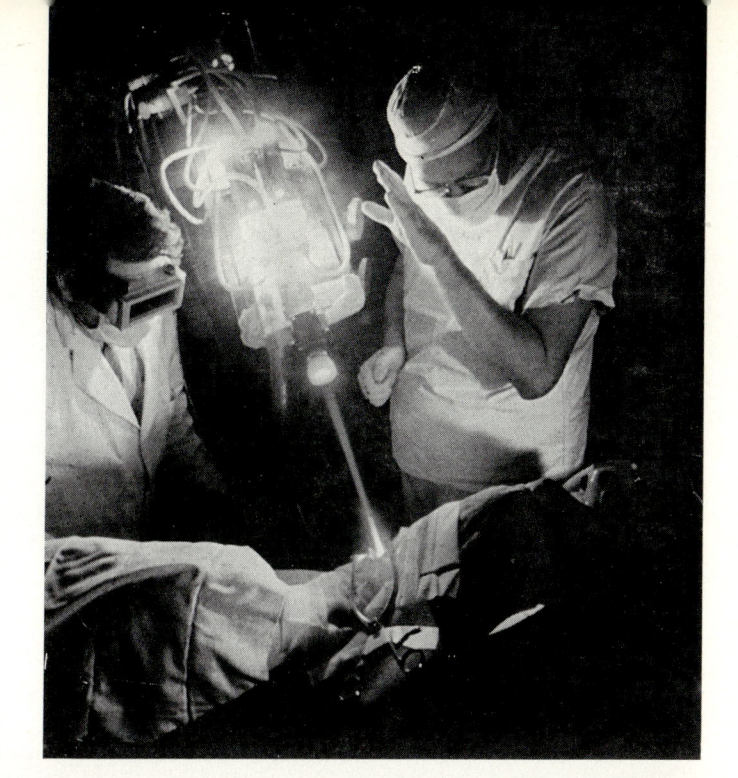

102 Medical science: operation with a laser-beam.

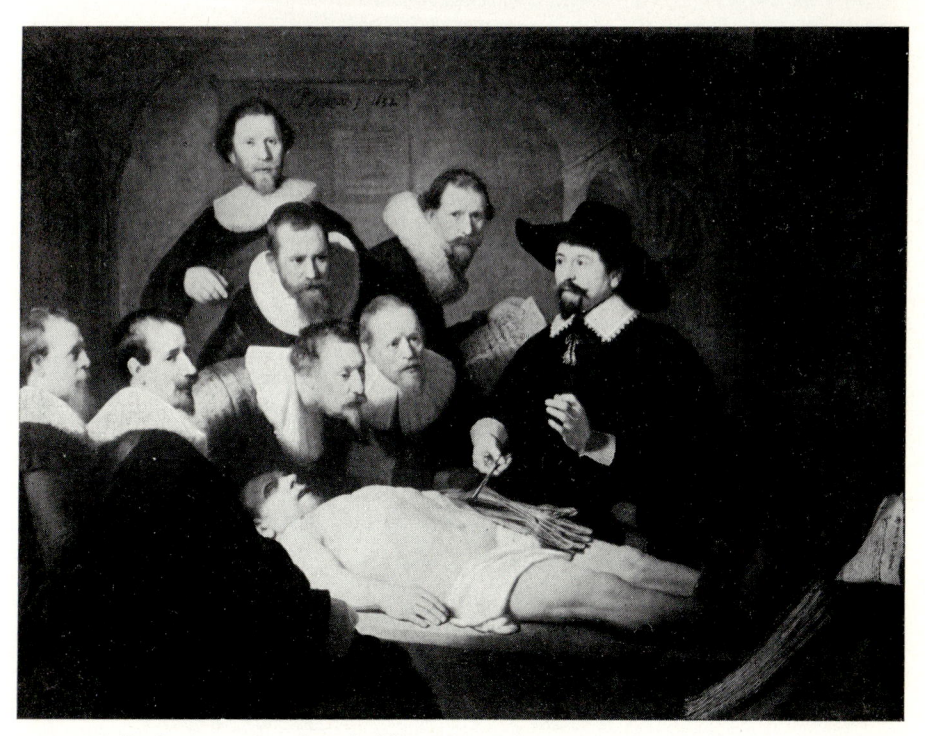

103 Medical science: Rembrandt, The anatomy lesson.

104 Mental science: Chinese scholars deciphering texts.

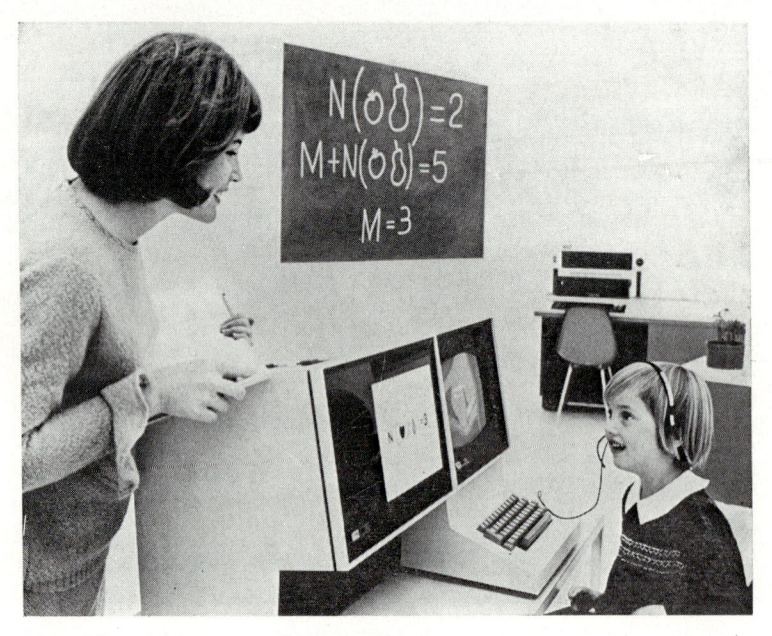

105 Mental science: teaching machines.

the unknown (urge to exploration, inquisitiveness). The two factors first mentioned have a very central position in the mythical world view and play a major role in the process of learning to vegetate. Myth unveils sexuality and death; it also regulates them. Primitive peoples' religious rites and forms of expression which modern man feels to be artistic in the highest degree, they all frequently relate, as also do social rules, to precisely these themes. In general the mythical world view has a rather closed character. Everything has its place, its locale, in space and time; whilst the world picture in a narrower, more geographical sense is likewise fenced in. The unknown is the dangerous thing, in mythical language sometimes even referred to as 'chaos' or 'nothingness'; and the stranger is felt to be sometimes an intruder, sometimes an awesome power. To us, therefore, it looks very much like a severe clamp-down on any possibilities of development. One could say that in this phase the urge to explore is ousted and suppressed.

This of course has social consequences too. The various classes in society are very little open to movement or change. In the higher orders, marked off by heredity or by the prescribed rules of religion – higher castes, tribal leaders, kings, medicine-men, shamans and so forth – the tribe or group finds an expression of its own power, its own existence. The conquest of hunger and death (the pharaoh, mummified, is proof against dissolution; ancestor-images), the power of fertility are given expression in these castes and classes, but not the urge to exploration. We can denote all this by a single term: prosperity; but then taking the word in a rather unusual sense, because it does not refer here primarily to wealth and the 'good things of life' (which is what 'prosperity' normally means) but links riches and victory in the struggle for existence to a particular class or condition determined by heredity and by mythical rules.

The ontological outlook assumes a disjunctive position vis-à-vis the reality that surrounds men, as we explained in some detail in the third chapter; so that here the vegetating process drops into the background, because a more indirect relationship to nature comes into play: production. In the learning-process associated with vegetating certain protoforms of production are already developing, for example, in the manufacture of tools and weapons as well as in a more and more systematic pursuit of agriculture. Within the ontological position people begin to operate with sciences and technologies. They try to discover the real nature of things, establish basic principles and laws; and this knowledge leads to the production of whatever fundamental thing has been learnt. This business of producing, which is to give rise eventually to industrial society, is also a major learning-process. Illustration 91 (p. 162) gives us a glimpse of the distance between learning to produce and the preceding phase.

At this juncture the really important indicators are no longer mythical symbols but scientific laws, religious and political tenets, objectively formulated moral norms.

Along with the ontological frame of mind goes an enormous expansion of man's view of the world: spatially, the world is opened up, strange countries are discovered, unaccustomed art extolled, political revolutions set in motion. The exploratory impulse, thrust aside in mythical thinking, is now given full play. Without it the learning-process of production, difficult to get going and extended over many centuries, would be inconceivable. New products and methods follow at an ever quickening pace, imbuing human history with a fierce dynamism. The motif of death persists and in some periods is even strikingly prominent in art and reflective consciousness, as in the theme of the dance of death, in which every distinction of rank and class falls away. Yet there are changes that belong to the more ontological approach: death is analysed, philosophers and anatomists are bent over the human body. But at the same time man still turns his attention to the conquest of death, not as myth once did but via distanced theory: proofs of the immortality of the soul, from Plato to Schopenhauer, are an illustration of this. To a much lesser extent, on the other hand, is there a place in the ontological mode of thought for sexuality. Philosophers, theologians and psychologists in this period often define sexuality as the purely biological, animal and irrational in man, sometimes as what is bad and unseemly. Sexuality does of course get a function assigned to it for the purpose of procreation, of begetting progeny – a function fitting perfectly into this phase for which producing is such a crucial factor. But as a result, the proper function of sexual experience disappears. In the culture of Western Europe this constriction culminates in the Victorian age with its prudish and cold-shouldering attitude to sexuality.

The business of producing has social consequences too. A feudal, caste-based society gives place to a capitalist one. Inheritance and traditional prescripts still have some influence but are no longer crucial factors in determining who the leading figures in any society are going to be. Fear and trembling before the 'that' of existence, so very characteristic of myth, sexuality and the hereditary transmission of authority give place to the 'what'. Authority passes to whoever commands the means of production. As the pace of history quickens, so the possessors of power can change more rapidly too. The process of learning to produce centres more and more, therefore, in the choice of those means which tend to increase wealth, because wealth is no longer a consequence of esteem, as in mythical society, but esteem is an outcome of wealth. In the business of social intercourse roles become more and more interchangeable; and the democratizing process that goes along with that ensures that more and more people are allowed to share in the benefits of the production process. By way of contrast to the vegetating phase, with its criterion of the 'prosperity', that is, the comfort and prestige of the few, in the productive learning-process, it is more a question of 'welfare', that is to say, of wealth and the amenities of life for the many.

In chapter IV we were arguing that man is today caught up in the transition from an ontological to a more functional posture. Agriculture has been perfected; and in one third of the world an industrial society is firmly established. Aid to less developed areas forms part of the programme of every industrial state. Learning processes concerned with making use of nature in a rational way and with increasing production on a scientific basis are gradually spreading to cover the entire world. After many centuries of effort man has gone a long way in the direction of efficient vegetating and producing. Yet it is precisely the highly developed areas of the world that are now faced with a third and enormous task: they still have to learn how to consume! In a more vegetating type of existence consuming constituted no problem. The bond with nature and its products was a direct one; and what is more, it was regulated by direction-setting mythical stories. The struggle for existence hardly ever resulted in superfluity. In the period of production-potentialities consumer goods are not, to begin with, much to the fore. Conditions are regulated by the sciences, within particular economics, as the science of scarcity, occupying an ever more central place. Only when welfare advances so far that society becomes one of plenty (Galbraith's 'affluent society') does the question arise as to whether positing and deciding upon alternatives ought perhaps to apply even with respect to consumption. Man's vision or the eye of the camera has all too easily familiarized itself with the world of consumer goods (ill. 92, p. 162). Man today is too little aware that he has in fact thrown up a consumer-barrier as a screen

106   From producer to consumer (cartoon by Gabriel Edme).

between himself and reality. Only at rare moments is this protective barrier rudely disturbed (ill. 106).

The impression one gets, right at the start of this new learning-process, is that the exploratory urge will come even more into its own. Scientific research, tourism, the use of leisure time, medical and psychic activity affecting our wellbeing, individually and collectively – all these fall within the range of interests on which public opinion on a world scale may be formed. Moreover, it is quite clear that sexuality, having been pushed out of the way, is once again coming to the surface. Aided by a new image of man, by theological interpretations and ideas, an ethics of sex, erotic techniques, medical intervention, the production of contraceptives and many other factors, a new way of experiencing sexuality is setting in, the centre of which is no longer 'productivity' but the erotic, valued in and for itself. This fits completely into the general consumer atmosphere; but it also presents us with a whole run of problems. Sex, sheer sex, appears as an article of consumption where the activity of consuming is accepted without direction or restraint, as might in principle have been the case with respect to vegetating and producing. But here too a learning-process is required; and questions with a wider bearing occur which are to receive more detailed consideration in the remaining chapters.

Finally, so far as the third elementary impulse is concerned (to uphold life in confrontation with death) we can say that in the consumer society it is death that is more and more being thrust aside. Whereas around the turn of the century conscious reflection on death and the public manifestation of death in a context of work, of the family and the street were still common, all this is becoming more and more effectively masked; outwardly, by social mechanisms which enshroud and conceal dying and mourning, inwardly by psychopharmaceutics designed to bring under control to an ever growing extent the state of mind of the dying and of those about them and to make death, at any rate as it appears when properly wrapped up, almost a 'consumable product'.

Diagram 107 sets out the following points: the three phases of learning and the role which the three elementary issues of death, sexuality and the urge to explore fulfil in them (the shaded panels indicate the suppression or dismissal of one or another such issue). With respect to sexuality this is also clarified with the help of illustrations. The Papyrus of illustration 97 (p. 171) shows how in the mythical mode of ex-

	mythical vegetating	ontological producing	functional consuming
death			▨▨▨▨▨
sex		▨▨▨▨▨	
exploration	▨▨▨▨▨		

107 Schematized diagram of the three phases of learning.

perience sexuality is a cosmic and indeed self-evident occurrence: the earth-god, Geb, attempts to have sexual intercourse with his spouse and sister, Nut, goddess of the vaulted dome of heaven. Victorian, however, is the covering of the specifically sexual features in sea-bathing as it was done by ladies at the beginning of this century (ill. 98, p. 171). A now open and liberated sexuality finds expression, for example, in the diversity of books on sexual enlightenment. From one such book we have taken illustration 96, which because of its artistic and open approach manages to avoid striking a pornographic note.

The social consequences of consuming as a learning-process are far-reaching and still almost incalculable. One part of them, at any rate, is a resistance to the 'consumer society', that is to say, to the kind of consumption which we have not so far got under control and which we allow to dictate our behaviour, nay, our very feelings and desires. Typically non-productive, antagonistic attitudes, such as the strike, demonstrations, tactical revolutions, begin to appear more and more as a means of forcing the consumer society to a reflective awareness and to some programme or policy of its own. Typically non-vegetative reactions too are geared into this, such as the hunger-strike, self-incineration, self-imposed austerity, voluntary tax-returns (self-tax movement). All such reactions are here included within the learning-process of consumption. It is a kind of sampling of possibilities (a process of trial and error), with a view to exposing within consumer behaviour alternatives which are so far still locked away inside an involuntary and undirected consumer activity.

All this goes hand in hand with the basic feature of the functional approach: the 'how'. We have to learn how to treat other people, how to handle tasks, processes and things. There is a plentiful supply of financial resources, free time, consumer goods, social contacts; but no one raises the question of how all this is to be used, applied, lived out in experience. When it comes to authority one is bound to notice changes, because authority no longer accrues to individuals by virtue of heredity or some other form of tradition, nor indeed because they own the means of production. Intermediate forms emerge, in which the 'how' is beginning to be the crucial factor, where the exercise of authority is concerned. Thus in large-scale industry it is the manager or chief executive who is coming increasingly to the fore, since it is he who can determine the 'how' of the organization-process. In the world of the publicity media it is the specialist in information who looms largest of all. In political groupings the party secretary is the most important figure. Those who give evidence of an ability to control processes, and therefore to give directives as to how to get things done, acquire a natural authority; so that this more functional type of authority passes to those who show that they deserve it: this is the meritocracy (M. Young).

However, all this still has to do with intermediate forms; for whilst it is true that the functional 'how' is already coming to the fore, still these structures are largely determined by an industrial society. The shift now taking place from people working in the industrial and commercial sector to those operating in the sphere of service activities generally is typical of a society that has to learn how to consume. Occupations connected with recreation, training and educational work, tourism, social-cum-international aid, the mental health of the public, publicity media, legal, pedagogical, artistic consultancy and advice centres and so on illustrate the need for fresh alternatives, that is, practicable, realisable possibilities, for society to learn to organize. Whereas, starting from simple vegetating – in the strict sense, something that never occurs in human culture – the process of learning to vegetate had to arrive at a purposive use of what nature and the environment had to offer, so a similar kind of limiting orientation needs to be learned with respect to consuming. The basic motivations, of which only the urge to explore, sexuality and the passion for life have been mentioned in this restricted three-phase model, must never be allowed to become a sort of natural force or energy, a legitimation of fate. Man has to learn, through responsible decision-making, to set these forces within the perspective of meaningful personal and social existence. In the vegetating mode of existence the hereditary or traditional leader played an exemplary role in this respect: prosperity, propitious circumstance. Within the context of learning to produce, it was welfare that became a kind of goal. In the period of learning to consume it will have to be wellbeing. A capitalist form of democracy is then replaced by a more functional one, in which it is not possessions or ownership but (moral and social) merit that gives authority and is recognized as a function of what it means to be human. Democracy must then involve an optimal participation, not excluding the spheres of education, religion, art and the pursuit of politics.

108 The film gives us Alpine mountaineering in close-up.

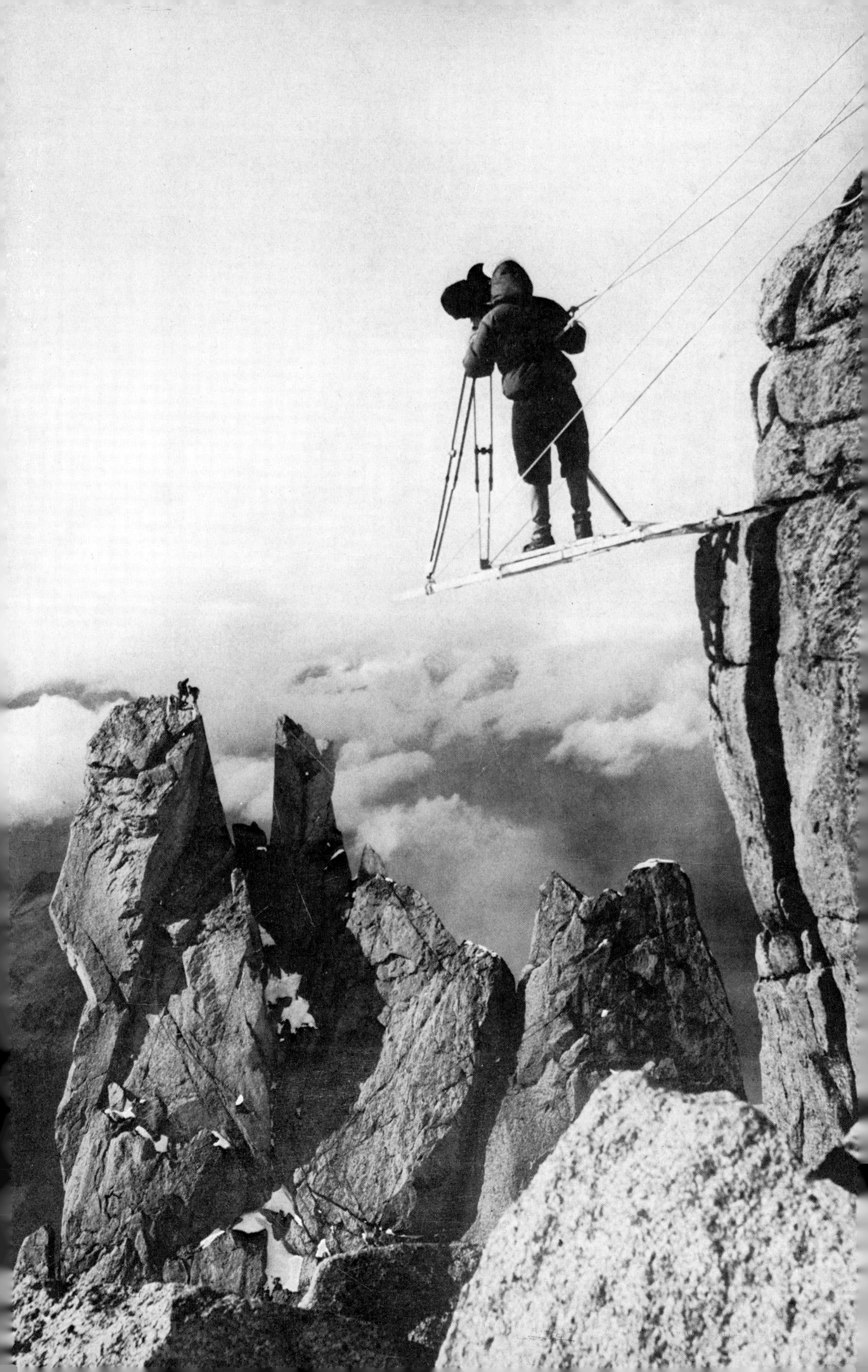

109 In a social drama an open situation is being delineated and developed.

110 Excursion then: Sin Yoon Bok, Excursion.

VII

From knowledge to ethics

Knowledge, technology, ethics

Our simple, developmental model, comprising the mythical, ontological and functional stances, was meant to characterize not only certain ways of knowing but also of acting and experiencing. That there is an intimate connection between knowledge and action finds most emphatic expression in the modern world in the question of the sciences and their ethical implications. Our sciences have transformed the patterns of daily life to such an extent that we can no longer simply ignore this question, as though it did not come into ordinary moral decisions. The fact is that the decisions which the individual keeps having to take (such as whether to give money to some cause or other, send in a letter to a newspaper, continue his children's education on the same basis as before) turn out to involve a mixture of moral and scientific considerations. As to the scientific factors, they may be present in the simplest forms, if only in the readiness of the individual concerned to accept information which reaches him in conversation or through the press and information media. Decisions without any backing of information must be as rare as information totally unaffected by scientific ideas. In a mythical society this unity of knowing and acting, of the mythical world picture, social relations and individual obligations, probably comes about much more as a matter of course. The ontological standpoint brings with it a sharper division between various areas of knowledge, moral values and so forth. In the modern period some integration becomes all the more exigent as the strands of society become more intricately interwoven.

There is another development which tends to make the whole question of ethics more central than ever before: the movement away from an individualist ethic toward one concentrated more on the group or indeed on mankind as a whole. This is very properly described as a transition from a micro- to a macro-ethics. Of course, it would be untrue to say that in times past the macro-ethical dimension has been entirely absent. In the mythical world, in ancient Greece, in Hebrew thought and Chinese philosophy, we encounter ethical rules extending far beyond the individual. Yet in the more recent history of Western ethics the central question is much more how *I* am to act with regard to my individual neighbour. Even now a lot of people think exclusively in terms of an ethics of personal relationships. A macro-ethics poses questions of another sort. It entails more than just a scaling-up of currently received ethical practice: moral requirements as they relate to cooperation for development are more than amplified norms regarding a concern for poor people, issues centred around weapons of total annihilation different from those that have to do with conventional warfare; and the ethical problems arising from modern medicine, with its ability to interfere with vital processes, are assuredly not just extensions of the family doctor's traditional ethics. We might perhaps define this changeover from micro- to macro-ethics as a transition from an ethics centred on persons to one that relates to structures.

It is precisely within this new dimension that the previous point becomes clearer than ever: we mean, the indispensability of scientific and technically reliable information. But this again is more than just a matter of adding an extra degree of insight which is assumed to be lacking in what are otherwise adequate grounds for the making of moral decisions. The ethics at issue here actually takes on a different character, not merely because of the changeover to a macroscale but also because the old certainties have disappeared. We are no longer in a position to start from norms laid down in advance. The need to command reliable information extends to the very heart of the ethics: ethical norms are the guidelines for action, but they emerge only as a critical reaction to that information. This interaction between norms and hard, concrete data, on which we propose to elaborate in the present chapter, signposts the transition from a more ontological ('what') ethics to a functional ('how') one.

As we shall see, the central problem of ethics is the question of a criterion for assimilating information into a context of action – a question that involves all the structures of society. This quest for a new dimension, for alternatives to existing rules and structures, is what gives its keenest edge to the question of an ethics for the future. This becomes most evident when we observe how via its technological applications man's knowledge results in the problem of modern ethics as stated. For convenience we shall work with a model articulated, as it were, in three parts: knowledge, technology, ethics. This should help shed more light on the problem as it has now been presented.

The sciences emerge within the ontological outlook because they require a disjunction or distancing vis-à-vis an environing nature, at any rate when it comes to sciences which have gained their autonomy. They concentrate on the theoretical explanation of phenomena (empirical sciences) and on purely regulative structures (formal sciences). Sometimes they, or their practitioners, even give the impression that such knowledge is an end in itself and is unconnected with other spheres, such as that of responsible, considered action. Values and moral criteria then come to be seen as factors lying wholly outside of science, coming up for consideration, if at all, only when some question of applying or misapplying science arises. Without going into all the difficult questions this raises, we can say that out of this ontological position a clear development does emerge: one in which knowledge expands and grows into technology, and that in turn develops into ethically relevant action. For a more functional approach it is precisely this development – a move forward from 'what' to 'how' – that matters most. We shall now try to show that it is in the 'how', that is, in ethics, that the true nature of all man's pursuits, including the scientific mode of knowing, is brought to light. A more functional way of seeing things can then be made to include the sciences and human knowing in general, so that any sharp division between value-free science and evaluative insight and action in religion, ethics or politics disappears. We can then assign to the term 'ethics' a wider signification than simply that of a moral doctrine or a system of moral norms: the whole of existence, whether of the individual or of society, is a matter of responsibility and is therefore ethical.

The mythical world is dominated by mysterious forces: nature, life, sexuality, fertility, death, inventiveness: all these are 'powers' of which man stands in awe. Knowledge, technology and ethics are part and parcel of this, and have not yet achieved their independence and autonomy. With the distancing which the ontological outlook involves knowledge moves more into the foreground. The alien powers or forces of the cosmos, the 'polis' (community) and the individual are now distinguished, analysed and so far as is possible explained. The sciences are the precipitate of this knowledge, which is however broader in some respects and also finds expression in, for instance, metaphysical systems and the art of politics. But it is most obvious of all in the sciences that what is happening is something like a takeover of power. The forces outside of man can be exposed to view by man's insight and understanding; indeed, their power can even be resolved into explicable 'laws'. Scientific explanation does give man's reason a certain control over the phenomena all around him.

We might put all this differently again. Man's knowledge is confronted with transcendent powers, that is to say, with powers lying beyond human compass. However, as such knowledge develops on its own independent lines, the effect is to render that transcendence increasingly immanent, that is to say, to bring it under man's control. This tendency shows up even more clearly when knowledge is made applicable. Francis Bacon, in describing the basic theme of his new outlook on the sciences, as embodied in his *Novum Organum,* stated that it had to do with the interpretation of nature or, in other words, with man's capacity for control: *"de interpretatione naturae sive de regno hominis".* A long course of development of ontological thinking led up to this and now culminates in this dictum. K. Fischer has drawn a parallel between Spinoza and Bacon. The former gives us a metaphysical system in which the transcendent and the immanent coincide: Nature is the Godhead. This idea has a liberating effect in that the dominating role of the passions and the power of things are both removed. Bacon's concern is with an idea that is heuristically organized, that is to say, is in pursuit of new discoveries and inventions. Whilst Spinoza's aim, as Fischer puts it, is to ensure that things cease to control us, Bacon's is that we should control things. The next step, therefore, is the empirical-cum-experimental realization of theoretical knowledge in technological power.

Envisaged in this way, technology is no accidental or adventitious circumstance but the consequence of knowledge. Initially alien, that is, transcendental, powers are rendered immanent in technology and made to serve the genius of man. The powers of nature and society, even those of the mind of man itself, are analysed, explained and finally forced to do man service in enlarging his own authority and control. 'Technology' is a term that covers a wider field, therefore, than simply that of the machine-, energy- and information technologies we were talking about earlier on. The regulating of society, making experiments with animals, applying science in various ways in the sphere of welfare and health services and so on – these also have to be included within the range of man's technologies.

It can sometimes be made to appear as though with a highly developed technology man's control is complete. Science-fiction writers often put forward a picture of the future in which the sole decisive factor is the perfecting of technology. But it is precisely in this advance of technology that a remarkable reversal makes itself felt. Instead of man's control increasing all the time, completely new and disconcerting problems appear as a result of this technological progress. Technology gives rise to new questions regarding man's work, his social relations, the domination of man by those very social structures and concentrations of power which made their entrance into human history along with technology itself. As it has turned out, the last word has not been spoken with technology by any means; for the question has now arisen as to *how* this technology is to be applied. At this juncture the third facet of our model looms into view: ethics.

Knowledge and technology have a tendency to bring the transcendence of the alien powers within man's compass: that is, to make them immanent. In ethics a new constellation emerges: the powers turn out to be both immanent and transcendent. Technological mastery of the powers is not, it would seem, an automatic or self-evident business; but it faces man with decisions regarding the ways (the 'how') in which he is to employ his technologies. Any attempt to avoid this has its repercussion on even the most objective knowledge. The Italian surrealist painter, Giorgio de Chirico, depicts the mathematician who is so little engaged with the world around him that he himself changes into a mathematical object (a good illustration too of the operationalist conception of man) and the world takes on an ominous astringency, because there is no longer anything happening in it (ill. 99, p. 172). A cartoon in *Punch* pushes home the point that the most abstract calculations imply a knowledge which, when technologically applied, may well lead to ethically shocking events (ill. 111).

What norms or criteria must man pursue if his policy for the technological moulding of nature and society is to have a positive outcome?

'Of course, if $\int_a^b v^2 du = \lim_{n\to\infty} \sum_{i=1}^{n}\left(\frac{v_i}{t_i}\right)^2 \cdot \frac{v_i}{t_i}$ we're done for.'

111 Mathematics and its results (cartoon by G. Wilson).

How indeed can this technological culture become a strategy that will make all men free participants in this cultural programme, instead of leaving them captive to impersonal forces conjured up by the technologist's skill and the ingenuity of the organizer? Manifestly, it calls for criteria which go above and beyond the immanence of technology itself. Ethics is what breaks open technology and confers a transcendent dimension – a dimension of menace and of expectancy, of critical evaluation and responsibility – upon the whole strategy of culture.

Natural, biological and cultural sciences

Man's objectively orientated knowledge develops through a line of successive sciences. This sequence is a systematic one: it takes us from the study of those areas more remote from man toward others in which man's position is a very central one. The same sequence will often be found in history too; but it may happen that because of social or other constellations the primary concern of science is not with nature outside of man; instead, it chooses man himself as its immediate subject. In the systematic sequence scientific knowledge first of all concentrates on the phenomena which are rather more easily repeatable and occur over a wide area: nature. Of course, man constitutes a part of that nature and from the standpoint of the natural sciences is aligned with all other natural phenomena. The sciences concerned with living nature have what is already a more restricted field for investigation. When Archimedes' law speaks of "a body submerged in a fluid . . ." then 'body' denotes any material object, whether it be Archimedes' own body, as he steps into his bath, or the volume of a golden crown that is dipped in water, or a piece of wood, floating in a river. When the biological sciences talk about a 'body', this has a narrower signification, as they deal only with organic – and therefore living – bodies. In the cultural sciences the terrain is more restricted still. The events and processes are much less repeatable here than in the natural sciences or even the biological ones. Often it is a question of once-only historical occurrences. Nature and (biological) life merely constitute a background to the transformations, no longer describable in purely physical or biological terms, which are effected through symbols and rules in human society.

In the succession of natural, biological and cultural sciences there is yet another sharp differentiation to be noted. Primitive man responds to the forces of nature with feelings of awe, at any rate at the nodal points of his existence. But there is a sense in which life-forces are even more drastic in their effects; for after all, we are here confronted with life and death, fecundity and disease. Still more directly does man feel himself involved with forces of a more social character: family and tribal ties, the rules of respect for and control over others. In a mythical society these three groups of forces are all meshed together, it is true; and it would be hardly possible to mark them off as separate terrains. But as history proceeds, distinctions of this sort stand out more clearly. The power of nature is detected and distinguished in all social contexts, primitive and modern. A fearful reverence for the life force finds specific expression in some ancient cultures, particularly that of India: the doctrine of 'ahimsa' or non-violence, for example, is part of that. An awareness of the 'powers' inherent in society is something very characteristic, of course, of the modern period, although it is to be found in innumerable ancient cultures as well. The feeling of most people nowadays, however, is that whilst in large measure the forces of nature have been examined and can be canalized, and the life forces have to some extent been identified and made manageable by technology, the 'powers' inherent in our social structures have only very incompletely been brought to consciousness and so far remain almost entirely beyond the range of human control.

All this stands out more sharply if we now take our three segments (knowledge, technology, ethics) and set them alongside the growing tendency of the sciences to converge on the area of man and society (ill. 124, p. 200). First, where the natural sciences are concerned, we can affirm that knowledge here has made enormous progress and to a very large extent the alien forces are accounted for and by means of symbols brought under control – one thinks of the application of mathematics to physics, of the use of symbols in chemistry, which in the setting of the periodic system of elements offers far-reaching possibilities of explanation, and so forth. The second segment, that of technological control, has likewise undergone a far-reaching development. Modern technology, up to and including information-technology, has come about mainly through various applications of the natural sciences. Natural forces, felt at one time to be a kind of blind fate, have in many respects become factors playing their part within the human strategy. This is especially striking, to use only this one illustration, in regard to the explosive energies in nature. The ability to control fire is in itself characteristic of man's mode of being; in ancient myths this power is described as being borrowed or even stolen from the gods, and in paleontology the use of fire is taken as a criterion for distinguishing proto-men or primitive men from the simian primates. However, natural science makes possible technological control over even more radically destructive forces – a development marked in energy-technology by the use of electricity and the internal combustion-engine and, in the most recent development, of nuclear forces too.

With respect to the third segment, that of ethics, we are still at the beginners' stage. It was about a hundred years ago that the ethical consequences of technology and of the resultant industrialization and mechanization began to command the attention of a wide circle of people. Thus modern physics and mechanics, among other things, begins in Galileo Galilei's room (in reconstructed form depicted in ill. 100, p. 172) at Pisa, where he was professor at the end of the 16th century and from the famous tower conducted his experiments connected with the laws of falling bodies. One result of the laws of mechanics was the industrialization of the last century. Gustave Doré has exposed in an artistic and yet

112 Excursion now: a Japanese bridal pair go off in a helicopter.

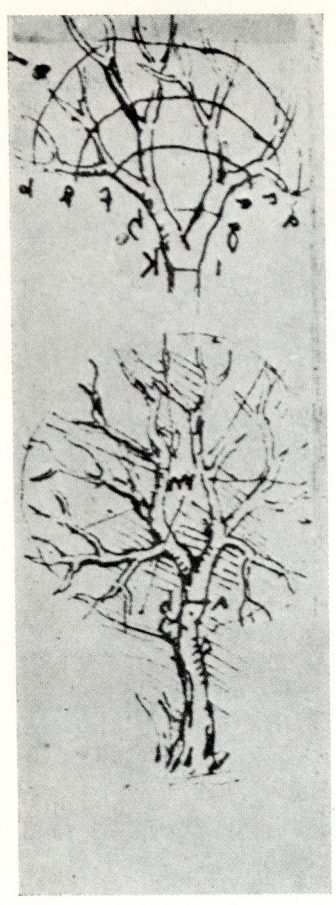

114 P. Mondriaan, The red tree.

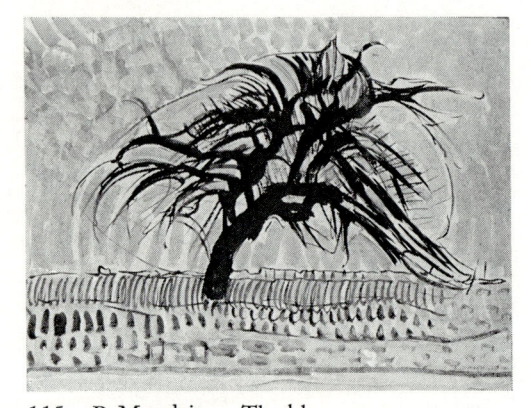

113 Leonardo da Vinci, diagram of the growth of a tree.

115 P. Mondriaan, The blue tree.

116 P. Mondriaan, The grey tree.

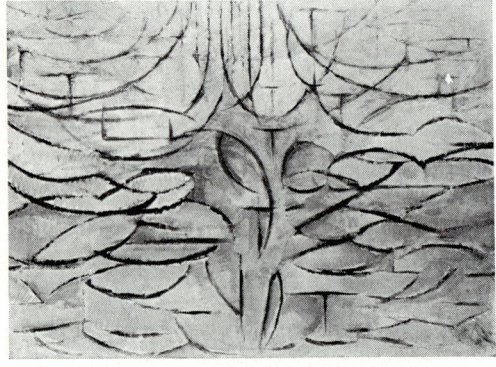

117 P. Mondriaan, Appletree in blossom.

118 Human countenance and grief (photo: Cas Oorthuys, from: *Family of man*).

119 Crucial events: a Buddhist monk burns himself to death in Vietnam.

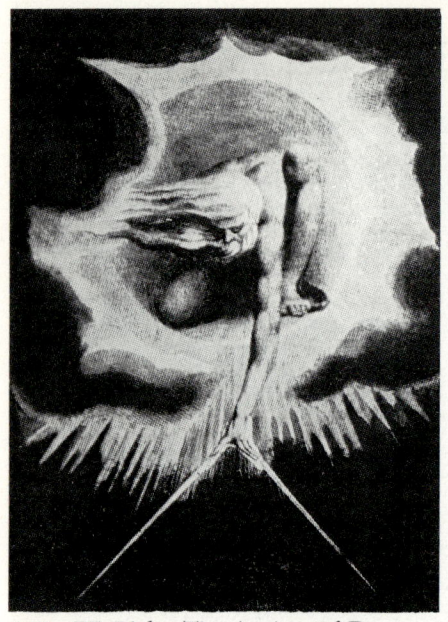

120 W. Blake, The Ancient of Days.

121 T. Zuccari, Conversion of Paul.

122 Crucial events: Martin Luther King: 'I had a dream'.

123 Human countenance and grief: C. Hofer, Das schwarze Zimmer.

extremely critical fashion the London slums, which again typify the socio-moral consequences of that same industrialization (ill. 101, p. 172).

Routine work threatened to turn man into 'a cog in the machine'. Heavy industries demanded enormous capital investment and put economic power in the hands of small groups. The emergence of a workers' proletariate led Marx to form the notion that there would be a progressive and inevitable descent into misery for the workers *(Verelendungstheorie)*. And indeed had a purely technological and industrial society given free play to calamitous forces, that would have been a defeat for the learning-process of the human race. A new form of control was needed: no longer a purely technological one, reducing everything to immanent processes, but a moral one which would establish more transcendent norms. This process of ethical structuring is an extremely broad one in that it embraces political and social changes as well as reforms in the sphere of labour-legislation. Yet it remains an ethical process, because it is not a question of technical, organizational, political measures and so on, but of a critical evaluation, the growth of a new sense of responsibility in all these areas. We today find ourselves in the middle of this development. The transition from welfare to wellbeing, from a technologically perfected consumer society to the need for learning how to consume within an ethically responsible selective procedure: all these issues, which we were discussing at the end of the preceding chapter, have now to be reckoned with.

This need to become ethically aware in order to achieve a responsible strategy for modern culture is thus becoming a central factor in the development of the natural sciences. This applies with even more force to the sciences concerned with life, since they are as it were one stage behind the natural sciences in the narrower sense. Among the sciences referred to are biology, genetics, the medical sciences. The growth of knowledge in these fields has been especially rapid over the last two hundred years; but its technical application is more recent. Rembrandt's famous 'Anatomy lesson' shows a stage at which knowledge is being acquired, a stage in which medical science was still more or less wholly immersed (ill. 103, p. 173). The photo of an operation carried out with the aid of a laser-beam (ill. 102, p. 173) reveals something of the rapid rate of recent development in the sphere of technological applications. The onlookers, psychologically so well typed by Rembrandt, are no longer visible here;

they are perhaps following the operation on a screen with which the operating theatre is connected via a closed television-circuit.

Major developments in medical practice are closely related to transplant techniques, the use of antibiotics, the manufacture of 'mind drugs' (psychopharmaceutics), interference in the mechanism of the cell and so forth. Here again, the regulation of explosive energies offers a good illustration of the extensive technical capability of these applied sciences. Discoveries in the field of biochemistry and genetics, whereby a start has been made with deciphering the genetic code, bring in prospect many techniques that will enable us to control, for instance, the explosive proliferation of cells which occurs in the case of diseases like cancer. More drastic still will be the ability to affect the genetic code itself, because in that way millions of cells, which arise later from the gene, nay, many genuses even, can be transformed in their hereditary structures.

This brief summary may serve to remind the reader about the many discussions which are taking place just now all over the world regarding the explosive possibilities that present themselves here and are causing such grave disquiet among so many experts in the bio-medical sciences. What this means is that the third segment, that of ethics, is as yet still in its infancy. Traditional ethical norms in medicine are turning out to be quite inadequate. At this very point, in fact, it becomes clear just how much man is able to transform what is given in nature and thus to bring it within the scope of his decision-making. In time past it was possible to hold life in respect as a purely natural mystery, nothing more or less. Now, however, medical techniques are opening up possibilities of prolonging life; so that the normative function of 'the natural' disappears and the ethical question as to whether it is admissible or not to prolong life in various situations becomes very acute. Obviously, ethics can no longer be envisaged as a 'what', as a list of self-subsistent norms, but has to assume the form of a 'how', of a continually revised normative assessment of medical techniques.

With the cultural sciences we leave the realm of purely natural data and enter that of the transforming activity of man. The need for critical evaluation as a hallmark of the strategy of culture will soon be more pressing than ever here, because these sciences follow in their turn behind those that deal with living things. Knowledge in this field of the cultural sciences – among which we reckon here the social sciences, the sciences of human behaviour, the systematic study of language and of history – is something recent. Thus psychology and sociology, as independent sciences, have so far existed for less than a century. Techniques are already part of the bidding, albeit in a less advanced state than in the biological sciences. By means of simple models, simulated situations, role games and the like some attempt is being made to trace the principles governing the mental and social life of man and then, by a process of adaptation, to regulate them. Recent research in linguistics has often resulted in a new programming of learning-processes, whilst even the study of history can prove instructive, resulting in the adoption of political techniques, including those that may help keep in check explosive situations likely to lead to war.

It is evident that what happened earlier on in the realm of the natural sciences and much more recently in that of the biological sciences as well will also arise in the cultural sciences: the need for some ethical control of the possibilities of technical application. On several scores this need is already becoming obvious: one has only to think of the brainwashing techniques which in fact have already become widespread within the power-structures of modern society (propaganda, advertisement, monopoly control of the media of mass communication). In many cultural milieus the 'knowledge' stage makes a very early start; and then it still has a markedly academic character – note the Chinese scholars depicted in an ancient drawing studying their texts (ill. 104, p. 174). But modern methods of education, of which the contemporary teaching-machine is a kind of precipitate (ill. 105, p. 174), make deep inroads into the growth and formation of the human mind.

One begins to suspect that one is confronted here with technical possibilities of influencing and regulating human behaviour and the inner life of the mind that are even more alarming than those presented by the medical sciences. That is hardly astonishing: in ancient times the powers of nature inspired in man a reverential awe, those inherent in the life force were soon more drastic still in their effect; but the powers of society are even more awe-inspiring. Perhaps this is because we are no longer concerned here with forces linked directly with nature, but with powers which in some fateful way man himself continues to invoke. Thus it must be the aim of a positive strategy to get these forces under control and to lead them in the right direction. Ethics as a responsible evaluation of the technological forces enshrined in the knowledge gained through the cultural sciences has still to be learned, in this new, more functional sense. Concentrations of political and economic power, impersonal social structures, the mood and spirit of the times, the mentality and life-style: all these are forces still elusive and incomprehensible in many respects. It may perhaps turn out to be more difficult to get these forces under control than those of nature. They constitute a self-enclosed, immanent field; and not until this has been broken open and a transcendent dimension unfolded in ethical reflection and consciousness can there be any question of a growth of freedom for man.

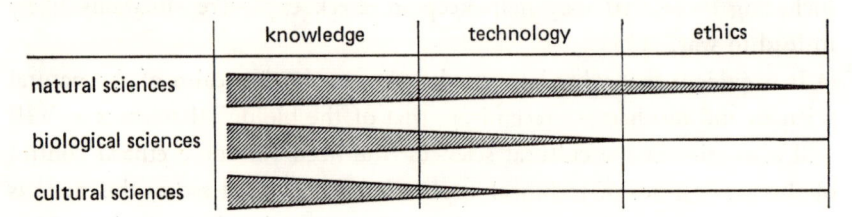

	knowledge	technology	ethics
natural sciences			
biological sciences			
cultural sciences			

124   Schematic diagram of the three phases of science.

An ethics of interaction

The preceding sections may have made two things clear. First, that mankind today is still at the beginning of a long process whereby the non-natural powers in particular have to be brought within the orbit of man's responsibility. When there is discussion about the future of mankind and culture, it centres far too much on questions regarding technological command of the forces of nature. The main items discussed relate on the one hand to the growth of technology and automation and on the other to man's increasing medico-biological resources. We have been contending that even in those areas the question of the ethical control of such processes is paramount and that this question has to be posed with still greater urgency in regard to the powers that are not simply given in nature. The very fact that these questions are so urgent and at the same time still so vast and wellnigh incalculable makes the significance of culture as a learning-process even clearer. The more rich and variegated our culture becomes, the less it would appear to be a finished product. Rather is it a confrontation with wholly new situations calling for a more far-reaching liberation of man. Thus culture is the mobile strategy by which man, employing what are often inventive innovations, tries to react in a more purposeful way to the reality around him. This reacting is in fact a response on his part, not just as a cognitive and technologically performative being, but more especially as a being committed to ethical evaluation, that is, to responsibility.

A further point that emerged is the need for a concrete ethics. Ethics, after all, is evidently not limited to purely moral prescriptions. It is rather man's total strategy for bringing impersonal forces, whether of nature or society, within the range of his own capacity for decision-making. Religious belief, political engagement, social activism, educational policy, the democratizing of society – ethics has to do with all these. At the same time this implies that ethics is not something self-contained; and it goes far beyond the ethical norms of a particular society. In the context of the ontological outlook it was still possible to speak of a system of self-subsistent, ethical values; and the value sometimes held to be the culmination of this was 'goodness'. These ethical values were then applied to concrete phenomena like human conduct or political policy. In that way ethics had an influence on the great diversity of historical events and human activities. Nowadays, in a more functionally orientated culture, all that is no longer feasible. Moral norms are not established a priori, before they are applied, but they emerge within the ethical programme, itself orientated upon a multiplicity of concrete events and problem-situations. An ethics has always to be substantiated, therefore, by concrete instances. It is no longer the case that we act on the basis of an ontological-cum-ethical kind of knowledge; but the ethics itself comes into being only in an interaction with what in fact occurs. We have here an ethics of interaction, of an interaction between the moral sense and concrete problems.

An illustration of this is afforded by the issue touched on in the previous section: that of the prolongation of life. Medical techniques have brought about a concretely given situation which was scarcely imaginable before. Life was, and in many countries still is, an extremely precarious business. The mortality rate shows just how few of the large numbers of children living in medically and hygienically poor conditions survive. In the case of many progressive diseases knowledge has fallen so far short that the doctor simply had no means of changing the course of the illness; the only thing he could do was to alleviate the suffering somewhat. As we have moved from that situation to one where rapidly improved medical understanding has led to a therapeutic and even preventive technique, giving rise to a drastic limitation of the mortality rate, so the ethical control of such a situation has come to present an immense problem. We must add here the innumerable possibilities for prolonging life in old people and the seriously ill. An already existing ethics, determined as it was by a natural reverence for the mystery of life and likewise by the need to preserve life, if it were at all possible, as a precarious asset, is now totally inadequate. It is not an a priori, given ethics that can any longer be the controlling factor where man seeks to act responsibly. The primary circumstance is the changed situation, in which the natural forces of life, disease and dying have come increasingly within the sphere of influence exerted by man through his culture. What is required is a breaking open, ethically speaking, of the forces which this technological power in its turn invokes; one thinks of the misery that results when we preserve, for the sake of preserving, the vital mechanism, where the individual concerned continues to be exposed to an advancing process of physical and mental suffering; or of the degrading situation that can arise when the cortex and with it the mental life of an individual are put permanently out of action, so that there is just a vegetating human organism witnessing to the onlooker from one day to the next to the moral impotence of this technical power of medicine.

This example can help to illustrate the fact that on the one hand ethics is a very comprehensive human strategy in that one is trying to regulate a whole series of situations in accordance with norms of humanity. But the example is also illuminating because it shows how ethical consciousness is pointed very concretely as responsible action and can only acquire form through interaction with very specific events and processes. This serves to remove ethics from the realm of purely intellectual contemplation or metaphysical (envisaged in detachment from empirical reality) constructions. Ethics needs to be keen-eyed if it is to perceive in any concrete circumstance where the rub will come. This ties in with a broader issue: the business of visualizing, in which the intellect and the senses perform together. In the sciences it is often the graphic model that serves this purpose, and in education it is personal example; in ethics it is the transformation of a situation into an 'eye-catcher' – an arresting spectacle –

that can achieve this effect.

Another example may help to drive home this point. At a particular spot on a motorway there is a 'reduce speed now' warning, put there because of some difficulty in obtaining a clear view of the overall situation. Generally speaking, motorists will to some extent heed such a warning notice. But if one day a car actually comes to grief at that spot and the wreckage is still lying there on the road, the drivers' behaviour will change, because the reduction they make in their speed will now be very obvious indeed. The visual warning provided by a car which has actually had an accident clearly has a far, far greater effect. Thus the visualizing is not just the picture with the warning – in fact the danger notices on the road are such an eye-catching visual factor in themselves – but the connection between the formulated rule (e.g., 'drive slowly') and the actual event (the car accident). In the same way ethics is only feasible in an interaction with factual occurrences and with whole constellations as they emerge under the influence of sciences and technologies.

Visualizing is coming to play a bigger and bigger role in our lives today. Television, audio-visual instruction, advertisement and so much else is deliberately concentrated on man's whole world of perception and representation, so as to be able to penetrate more deeply into the human psyche. The close-up, as employed in filming, brings whatever may be happening right up to the spectator: an exciting mountain-climb (ill. 108, p. 183) takes place in front of our noses, making us conscious of our own resistances as well as of our impulse to go on.

Teaching, the educational process, will have to take full advantage of these opportunities for visualizing. Where the future is concerned, the functional character of education, especially of higher education, requires what are really two separate and distinct components. On the one hand it will become more and more necessary to formalize. This means in fact eschewing everything concrete and representable, so that what are acquired are just methods of operating with data, as happens in symbolic logic and mathematics. Thus these formal sciences are coming to have more and more bearing on certain areas of the sciences concerned with life and culture, and no longer simply on that of the natural sciences. By formalizing we concentrate on the 'how' of the data to be investigated (these points have been discussed in rather more detail already in chapter IV). But there is a second component; and that is visualizing. Purely formal rules are the blueprints, as it were, for a possible ordering or organizing of knowledge (as in the natural, biological and cultural sciences) and for possible procedures (as in technologies). But this leaves so many courses still open to us. In technical language we say that such formal systems (mathematics, for instance) have not yet been interpreted. They have, then, to be interpreted; which means that they have somehow to be linked up with concrete events. How do we interpret them? How do we use them to try and extend or transform existing situations in a justifiable way? It is here that along with our ethical questioning there also emerges the need to visualize.

By laying methodical emphasis on the 'how' in the teaching process we should be able to achieve a new approach to education that will do justice to the formal as well as the visual aspect and so eventually draw a line of connection from knowledge to ethics and from teaching to character-training. In the latter kind of activity theoretical cases are sometimes delineated in socio-drama by the participants themselves and so are 'lived out' in terms of moral experience (ill. 109, p. 184).

Another example of pointing ethics sharply and concretely may help to illuminate what we have just been propounding from yet a different angle. The big city has created a new constellation in which the old norms for human social intercourse are no longer valid. The fact that people now live in enormous blocks of flats (to take only this one point) makes the contacts between individuals quite different, to say the least. People talk, and rightly so, of the anonymity of the large city. Yet this is by no means in every respect a bad thing. In certain regions of India and in parts of Africa the man who migrates to the big town often feels this anonymity to be a liberating experience: a deliverance from the increasingly restrictive bonds of caste or tribe. Ethically, however, the anonymity of the big town or metropolis and the patterns presented by a mass society have somehow to be taken in hand and dealt with. Otherwise there is the danger of loneliness, or of the isolation of small protest-groups, or of a total conformism in which the individual loses his own identity, or of flight into an illusory world of opiates or of an irrational urge to destroy, and all the other disruptive tendencies which many social psychologists have already pointed out. Such an ethics must consist in an active process of gearing the individual and the family unit into the forces constituted by urban society.

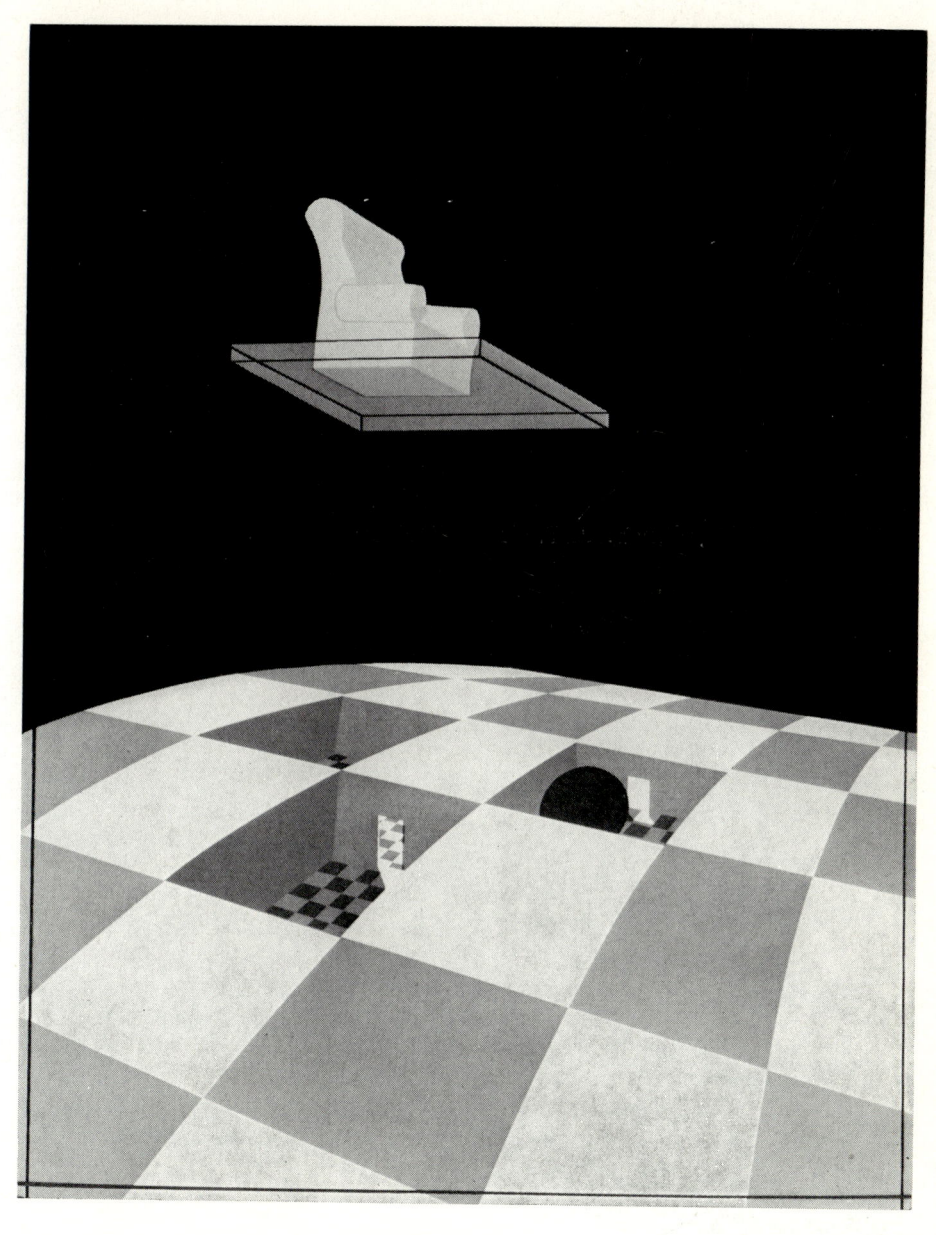

125 Disengaged existence: J. Henneman, The floating armchair.

126 Mankind has dirty hands: P. Picasso, Guernica.

127 A. Robida, a picture forecasting the emancipation of women, 'Women's Lib'.

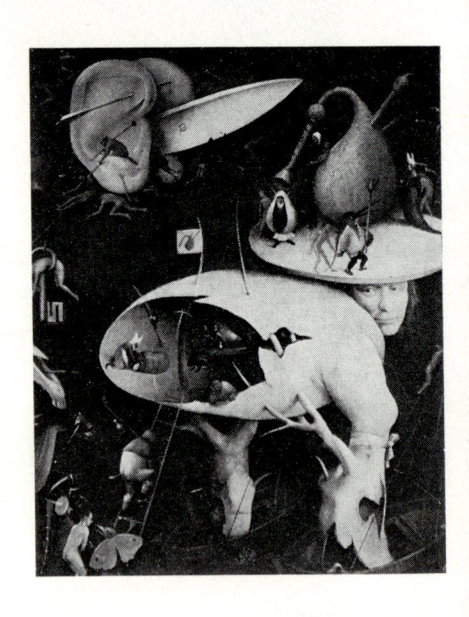

128 J. Bosch, Hell (detail).

But this in turn has to be made concrete through interaction with what is actually happening in that social structure. Thus, to give an example, anyone and everyone must surely benefit from the building up of defence mechanisms against the innumerable daily contacts they have with other people: fellow residents, visitors, tradesmen, officials, investigators and so forth. The approach we adopt to one another must often be operational, simply in the quality of the various roles in which our mutual encounters occur. A personal relationship is bound to be quite deliberately excluded in cases of this sort. On the other hand, amid these contacts we must nevertheless construct some relationships which *are* specific and personal. 'Face to face' contacts are not possible in large numbers, but in specific cases they are necessary. A medical specialist, hard pressed every day during consulting hours, expressed this by saying that he was unable to give more than two minutes to each patient, but each day he paid a great deal of attention to one patient and spent a much longer time with that one, partly with his attitude toward his other patients in mind, so that in one instance, at least, he could develop and maintain a real personal contact. This applies with even more force in, say, a housing situation – that kind of constellation – where it is not so much operationally conditioned as in the context of a 'job' or a profession. Of course, these kinds of personal contacts can no longer be made just haphazardly with someone; but then an ethical strategy of this sort entails our learning to pick and choose. This one example, therefore, leads us to conclude that what people need, at any rate, is to cultivate, as they have not as yet been accustomed to do, discrimination in their choice of friendships, if a supportable pattern of society is to be achieved in the mass structure of the metropolis.

The examples already given have helped in a number of respects to define more precisely the nature of the interaction. Some acquaintance, often in an interdisciplinary context (e.g., doctors, psychologists, welfare workers), with the concrete, ethically relevant events (the 'eye-catcher' transformation) is necessary, as well as a formally operational approach combined with visualizing, whilst at the same time learning how to be selective is indispensable too. To this one might add a training in the discovery of alternatives, sometimes even of a new system of rules. This point came up in an earlier chapter, when we were talking about the highest form of learning process: that of inventive restructuring. That may be realized in quite simple practices and customs. Compare the boating expedition painted in the 18th century by the Korean artist, Sin Yoon Bok (ill. 110, p. 184) with a modern excursion which technology as it were integrates into a new system of rules: the Japanese honeymoon, for which use is frequently made of a helicopter (ill. 112, p. 193).

In this sense the whole of culture would seem to have the character of a strategy which is never self-evident and never concluded.

Selectivity provides a new rule just where an excess of information, consumer articles, leisure time and personal contacts might be supposed to be stifling life. Alternatives give us a new rule by opening up new possibilities beyond the existing ones, that is, beyond those now accepted or recognized by everybody. In the business of learning how to consume, which we were discussing in the previous chapter, man's inventiveness proves so far seriously inadequate; and so the strategy of culture has been developed more on technological than on ethical lines. A selective approach to the acquisition of goods and the use of money and free time is something that comes about less in the course of things than we are wont to believe: on the contrary, it is something that has still to be learned. Again, discovering alternatives that lie outside the range of known possibilities calls for a new attitude in which what is technologically practicable, for instance, in the spheres of economics and recreation, comes more and more under the regulative control of ethics. Here too the application of norms of a transcendent character – that is, one neither self-evident nor natural nor given on technological grounds, but emerging from political ideals or social commitment or religious belief – is needed to break open the immanent sphere of possibilities.

It is especially difficult to envisage alternatives in any concrete terms, not only because one has to create new rules of the game, as it were, but also because it is all too easy to leave out of account various resistances and obstacles. We could even say that the greatest degree of inventiveness is necessary to envisage the effort required to make an alternative a reality. In a utopia things are quite different; for it criticizes an existing situation from the vantage-point of an ideal notion of society, posited in such absolute terms that whilst on the one hand the critique may be very radical, on the other hand this kind of utopia offers no realizable alternative. And when some attempt is made to bring about a utopia, it can only succeed by dint of forcing the situation and doing violence to it, so that demonism and dictatorship may well be its concomitants. Why is this? Because a utopia takes no account of the 'gravitational pull' of social reality, that is to say, of human impotence, moral failure. Genuine alternatives demand the recognition that the liberation of man and his self-realization must always involve a great deal of painful effort: an alternative to a given social constellation must not ignore suffering, guilt, antagonism, but meet and assimilate them.

A few examples may help to illustrate this. In a situation where there is a persisting threat of war moral inventiveness is needed to provide an alternative which will be a guide to political action. But such an alternative must be more than a utopia in which 'peace', as a polar opposite to war, is posited as an absence of war, aggression and conflicts. What has somehow to be attained is a positive assimilation of aggressiveness, the potential varieties of conflict and so on. New rules for society can be realized only when these kind of forces, which may even have their biological roots (K. L. Lorenz), have been fully allowed for: they are not just negative, but in the context of a different sort of rules can assume a more positive function in human society. It is precisely in dealing with 'aggression' and 'conflict' that a great deal of modern research in the biological and human sciences points in that direction.

To this we might add quite a number of other examples. One thinks of the protest levelled at the family structure because of the authoritarian style of its influence on the growing child. Here again, a utopian rejection of the family is unrealistic: what is needed is for the biological kinship-relation to be repeatedly opened up in a critical, that is, an ethically warranted fashion within a new set of 'rules'. In the same way, the utopia represented by a world without work, a world of leisure pure and simple, is quite inane, unless as a real alternative to the present situation we begin to reflect seriously about difficulty and effort as factors indispensable to any genuine recreation. This calls for a whole programme that would deliberately eschew the tendency of the modern recreation industry to superficialize everything.

Within the present structuring of labour, too, alternatives are conceivable. One of the principal motivations for doing a job of work in society is still the financial reward. Some of the other incentives are job satisfaction, status, the free time made available, and so on. Where these factors are concerned, the incentive of responsibility is a genuine alternative, even though it does not rule out the rest altogether as contributing factors. If we want to make a sense of responsibility a principal incentive or motive for taking on this or that function in society, this must have far-reaching consequences. It presupposes at the very least a further spread of education and, in that process, a greater emphasis on upbringing and training; this is already a chapter to itself. Then it must also have an effect on incomes and the distribution of earnings, which will be determined less directly by the status attaching to this or that particular function. Again, it will entail a greater degree of participation by all the workpeople in the task of shaping the policies that involve and affect their own jobs. Finally, one would expect to see a direct and positive effect on job satisfaction and performance. This does not mean that the situation thus achieved would be a kind of static 'ideal'; for just such a sense of responsibility for the job would very likely go hand in hand with greater expertise, a better command of 'know how', even a new form of status. This would entail social difficulties that would themselves constitute a challenge demanding a progressive, ongoing ethical programme. It has not been our concern, however, to offer a detailed and persuasive exposition of alternatives to the present situation of labour in its psycho-social aspects, but merely to call attention to a possible item for discussion, as an illustration of what we are to understand by 'alternative rules'.

All the examples cited have this in common: that, first of all, they demand a more intensive interdisciplinary contact (educationists, politicians, scientists, and so forth) and, secondly, that they are bound to lead to greater integration of the various sectors of life within the unity of the individual person. One can also express this – and we shall return to the point in more detail in the next chapter – by saying that they are bound to contribute to the identity of the person. Man must not be allowed to get himself lost in the fatal forces of nature, but must take them under his own control. In so doing, he does not render them immanent, he does not become the autonomous master, for that would mean his being once more absorbed into his technological attainments. No; what he really needs is to assign and operate with norms, that is, to open up the structure and ordering of his life in a process that reaches beyond his own being as man, in order to arrive at an ethical and warranted regulation.

For man the normative is as it were 'the other side', the opposing player. Thus in religion the norm-originating authority, signified by the term 'God', does not derive from human insight or human feelings but stands over and above them; and in that sense, therefore, it functions as a perpetually new criterion for what is to be understood by such concepts as 'humanity', 'justice', 'trustworthiness', 'renewal'. This 'counterplay', this correction, whether its context happens to be religious or political or social, always has to be embodied in concrete constellations that have been made ethically relevant. One thing that should be mentioned in this connection is the need to ensure that criticism and alternatives are continually being brought up to date through (in politics) the existence of an opposition. There can be a genuine political opposition only where a group or a party is functioning in such a way as to provide real alternatives to existing policy. If this is not the situation, there is no genuine opposition, not even though the country in question may have 'opposition parties'. 'Democracy' too is basically determined by the existence of a constructive but critical opposition.

The foregoing illustrations have been so many items for discussion, taken from a variety of fields: medical care, urbanization, consumer habits, work motivation, political opposition. They are an attempt to show that extending the line from knowledge through technology to ethics can have relevance for a large number of distinct areas on each of which, severally, closer detailed study must be carried out and actually is being carried out in quite a number of publications. Our main purpose has been to elucidate the strategy of culture, which can develop in greater freedom only as the transcendent dimension — that of a wise ethical policy — is opened up. All this gives added emphasis to the functional character of our present culture. It has made it possible to distinguish more precisely the tension we described earlier on between a more operationalist tendency and the functional approach. As it turns out, therefore, a functional approach is by no means just a positive phase in the strategy of culture, but rather a new prospect in the learning process that is human history.

VIII

Possible and impossible worlds

The world's structures

In many sciences the term 'structure' has come to occupy a central place in both method and research. Structure is something that had in fact attracted the interest of research workers in, for example, botany a great deal earlier. M. Foucault makes the point that botanists in the 18th century define 'structure' as the composition, the fitting together, of the parts of a plant-organ. They take sometimes geometrical forms, sometimes those of parts of the human body (as Linnaeus did) as models for tracing organic structures, so that names could be assigned to them. Foucault concludes that by 'demarcating and filtering what is to be seen, the structure offers the possibility of being transcribed into language'.

Indeed, a structure is more than something given in the external world, because it is at the same time an organizing principle for our knowledge concerning that world. The cohesive relation between parts of an organism or between elements of a language may evince a particular pattern which for the scientist makes that cohesion accessible and manageable. As early as the first half of this century the *'Gestalt'* psychologists, so called, were talking about the distinction between a conjunction of parts and a sum of parts. At about the same period the linguists of the Prague school, including the Russian, R. Jakobson, were asserting that the sensorily perceptible import of a language, for instance, of the phonological elements, is less relevant than their reciprocal relations within the system. Thus the modern linguist, E. Benveniste, argues that the doctrine of structuralism stands for the ascendancy of the system over the elements and tries to trace the structure of the system through the relations of the elements.

Very recent developments have brought out yet another aspect of structure: the possibility of transformations. The network of relations is, after all, more important than the component elements; which means that the elements are interchangeable or can be replaced without the structure disintegrating. Leonardo da Vinci's diagram of the growth of trees (ill. 113, p. 194) presents a growth process as a network that is no longer tied to one particular exemplar. We find something analogous to this in the process of formalizing the tree, reflected in the series of four paintings by Mondriaan (ill. 114, 115, 116, 117, p. 194). Progressively, the 'red tree' (1908–1910), the 'blue tree' (1909–1910), the 'grey tree' (1912) and the 'appletree in blossom' (1912) lose their substantial and concrete character and turn into a process of transformation in which an abstract network emerges.

There are then describable structures that yield rules according to which the transformations will take place. In this way the same sort of structures can be revealed in extremely diverse data. In linguistics the school of N. Chomsky is trying to show this, whilst in a different fashion C. Lévi-Strauss's cultural anthropology is bent on bringing to light the same structures in differing cultures. Various interpretations of these structures are possible: are they timelessly valid rules, so to speak, or is it rather that they come about gradually, in a historical process? We are not going into those technical issues here, because whatever the answers may or may not be, the structure – in the words of J. Piaget – can be defined as a system of transformations which happen in accordance with certain rules, so that the system is maintained or expanded. This latter point arises particularly in connection with structures of living nature or of the human social world; yet all these features can be extended to include even mathematical structures which do, after all, exhibit basic patterns, continued or enlarged in countless possible adaptations.

The 'structure' concept is one on which a whole variety of penetrating studies have been written; but these introductory paragraphs on the subject were needed to enable us to table a more practical problem: that of modern man as the prisoner of social and political structures. It is true that in this very popular sense the term 'structure' is being taken in a somewhat less exactly defined signification, because what is denoted here is the ascendancy of all environing constellations over the individual. Yet it would seem that even here we are dealing with structures that can be analysed, described by means of rules and sometimes even formulated in the language of mathematics. And this is a point to which we must pay some attention and which will come up again later on: if we can recognize rule-structures, this implies the possibility of manipulating and of controlling future situations through them.

The simplest way of making this clear is with the help of what is now the classic phrase of earlier philosopher-logicians (like G. W. Leibniz) as well as of modern ones (like H. Scholz): 'all possible worlds'. What is meant by this is the infinite range of possibilities which is opened up by purely logical rules. These rules mark off what is possible from what is not; and there are innumerable ways of filling in formally conceived possibilities of this sort. Thus under an algebraic rule such as '$a + b = b + a$' one can comprehend all possibilities, such as $3 + 2 = 2 + 3$, $155 + 2375 = 2375 + 155$, and so on ($3 - 2 = 2 - 3$, for instance, being then ruled out). A logical rule such as 'A is not non-A' entails among other things that a person cannot cross a river and at the same time *not* cross it – which holds true if we fill out this abstract rule with the historical event of Caesar's crossing the Rubicon, and would still hold true, had Caesar not crossed the Rubicon. But according to Leibniz, this last case would imply that this historical world would have been a different one; for two logically conflicting circumstances cannot both be realized in one and the same world. Thus logical rules (logic, mathematics, pure structures) form as it were networks which can be filled in in innumerable ways. As regards the structures, the implication is that we can not only transpose what is visible into language but even into a symbol-language which is completely 'blank' and can therefore indicate something of all possible worlds that we might conceive of as filling in such a network. William Blake's engraving, dated 1794, presents a sort of vision of the creation of the world (ill. 120, p. 196). It is as though the mathematical, so far empty, area of all possible worlds is first spaced out with the pair of compasses; and then the world actually to be formed must be made to fit into it. Blake's work shows a resemblance to earlier works by Michelangelo and especially to the work by Taddeo Zuccari (about 1550), reproduced here (ill. 121, p. 196), which depicts the conversion of Paul. Even so, for Zuccari it is a question of a divine intervention in the history of this actual world; whereas Blake's concern is with the whirlwind motion of the divine Power, which has first to lay out geometrical space before time and history come into being as a framework for *this* actual world. That is why Blake's imagination is much more 'surrealistic' and the more 'vacant' gesture spans all possible constellations of fact.

Perhaps this line of argument will help to clarify the force of modern structural analyses. Through the study of a particular language, a particular culture, and so on, we are in fact aiming for rules that will hold good for all possible constellations in these fields. By so doing we arrive at an organizational scheme which is very comprehensive and is even expressible in mathematical terms. What is more, we can not only get to know the phenomena under examination much better in this way, but also predict future phenomena and so eventually control them.

At this point, however, we are ready to raise a fundamental question. Does not all this imply in advance that any future development is bound to fit into the structures we recognize here and now? In the detailed discussions on the theme of structuralism a number of finer distinctions have been drawn, it is true. Some acknowledge that the structures in themselves are subject to a particular course of development. Others believe that every change or transformation of structures is tied to certain underlying rules of transformation. We shall not be going into all those more technical discussions here; for our concern is more with the practical question as to whether structures of this sort do not stand in the way of a real development and renewal of culture. After all, each and every possibility must still comply with certain rules, rules that in one way or another exist. This we may construe in two ways. The first entails adopting a sort of cultural determinism: there are immutable laws, just as in nature, that determine the course of history. The second alternative is to envisage these structures not so much as an account of laws governing culture but as human rules which do not so much describe culture as seek to push it in a particular direction.

There is a good deal that argues in favour of the latter notion. The natural sciences identify the laws of nature. The sciences concerned with life concentrate on living phenomena. But the cultural sciences study those forces of a social character which man has himself called into being. That is why at the end of chapter VI we remarked that here especially it is never possible to speak of nature's 'fatal' forces, because man has to learn for himself how to control such powers in a responsible fashion: the strategy of culture.

One might start from very formal, for instance, mathematically formulated, structures (the network) in order subsequently to work them out in concretely given situations; this is very properly described as 'interpreting' a structure (in an earlier paragraph we referred to the 'filling in' of a network). As a further test of these propositions we propose to reverse the process and begin with the interpreted structures; that is, with the previously mentioned power structures of a social, political and organizational nature, in which modern man finds himself situated. It is often impossible to get a grasp of these power structures. Does power rest with a small group of big industrialists? But closer investigation reveals that they too in many cases are simply carrying out orders imposed on them, as it were, by international economic rules, advertising consultants, public opinion and so on. Does power reside with the legislative, with Parliament? But this again feels itself in many respects to be simply carrying out the recommendations of party experts, planning offices, publicity media. And so one ends up in a circle, because each group has a sense of giving effect to other influences. Therefore the structures of power are not in fact in the hands of a particular group, but are the deposit of the total interplay of groups, interests, mental outlooks, which results in a more or less elusive, impersonal power. As long as we are unable to regulate it on an ethical basis, for just so long will this power as a kind of fatality obscure our gaze and vision of the future.

The central question, therefore, is how socio-cultural structures are to be brought within the responsible control of concrete human beings. So long as those human beings are envisaged purely as a role, as a social function, there can be no prospect of success. Here we have a clear expression of operationalism, as described in chapter IV. The identity of individuals is wholly defined by the pattern of expectation within existing structures. They merge into the role laid upon them. That is why it is like clutching at emptiness to try and pin down the individuals who wield power in a society or group: they are merely exponents of invisible, omnipresent structures. Thus the only feasible solution lies in breaking out of this operationalist mechanism by re-establishing the functional stance of the person. This must mean that the individual will fulfil his roles, not by being absorbed into structures but by taking them in hand. Mere knowledge of these structures will not suffice. Even technical control only serves to enhance the power of such structures, because people and groups proceed to manipulate them simply on the basis of the technical possibilities implicit in them. Just as in chapter VII, the term 'technical' is used here in a broad sense, because it has to do with a variety of applications in such widely different fields as the organization of society, ways of influencing people's mental outlook, methods of escalation in politics, persuasion-patterns in advertising, manifestors, propaganda and so forth. Not until we achieve some ethical control can the power of the structures be taken in hand; but that requires us to qualify the structures and evaluate them. They are not just simply rules for all possible worlds and constellations; but then this raises the whole question of power structures, of what is neither admissible nor morally feasible in them.

The blind spot

In chapter VI we were expatiating on the action of a trigger-mechanism. It turned out that this involves a physical process which measured by certain rules has disproportionately large-scale consequences. This trigger-mechanism also plays a role in social structures. We are concerned here with some event which may be recorded in empirical and social terms but which acquires a far-reaching significance only when assessed within a system of moral rules. To put it another way: action on the part of the individual may have far-reaching consequences (can function as a trigger-mechanism), if such action can be made morally relevant. How does this come about? In the preceding chapter we defined ethics as a process of breaking through an immanent situation; the transcendent dimension of any ethical activity consists in assigning and applying norms, that is, in the critical evaluation of a given constellation. Determinateness, whether scientific (knowledge) or practical (technology), is no longer something we accept as a kind of fate. On the contrary, it is recognized as an impasse, so that the way is cleared for a wholly new sort of questioning, a new, only now truly warranted, strategy of culture.

Examples of such a trigger-mechanism are easy, the rules they bring into play extremely difficult, to indicate. In the case of panic arising in a difficult situation, say, in an aircraft, calm behaviour on the part of one person can mean the salvation of a large number; the fact that one person burns himself to death may alter a whole political situation; a small group of people who deliberately and persistently abrogate the tacitly acknowledged demarcation-lines between races and/or sub-cultures, say, in certain parts of a city, can bring about changes in society; a country which in its foreign policy sacrifices some economic or diplomatic advantage on moral grounds, so making – from a rational and prudential political standpoint – a wrong move, may produce for that very reason a general relaxation of tension. These examples could easily be supplemented with many others. Who could ignore in this connection Martin Luther King's famous speech beginning 'I had a dream' (ill. 122, p. 196) or the self-inflicted death by burning of a Buddhist monk in South Vietnam (ill. 119, p. 195), events that had far-reaching political consequences?

More difficult, however, is the business of analysing the rules by virtue of which such actions become relevant and actually have such far-reaching consequences. Some cases of people burning themselves to death achieve a result, others do not; these are quite often the acts of mentally disturbed individuals, and this has of course a bearing on the impossibility of attributing any moral relevance to them. That would apply to all the examples we have mentioned. Such actions are relevant only when the individual or group concerned has a proper insight into the existing rules and structures and they are recognized as forming an impasse. Only then can a social process be transformed into a trigger-mechanism and a situation into a real moral 'eye-catcher'.

The condition that makes this whole strategy feasible is that we should start, not from the abstract structure, still less from the analysed form it is given in the sciences, but from the interpreted structure, that is to say, from concrete situations. As a typical feature of how man operates, culturally speaking, we instanced in some of the earlier chapters the setting of events within the perspective of meaning or purpose. The question of the meaning of life, of society, of happiness, sorrow and so forth is a comprehensive one, the answer to which may be found in religion, in moral conviction, in this or that view of the world. But then this has nothing at all to do with conclusive answers to scientifically defined questions; it is a whole 'answering' situation which entails a continual transforming of starting-situations. Religious belief, moral conviction, the political objective, these are ways of viewing transcendent potentialities in the existence of man and the world. In a context of evaluations natural data are qualified as good, bad, culpable, propitiated, a forewarning, a sign of expectancy and so on. Now all this results in a particular way of approaching things and people, in a programme aimed at opening up impasses and renewing situations. This is always centred on concrete persons and groups and on existing situations and events; and so it is a way of going about things which will invariably occur as an ethics of interaction. Structures in the more formal sense of rules disclosed within the various sciences may serve as instruments, as points of orientation, but can never supersede the concrete structural situation. On the other hand the impersonal power-structures of society are real data which in the ethical interaction and via the trigger-mechanism of personal conduct have to be stripped of their anonymity.

As we observed before, this trigger-mechanism can only function against a background of ethical rules. Then again, it will always involve a breakthrough to new rules, which themselves break through this or that existing impasse. In this respect, therefore, it brings us back to the inventiveness we were discussing in chapter VI. We described it there as characteristic of a supreme form of learning process by means of which new rules are discovered which reveal unexpected possibilities. It appeared that this learning process, of such great importance to the advance of human culture, goes along with a feeling for the problematical, which transcends the already existing system of rules. Now it is precisely the ethical factors in the renewal of a situation that involve this sort of inventiveness; and this also means that the individual, initially imprisoned in the power structures, becomes free once again. He moves from operational role to responsible functioning, so acquiring a new and distinctive identity. The strategy of culture is bound in future to develop this learning process even further and so, through education, training, political maturity, an enhanced authenticity of religious conviction and artistic expression, in short, through the manifold ways in which man responds to problem situations, will further the progress of creative humanity and a responsible society.

Sensitivity to what is problematical about a given constellation is impeded by the 'blind spot', as one might call it, in man's way of seeing things. It is not really at all simple to point to those aspects of one's own situation which ought to be adjudged inadmissible or at any rate to be seen as calling for some revision. In the labyrinth of historical constellations man is more inclined to see the familiar situation as a way out than as an impasse. The ills and abuses of the past are the more easy to pinpoint, the further they are away from us. That slavery is a bad thing everyone is now agreed; but of the people living in those days those who saw any injustice in it were few indeed. In fact, among the slaves in the ancient world and during the 18th century there were very many who accepted their lot as being simply in the nature of things. Until recently, poverty in India, even for those who were its victims, was something taken wholly for granted; poverty and suffering were frequently justified on ideological grounds. The discovery that a situation of this kind is inadmissible transforms such a situation in toto. For all those around the situation becomes a challenge; it is as though the scales have fallen from their eyes. For those involved the protest against their situation is interiorized, becomes an inward sense of displeasure: the abandoned acceptance turns into revolt and their distinctive identity becomes a different identity, nay, is properly discovered only in the situation of duress.

But why do blind spots prevent us from seeing properly things that lie right under our noses? It can sometimes happen that action on the part of a few journalists or television people suddenly reveals the intolerable atmosphere of some slum, even though we have been personally familiar with the neighbourhood for a long time past. It may even happen that those involved do not accept the negative verdict and want to keep their old, unperturbed identity: thus the clearance of shanty towns and the removal of the occupants to better accommodation sometimes meets with fierce resistance in certain parts of Africa, not so much because people are unwilling to surrender a wretched but familiar milieu, but because they do not want to be torn out of the identity which they have for so long accepted as their own. The educative process here is always a two-sided one. Learning to help is easier sometimes than learning to be helped. To that we must add immediately that one should never think in this context of two parties, the one active and the other passive. Being helped, letting oneself be helped, does not mean passively submitting to various benevolent actions; it means taking strong action in order to teach the other party what the two-sided process of helping really is.

The blind spot vanishes when man discovers suffering. But that has to happen concretely, as it were, not as a general and abstract conviction about suffering as something that just happens to be in the world. Grief we can only really discover, says the philosopher, E. Levinas, on the face of another human being. He speaks of the transcendent as being opened up, indeed as bursting open, when the look of appeal on another person's face makes its impact upon us. Carl Hofer's painting, 'The black room', shows a drummer whom even in the first version of this picture, painted during the twenties, he had depicted as a kind of mute intimation of the fascist revolution. In this version, dated 1943, Hofer has become familiar with the concentration camps; and bitter sorrow begins to appear already on the face and in the silhouettes of the surrounding figures (ill. 123, p. 196). Striking too is the dimension of grief imprinted on the face in Cas Oorthuys' photo, included in 'Family of Man' (ill. 118, p. 195).

Even amid the mass-like structures of social patterns, economic organizations and the media of more psychic persuasion, it is just this concrete relation to the sorrow of another human being that can make us once more human, once more free persons. Remember that the individual human person has to be envisaged functionally and so not as a totally self-subsistent individual. Thus when we discover the countenance of a fellow human being, this is seldom a strictly personal event. In the context of an ethics of interaction, it will arise for the most part from contact with others, including other occupations, as well as being fostered by an accurate and reliable supply of information. The personal is in no way opposed to the communal; but it is the crystallization-point, so to speak, the point of recovery of one's own identity from one's fellow being.

The disappearance of the blind spot is not something that occurs spontaneously or with the help of a little goodwill here and there. Here again, a process of learning and education is required that will prescribe the unfolding of the strategy of culture and for which the assistance of scientific insight, social organization and so on is just as necessary as personal, conscientious commitment. This new ethical view of real circumstances entails a recognition, therefore, that any given situation is essentially incomplete, imperfect. Man has need of pain, at any rate of being able to recognize suffering, in order to be himself and at the same time to revise and alter situations. The enigma of pain and of moral evil runs like a crimson thread through the reflective consciousness of every age. Religion speaks of human sin, a philosopher like Kant of radical evil, Sartre of man as the one who in acting as he does, invariably dirties his hands. The celebrated canvas entitled 'Guernica', in which Pablo Picasso rearranges structures and figures from much earlier work, thereby giving them a new significance in the setting of the menacing power inherent in the violence of war, expresses moral evil and disjointing grief with an almost metaphysical power of utterance (ill. 126, p. 206).

Pain is nearly always brought into some relation or other with moral evil; and indeed it is just this discovery of suffering in someone else that may lead a man suddenly to perceive the moral deficiency in himself.

A programme for the future

Culture forms a strategy of man that is focussed on the future. So that this future may be planned some attempt is being made to predict specific developments. Innumerable interdisciplinary groups, spread around the world, are engaged on this task. Indeed, scientific analyses do make it possible to extrapolate trends which are happening at the moment, that is to say, to carry them through into the future. The sciences are able to uncover rules that extend beyond current situations and so can contribute to a course of action centred on the future. Moreover, the formal sciences such as mathematics make it possible to achieve very exact methods which enable one to assess the degree of probability attaching to various possibilities in their chance character. New forms of 'game theory' are thus able to allow for unexpected events or for the sort of moves an opponent will make in this or that conflict situation.

Yet we are bound to point out a fundamental limitation intrinsic to all these methods. One never foretells the actual future, but assigns a general structure to what may occur in the future. That is to say, we do not prognosticate this de facto world but describe all possible worlds: in a logically consistent way we produce lines that are revealed in the contemporary situation. We start from axioms and rules which are generally acknowledged here and now, so that via deductions we may arrive at inferred rules which might hold good in the future. The earlier part of this chapter served to show that all this, while not useless, is certainly inadequate. Merely to produce lines toward all possible worlds might well make contemporary man blind to what is inadmissible (morally 'not feasible') in this present world-constellation. And a view of what must be evaluated as an impasse in the given situation turned out to be the very thing needed as a precondition for an inventive programme. Without the

P. Delvaux, The man in the street.

P. Blume, The eternal city.

131 John dictating his vision of history (Russian icon).

132 C. Kneulman, Jacob wrestling with the angel.

ethical qualification of this world's 'impossibility' one cannot reach a responsible view of future interpretations (fillings in, realizations) of all possible worlds. Indeed, it might even be that all possible worlds are only tangents to a future world, because a different – and 'different' here does not in itself imply 'contradictory' – sort of structures and logically expressible rules apply in it than apply in the present one.

We made the point in the previous chapter that it is difficult to establish alternatives which are not purely utopian. In alternative systems for living which are open for man there are always resistances and tensions which will have to be assimilated. All this is more evident now, because in fact one can arrive at a real alternative only as one discovers something of the structural unacceptability of one's own situation. Without such an ethical criterion one can never get beyond predicting new and future worlds which in essentials fit completely into the system of rules covering a world constellation as that exists here and now. In the diagram printed below, the existing world, the given situation of culture, is represented by a small black, compartmented area: the filling in of one compartment within an enveloping network in which the empty spaces represent all possible worlds. Any filling in, in futurology and planology, of other possibilities remains inside the total structure, the general 'logic' of the network. Yet it might not be so. A second diagram shows that the filled in area may also become part of quite different structures, of networks that exhibit a curve in respect of the existing and accepted system of

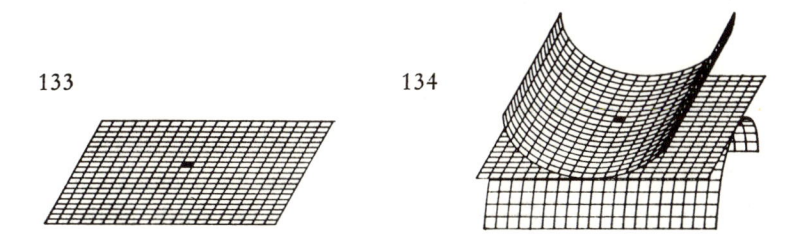

133

134

rules. (In strictly mathematical terms the element common to all these planes is either a point or an extended figure with three dimensions.) An ethical and critical stance enables one to begin to alter one's own situation, even structurally. Illustration 125 (p. 205) is a work by J. Henneman, 'The suspended armchair'. This armchair floats like a utopia above existing reality. Just as a utopia would do, it reveals the inner

135 Fashion designs of 1880.

structure of that reality and affords a critical viewpoint in that, remaining detached from the actual force of gravity, it hovers above its own point of departure. But if it alights anywhere else, then it will fit back into a compartment of like structure: its strategy stays imprisoned within the possibilities which in extended form constitute the chess-board pattern of its own world, so that whilst other squares may be discovered, the total structure remains unchanged.

This may also be illustrated by a few simple examples taken from a book by Robida, published in the last century. In it one finds prognostications regarding fashion, urban building and so forth, as they will be in 75 to 100 years' time. We can now check those predictions against the facts. Looking at these pictures now, one is struck by two things. The first is that they seem to us extremely quaint and in no sense whatever an accurate prediction of fashion, urban architecture and so on, as they are today; but secondly, that in certain subsidiary aspects they differ from fashion and architecture as they were at the time the book was written. The art historian, H. van de Waal, has pointed to a number of remarkable features here. How were people then able to forecast the fashions of today? By looking at the fashions of their own day and then exaggerating certain traits which they considered very modern. But this business of emphasizing aspects considered to be modern takes place within the generally accepted structure of the fashion in question. That becomes clear from the illustrations as soon as Van de Waal sets off the 'forecasts' against the structures typical of the fashions of that period: it then appears that the models thought to be futuristic can be fitted straight into the structures prevailing at that time. In illustration 127 (p. 206) we have Robida's comic forecast of woman's supremacy at around the year 1950; the (then) futuristic dress worn by the leader of these Women's Liberationists (at the barricades of a revolution on the streets of Paris, which Robida expected to occur around 1950) obviously fits perfectly into the design of 1880 (ill. 135) (Van de Waal took this picture from *Der Kinderen-Besier*): Robida published his book in 1879.

The same thing applies, even more obviously, to urbanized utopias. These too plainly exude the atmosphere of that bygone age. Within the structure of the last century they are of course fantastic; but the modern

136 Robida's drawing (1879) to illustrate the future effects of chemistry.

137 A. Robida, drawing of the city of the future: 'sur les toits'.

observer will see them as entirely determined by the technological and stylistic possibilities available at that time. Borrowed from the same book of Robida's are the prognostications regarding urban architecture around the middle of this present century: these depict a European town and an African town of about 1950 and are to be found here as illustrations 137 and 138.

We may conclude, therefore, that in these forecasts of the future no authentic, that is, unexpected, future is predicted; people have merely exaggerated and emphasized their own expectations regarding what the future would be like. They projected, as it were, a scheme for all possible worlds and in it depicted a future world (by 'filling in', interpretation); but all such possible worlds turn out in fact to be only extrapolations and extensions of the world which then existed. People accepted that existing world in its general structures – they seemed devoid of fantasy, or as we have now more accurately expressed it, of ethical inventiveness – in order to put themselves at a distance, on certain fundamental points, from the rules of their own world.

One can take these illustrations and apply them to yet other contexts. When we read modern reports that deal with the year 2000, no doubt there are possibilities predicted there which could very well happen. Even so, such predictions stay within the total, given structures of the constellations obtaining here and now. That much is clear from the fact that in such reports, naturally enough, an especially important function is assigned to the currently most relevant sciences, that is, to such disciplines

138 A. Robida, drawing of the city of the future: 'les boulevards de Gondskoro, capitale de la grande république Niam-Niam'.

as biochemistry and transplant-biology, which are just now experiencing the biggest breakthrough to new areas of research; which, again quite naturally, is not the case with sciences held at this moment to be of far less importance. On that basis might not current predictions appear just as quaint in the year 2000 as those of the illustrations we have been talking about? Admittedly, the assertions in this case have more of a scientific basis; but it is still true to say that those trends are extrapolated and given special emphasis which are reckoned to be important at this moment. Scientific predictions will be valid on those points in particular where developments are continuous and straightforward; but on other points they will be defective, especially where restructurings, unexpected discoveries and inventive renovations are going to occur. On these points our view of the future will yield more information in 2000 about what was found important around 1970 than about what is currently happening in 2000.

What is it, then, that such predictions primarily lack? An ethical evaluation of the present. This it is that stops us from simply projecting all possible worlds on the basis of currently prevailing patterns of thought. Surrealism focusses, with photographic attention to detail, on this de facto world, but does so in order to disclose strange, almost impossible combinations within it. The objectivity of the world and the subjectivity of semi-conscious psychic life appear to become a single whole. Thus the Belgian, Paul Delvaux, portrays strange landscapes with classical and neo-classical buildings – and this as a decor for nude female figures and men in evening dress who make vacuous and boorish gestures (ill. 129, p. 223). Such frozen eroticism gives an impression of decadence. Yet there is still no ethical evaluation here, because the whole scene is overlaid by an atmosphere of paralyzing doom. Things are quite different with the American painter, Peter Blume. His painting, 'La vie éternelle', contains the same ingredients as Delvaux' canvasses and interprets the painter's impressions after a stay in Rome between 1934 and 1937 (ill. 130, p. 223). That is to say, his scene is no longer situated in a surrealistic world, but reveals the decadence of a seemingly prosperous Rome. The head of Mussolini, appearing as a jack-in-the-box in the foreground, symbolizes the moral-cum-political critique whereby the fatal quality of this concrete world is to some extent annulled. When the writer we mentioned before, Robida, gives a social and economic critique of the future, with its artificial foodstuffs, poisoning alike of atmosphere and intestines, introduction of artificial organs and so forth, then his drawing (ill. 136, p. 227) at once assumes a topical and apocalyptical perspective.

An ethical evaluation, more especially of the results yielded by the modern sciences and organization-techniques, causes blind spots to disappear and thus reveals a glimpse of impossibilities in the given situation. This glimpse of the 'ethically impossible world' can then clear the way for inventiveness. A proverb reminds us that love will make shift somehow to gain its end. A sense of ethical responsibility can help put our thinking, even in the sphere of methodology and science, on a new track. The 'impossibility' prompts us to discover possibilities – a process which breaks out of and transcends the methodological immanence of 'all possible worlds'. Unnoticed ways out, new methods of thinking, different ways of organizing research and inquiry, reaching subtler, better differentiated conclusions, a more creative programme: all that can be developed within the strategy of culture, as man's learning process, at least, works itself out in the context of a sense of moral responsibility.

But surely, it will be objected, it is not possible to alter the laws, the methodological rules, of human thinking, as they are deposited, for instance, in the sciences? All the same, it becomes evident in the learning process that inventive restructurings can and do occur, as we were arguing in chapter VI. We pointed, among other things, to the real possibility of arriving at new methodological rules, even at whole new systems (the Copernican universe, non-Euclidean geometries, and so forth) from which we may derive propositions (as that the sum of the three angles of a triangle can be more or less than 180°) that were inadmissible within the old framework. A new structure of logical rules is then opened up. That need not involve discarding the old one, which can be incorporated into the new, logically more ample system as a special case: it is not discarded, but it *is* curtailed.

This becomes clear even from a quite different viewpoint. In the chapter to which we referred a moment ago, chapter VI, we drew attention to the structural growth of man's cerebral cortex. The rules by which man reasons, organizes and settles on this or that programme of action are undoubtedly correlated with neurophysiological processes and combinations in the CNS. In this respect the brain would seem to be a specific means of regulating our behaviour. Such regulative activity, and likewise therefore the neuronal network, forms a system which impinges upon the world around and is more or less attuned and assimilated to that world. The growth of the neuronal network goes hand in hand with a way of thinking and acting capable of giving man increasing control over his natural environment: man organizes processes and things via the instruments and agencies provided by his methods in science, technology and ordinary, day-to-day procedures. To the extent that he is able to analyse and evaluate that world correctly – or more correctly than before – to that extent will his behaviour-pattern, and with it his CNS as well, be developed in the right direction.

The world that forms man's environment is not simply the natural milieu, as it is with the animals, but the world of culture. Certainly, nature is involved – but nature as interpreted by man and 'processed' within the question of meaning. This question of the meaning of existence, as we have stressed a number of times already, is never a loose, general sort of question; it needs always to be concretized. The ethics of interaction does precisely that, because very specific and identifiable constellations or developments then become the starting-point for applying ethical norms. The world of man is not something fixed once and for all, therefore, but is susceptible of reinterpretation and renewal as well as of misunderstanding and disorganization. One such reinterpretation has been given by Jeroen Bosch (about 1500). The pains of hell from the 'Garden of lusts' (ill. 128, p. 206) have been the subject of much discussion; and people have succeeded in discovering a great deal of psychoanalytical symbolism here. Even more than with a surrealist like Delvaux (ill. 129, p. 223), the outer world here has come to be a reflection or interpretation of man's inner life. But in Bosch's case that goes beyond a symbolism arising simply out of depth-psychology. He wishes to offer moral criticism and to expose the hidden seducers in man as well as the false evaluations of the society that surrounds him, in the language of religious fantasy.

A wrong evaluation, or even a total unwillingness to evaluate a situation, in the long run evokes the wrong sort of programme and, at the same time, misleading rules; all of which implies that the CNS is capable of evolving in a wrong direction or in a good one. The world with which the human brain engages and toward which it grows is, after all, the world that is being evaluated in one way or another. The same physical world can acquire a different significance in the context of a particular cultural programme and system of symbols. It is by means of symbols that man both interprets and transforms the world. On the one hand certain perspectives are opened up in this way and specific tendencies are exposed, because man is not dealing with a natural world any more, but through his decisions is all the time transforming it into culture. On the other hand such tendencies and perspectives must have their effect on man's pattern of thought and action. The world of culture is an evaluated world — even if man thinks he has to do with a purely objective, given 'nature' — and man's existence, including his CNS and his everyday conduct of his affairs, evolves in the direction of those evaluations. It is in the interaction between symbolic transformations (the policy man adopts) and the perspectives opened up (tendencies, whether meaningful or not, in the reality around him) that culture, nay, and man himself, acquire their functional mode of being.

This interaction was outlined back in the first chapter, where it was said to be the fundamental relation between the human subject and the powers all around him. The strategy of culture is man's way of shaping that relation, which has a perpetually changing structure and yet always has as its core and centre one and the same confrontation. It is a good thing, perhaps, to point out once again that the symbols referred to in the previous paragraph are more than just signs — as it might be mythical,

139 Kravtshenko, Barricades 1905.   140   José Venturelli, Tod auf dem Platz.

artistic, algebraic symbols, gestures, linguistic signs, traffic signs and so on. We have to envisage the symbols which always constitute definite regulative systems as the precipitate of actions, directions, decisions, interpretations, in brief, as the expression of a strategy of culture. They are an exteriorization or externalizing of rules which define the structure of man's CNS and are in turn a result of man's adjustment and accommodation to his world. In that world 'nature' is never the sole determining factor. Human culture is one long story of man's efforts to disclose, always in ways that are new, what is meaningful and what is meaningless. His symbols are a kind of clue to those processes which in fact occur within human history.

This evaluating of situations and interpreting of symbols should not be taken to be a non-committal, theoretical activity. Marxism lays special emphasis on the connection between theory and practice. A. I. Kravtshenko's woodcut, 'Barricades 1905' (dating from 1925), not only displays revolutionary action but also, as a piece of socialist realism, serves to consolidate the identity of the labouring masses (ill. 139). Not so animated, perhaps, but at least equally enthusiastic in its feeling is José Venturelli's keen protest at the killing of demonstrators, embodied in his woodcut of

1946: 'Death in the square' (ill. 140). Both show the need for taking a hand in corrupt situations.

Calling a 'slave' a 'free man', qualifying the prolongation of life, in a concrete constellation, as 'inhuman', proceeding to define ownership on a more functional basis, characterizing an 'objective' documentary as a form of persuasion: all that implies a need to take a hand in situations and, if a given line of conduct has in fact been followed, to bring it to consciousness and make it pliable. A purely theoretical and sociological interpretation of 'slavery', 'freedom', 'power structures' yields mere marginal comments on the line being pursued. We must even be careful not to use theoretical interpretations in order to avoid taking action. This danger arises not because theory stands over against practical courses of action, but because by setting up 'all possible worlds' we create a wide field of logically acceptable possibilities which in fact, however, are limited by the acceptance of existing constellations and ways of thinking. As we were arguing earlier on in this chapter, such theoretical interpretations in fact lead only to lines of direction that have to be seen as tangential to de facto developments.

If however we may ascribe to such a scheme of 'all possible worlds' a more restricted function, then it can be understood as a model with an undoubted orientating value. The gravitational centre will then lie in the recognition of what is *not* admissible, in the vision of the ethical 'impossibility' of this or that particular world. Only then is a programme for the future possible that will be able to bring about an inventive renewal of our methods of thinking and our theories. Only then too will man achieve a sense of his own responsibility and with it acquire an identity of his own. Such an identity presupposes, as we said before, the discovery of suffering in other men. Only when man comes to recognize something that runs counter to his own current line of action and cherished reasoning is room made for changes in his strategy. The recognition of 'impossibilities' (always in the sense of what is morally inadmissible) stimulates the discovery of new possibilities. In that way the 'impossibilities' from being an adversary turn into a mysterious companion, as in the ancient story of the patriarch Jacob's wrestling with a mysterious Power. In that contest, and not before, he acquired his own moral identity – his name from that moment on became 'Israel' – and so it structured his existence, as C. Kneulman's sculpture and Friso ten Holt's drawing so hand-

141 F. ten Holt, Jacob wrestling with the angel.

somely portray (ill. 132, p. 224; and ill. 141). Thus these images of a personal involvement with a readiness to capitulate give a complementary dimension to the revolutionary élan to which illustrations 139 and 140 are meant to testify. That is why over and over again in human history inventive capitulations are needed to overcome the future. Inventive capitulations mean the liberation of the actual person from stultifying, 'self-evident' assumptions, and the integration of any policy for the future within a more meaningful perspective.

As we were contending at the outset of this book, one can see the quest for the right relation between man and powers as the basic pattern of every phase of culture. That relation is never fixed in advance; so that there is no instinctive, natural and inbuilt regulative process in man, as is the case with the animal kingdom. That is why human history has as its hallmark the strategy of culture: religion, art, science, technological performance, the growth to ethical consciousness – these are the perspectives where transcendence can become visible within the immanence of human thought and action. The very restlessness of history entails that this same confrontation must be realized over and over again in new and different ways: the strategy involves changing patterns of policy, of conduct, introduced in this work as a model comprising phases marked by the mythical, ontological and functional postures. In so far as there are inbuilt regulative factors present in man – a neuronal network in the CNS, laws of thinking, fixed patterns of action, socio-cultural tradition – they are all the time having to be broken open and developed by means of learning processes which extend much further than is ever the case with animal learning. The human CNS, as well as the rules of thought and action, must be kept under pressure, so that they remain flexible and are able to develop in the right direction. Inventiveness is the restricting of all existing rules so as to make possible a more responsible, a more original committal of the human individual and group. An elastic strategy means that in every phase of development the existing rules are concretized, and the basic relation of man and powers is brought within a transcendent perspective. Instead of being an automaton or the product of tradition, man is a free person, always having to achieve a programme of action that is truly his own.

In the functional position openness and isolation, inventive capitulations and a rigidifying autonomy are just as much present as in all other forms of cultural strategy. Here operationalism is the tendency to arbitrary, highhanded attitudes and conduct, which has to be recognized as a component of the functional approach to things. In an extreme operationalist culture human happiness is wholly defined by welfare activities, moral norms by social utility, religious convictions by their definability in scientific terms (psychological, cultural-historical, sociological), love by the pleasures and enjoyments it provides, and finally man himself by his openness to manipulation. Only when 'inventiveness' and 'future' are no longer identified simply as categories of knowledge and are seen primarily as moral categories can mankind *and* its systems of rules be set under such pressure that liberation into a proper experience of responsibility is possible. The 'meaning' of science, technology, ethical reflection and a policy vis-à-vis the future then breaks open the determinate character of an operationalist strategy and makes possible the renewal of personal and social response. Many of the illustrations in this book are the deposit, so to speak, of such a moral struggle, running like a thread through all of human history. So John, the visionary, dictates apocalyptic history – the theme of the Russian icon reproduced as illustration 131,

p. 224 (school of Novgorod, beginning of 15th century).

The responsible society arises through learning how to respond to the purposive, meaningful tendencies and trends within history; and mankind will be able to continue its story: the story of a liberation which is what, in his heart of hearts, every man longs for.

How to use this book

This book does not present a description, much less an explanation, of the enormous cultural shift through which mankind today is going. The purpose of this book is more limited: a simplified representation of the development of culture, a schema that may be useful in the changing situations we ourselves experience.

The schematic approach has been elaborated in a model comprising three stages in the development of culture: the mythical, where man is still part and parcel of the world around him; the ontological, where he acquires a more aloof attitude towards the surrounding world and towards himself; the functional, where he acquires insight into relations and so attempts to assess traditional data (nature, God, his fellow man, his own identity) in a new way. In these three stages it is not a matter of ascending to higher levels. No, each phase has its positive and its negative tendencies. That is why one should not go 'romancing' after a pattern of culture long past; nor yet should one take only a 'utopian' view, looking forward to a not yet existent form of society.

Thus the basic idea of this book emerges: 'culture' is not a noun, but a verb, or in other words, 'culture' is of our own making, is our own responsibility. So our account of culture is a 'functional' one, relating it to our own policy of life. This means that cultural development does not take place above and beyond us, but that man himself must find a strategy of culture. How is he to do this? The model having been developed in the first four chapters, those that follow present an elaboration of such a possible strategy and thus enable the reader, while treating the material in a critical spirit, to go to work on it in his own way. Let us sum up the points so far discussed: our attitude towards technology in our society, our work, our home. This technology is an extension of our own body, indeed, of our own brain (information technology). We increase our grip on the world; and then the issue becomes the role of the human capacity to organize, with its power and its impotence, the compulsion laid upon it to make considered decisions.

Another point is the increasing use of symbols in science, and also in the whole field of social interaction. A process of continuing education is needed here, that will enable us to look at these symbols as so many sign-posts for orientation and not as foreign, didactorial signals. In a broader context our cultural development can be regarded as shifting the focal point towards learning processes. Unless they serve to stimulate man's creative and inventive powers, they may well be used to manipulate him instead. Moreover, we must bear in mind that stimulating inventiveness in scientific research, in business and the professions, involves not only reason and emotion, but also a moral stance. Other questions arise when one views the history of human culture as a learning process, where the fear of death, sexual passion and the urge to explore can sometimes be repressed and sometimes be overaccentuated. The role of these factors in society should be analysed in aid of the necessary shift from welfare to well-being.

Finally, a group of problems are posited, that occur when one attempts to arrive at a new ethics, and an ethics at that, not emanating from abstract norms but from concrete problem-situations, in order to design on that basis some reliable 'policies'. We name a few of these problem-situations: the increasing influence, for instance, in education, of visualisation; urbanisation and the lack of direct contact with one's fellow man; the role of the opposition in politics; work motivation and new forms of reward; medical care and the prolongation of life; the influence the individual may possibly exert on power structures (the 'trigger-mechanism'); the growing awareness of the blind spot in our moral field of view; 'inventive capitulation'.

In a sense the reader, individually and collectively, should go on writing this book from his own experience. For this purpose all kinds of modern methods are available. We give here, in brief, some suggestions that may be of use to the individual reader and in some cases to groups as well (adult education and managerial courses, study groups).

(a) Describe how 'authority' makes its appearance in the three phases; take due note of the negative aspects (magical, substantialist, operational); give the term 'authority' concrete form by delineating an authoritative figure – e.g. a doctor, from medicine man to the present time; then do the same for your own profession; see whether directives for the future come out of this.

(b) A group working in large industries. Set the working procedure (possibly the mentality) of an unrelated industry (or it can be a service institution) within the three phases; analyse the various hazards; now do the same with your own occupation, but quite independently of the de facto situation; then compare the actual situation to the schema thus obtained.

(c) With regard to theological questions: horizontalism (emphasis on social effort) versus verticalism (emphasis on man's direct relationship to God). Try to locate the controversy between horizontalists and verticalists in the phase model. Which antitheses are invloved? Ontological–functional? Ontological–operational? Substantialist–functional? Substantialist–operational? See how each of these four possibilities represents a specific choice and can induce a specific policy.

(d) Try to illustrate the various basic concepts of the first four chapters by selecting cartoons to go with them, thereby at the same time relativizing the corresponding situations. (There are various collections of cartoons on the market.)

(e) Analyse and criticise the 'model of the learning process' of vegetating/producing/consuming: try to draft another model; compare advantages and disadvantages.

(f) What serious problems and what new possibilities arise when one considers e.g. the role of sexuality in each of the three learning processes mentioned?

(g) What is 'selective consumption'? Find advertisements to go with it as illustrative material; compare with an avarage housekeeping account; analyse a survey of what is being produced in your country in one year and what is being bought; try to evaluate critically.

(h) What is a 'trigger-mechanism' in a social sense? Find articles from weekly journals evidencing such a mechanism. Compare which weekly and illustrated journals assess the one case, and which the other case positively as a kind of trigger-mechanism.

(i) Do the same with 'inventive capitulation'. This can take place also, for example, during a course, without discussion, by purely 'meditative' observation of e.g. film excerpts or documentaries (M. L. King, etc.); record experience immediately in diary notes; these, probably at another time, can be read out as anonymous contributions.

(j) The 'blind spot'; on what does one reach quick agreement; in what respects does the affair turn out to be more complicated when thoroughly analysed (no cultivating of a simplistic, critical attitude); how, then, in the fields of political policy, managerial organisation, etc., can one take into account the removal of the blind spot?

(k) Find concrete points of engagement, that are recognizable in one's own occupational sphere, for an ethics of interaction. What policy does one propose? Analyse also T.V. and radio-programmes that can be illustrative and exemplary.

Readers can amplify and improve this list in order to go back thereafter to the actual text of the book. Additions, experiences with these or other techniques, critical remarks, proposals for further elaboration – you can, if you so wish, send them all to the publisher, so that a fund of experiences can be built up: a pool of suggestions and advice available to those who want to work with this book.

Literature

Chapter I

H. Arendt, The human condition. Chicago 1958.
J. Baillie, The belief in progress. London 1950.
D. Bidney, Theoretical anthropology. New York 1964^4.
M. Black, Models and metaphors. Ithaca 1962.
W. Dilthey, Die Typen der Weltanschauung. Leipzig-Berlin 1911.
Th. Dobzhansky, Mankind evolving. New Haven 1962.
N. Elias, Über den Prozess der Zivilisation. 2 Vols., Berne-Munich 1968^2.
H. Freudenthal (ed.), The concept and the role of the model in mathematics and the natural sciences and social sciences. Dordrecht 1961.
H. Freyer, Theorie des gegenwartigen Zeitalters. Stuttgart 1955.
E. Gellner, Thought and change. London 1964.
M. Ginsberg, Evolution and progress. Melbourne 1961.
H. Gomperz, Weltanschauungslehre I, II. Jena-Leipzig 1905-1908.
A. A. Grünbaum, Herrschen und Lieben als Grundmotive der philosophischen Weltanschauungen. Bonn 1925.
M. J. Herskovits, Cultural anthropology. New York 1955.
K. Jaspers, Psychologie der Weltanschauungen. Berlin (1919) 1922^2.
A. Kaplan, The conduct of enquiry. San Francisco 1964.
A. L. Kroeber, Cl. Kluckhohn, Culture. New York 1963^2.
M. Landmann, Der Mensch als Schöpfer und Geschöpf der Kultur. Munich-Basle 1961.
R. Linton, The tree of culture. New York 1955.
A. Malraux, Les voix du silence. Paris 1952.
I. T. Ramsey, Models and mystery. Oxford 1964.
M. Rokeach, The open and the closed mind. New York 1960.
E. Rothacker, Probleme der Kulturanthropologie. Bonn 1948.
G. G. Simpson, This view of life (new edition). New York 1964.
E. Spranger, Lebensformen. Tübingen 1965.
C. H. Waddington, The ethical animal. London 1960.
L. A. White, The science of culture. New York 1949.
B. L. Whorf, Language, thought, reality. New York 1956.

Chapter II

L. Adam, Primitive art. London 1954⁴.
R. Allier, Magie et religion. Paris 1935.
R. Benedict, Patterns of culture (1934). New York 1946.
H. Bergson, Les deux sources de la morale et de la religion. Paris 1932.
F. Boas, Primitive art. Oslo 1927.
R. Callois, L'Homme et le Sacré. Paris 1939.
E. Cassirer, An essay on man. New Haven 1944.
E. R. Dodds, The Greeks and the irrational. Berkeley-Los Angeles 1951.
E. Durkheim, Les formes élémentaires de la religion. Paris 1912.
M. Eliade, Le mythe de l'éternel retour. Paris 1949.
M. Eliade, Images and symbols (trans. Mairet). London 1961.
H. Fränkel, Dichtung und Philosophie des frühen Griechentums. New York 1951.
H. Frankfort et al., Intellectual adventure of ancient man. Chicago 1946 (later publ. as: Before Philosophy. Pelican Books 1949).
G. Gusdorf, Mythe et métaphysique. Paris 1953.
E. O. James, Prehistoric religion. London.
A. E. Jensen, Das religiöse Weltbild einer frühen Kultur. Stuttgart 1948.
C. Kluckhohn, Mirror for man. New York 1949.
A. L. Kroeber (ed.), Anthropology today. Chicago 1953.
A. L. Kroeber, Self, society and culture in phylogenetic perspective. Chicago 1960.
S. K. Langer, Philosophy in a new key. Cambridge, Mass. 1960.
M. Leenhardt, Do Kamo. Paris 1947.
G. van der Leeuw, Religion in its essence and manifestations. London 1964². (Trans. of: Phänomenologie der Religion. Tübingen 1956²).
G. van der Leeuw, L'Homme primitif et la religion. Paris 1941.
L. Lévy-Bruhl, La mentalité primitive. Paris 1922.
L. Lévy-Bruhl, Les Carnets. Paris 1949.
C. Lévi-Strauss, Les structures élémentaires de la parenté. Paris 1949.
C. Lévi-Strauss, La pensée sauvage. Paris 1962.
B. Malinowski, Magic, science and religion. New York 1948.
E. de Martino, Il mondo magico. Rome 1948.
M. Mauss, Sociologie et anthropologie. Paris 1950.
M. Mead, From the South Seas. New York 1939.
F. M. Müller, Last essays. 2 vols. New York 1901.
W. F. Otto, Die Götter Griechenlands. Frankfurt a.M. 1947³.
R. Pettazzoni, Miti e leggendi I. Turin 1948.
K. Th. Preuss, Die geistige Kultur der Naturvölker. Leipzig-Berlin 1923².
P. Ricoeur, Finitude et culpabilité II. Paris 1960.
F. W. J. von Schelling, Philosophie der Mythologie. 2 vols. (1856), reprint:

Darmstadt 1957.
B. Snell, Discovery of the mind. Oxford 1953. (Eng. trans. of: Die Entdeckung des Geistes. Hamburg 1948².
J. Wach, The comparative study of religion. New York 1958.

Chapter III

H. Conrad-Martinus, Das Sein. 1957.
P. Deussen, Das System des Vedanta. Leipzig 1883.
E. J. Dijksterhuis, De mechanisering van het wereldbeeld. Amsterdam 1950.
H. von Glasenapp, Die Philosophie der Inder. Stuttgart 1949.
O. F. Gruppe, Antäus (Ed. F. Mauthner). Munich 1914.
N. Hartmann, Zur Grundlegung der Ontologie. Meisenheim 1948.
R. Havemann, Dialektik ohne Dogma. Hamburg 1964.
M. Hiriyanna, Outlines of Indian philosophy. London 1932.
G. Huber, Das Sein und das Absolute. Basle 1955.
O. Lacombe, L'absolu selon le Vedanta. Paris 1937.
A. Malraux, La métamorphose des dieux. Paris.
J. Maritain, Distinguer pour unir, ou les degrés du savoir. Paris 1932.
G. Martin, Einleitung in die allgemeine Metaphysik. Cologne 1957.
F. Nietzsche, Jenseits vom Gut und Böse (1886). In: Werke (ed. K. Schleckta). Munich 1956.
C. Nink, Ontologie. Freiburg i.B. 1952.
S. Radhakrishnan, An idealist view of life. London.
P. T. Raju, Idealistic thought of India. London 1953.
Spinoza, Ethica. 1677.
R. Taylor, Metaphysics. Englewood Cliffs 1964.
Thomas Aquinas, De ente et essentia (1256); Caietanus, In de ente et essentia Thomae Aquinatis commentaria (1494).
E. Topitsch, Vom Ursprung und Ende der Metaphysik. Vienna 1958.
C. J. de Vogel, Antike Seinsphilosophie und Christentum im Wandel der Jahrhunderte. Baden-Baden 1958.
A. N. Whitehead, Science and the modern world. New York 1925.
Chr. Wolff, Philosophia prima sive ontologia. 1736.

Chapter IV

P. W. Bridgman, The logic of modern physics. New York 1928.
F. J. J. Buytendijk, Attitudes et mouvements. Bruges-Paris 1957 (trans.).
E. Cassirer, An essay on man. New Haven 1944.
E. Cassirer, Substanzbegriff und Funktionsbegriff. Berlin 1910.

H. G. Cox, The secular city. New York 1965.
J. Dewey, Logic. The theory of inquiry. London 1939.
D. Emmet, Rules, roles and relations. London 1966.
E. Fink, Sein, Wahrheit, Welt. The Hague 1958.
E. H. Gombrich, Art and illusion. London 1959.
M. Grene, The knower and the known. New York 1966.
S. Hampshire, Thought and action. London 1959.
M. Heidegger, Der Ursprung des Kunstwerkes. In: Holzwege. Frankfurt a.M. 1950.
W. Heisenberg, Physik und Philosophie. Stuttgart 1959.
D. Jenkins, Beyond religion. Philadelphia 1962.
L. Landgrebe, Der Weg der Phänomenologie. Gütersloh 1963.
S. Langer, Philosophy in a new key. Cambridge, Mass. 1942.
A. Th. van Leeuwen, Christianity in world history. London 1964.
J. Macmurray, The self as agent. London 1957.
M. Merleau-Ponty, Phénoménologie de la perception. Paris 1942.
D. von Oppen, Das personale Zeitalter. Stuttgart 1960.
J. Piaget, Biologie et connaissance. Paris 1967.
M. Polanyi, Personal knowledge. London 1958.
B. Radofsky, Architecture without architects. New York 1965[2].
A. Rapoport, Operational philosophy. New York 1953.
P. Ricoeur, Histoire et vérité. Paris 1955.
J. A. T. Robinson, Honest to God. London 1963.
G. Ryle, The concept of mind. London 1949.
J. Selz, Découverte de la sculpture moderne. Lausanne 1963 (Eng. trans. New York 1963).
B. F. Skinner, Science and human behavior. New York 1953.
W. H. Thorpe, Biology and the nature of man. London 1963.
H. Vaihinger, Philosophie des Als-Ob. Leipzig 1918[3].
C. H. Waddington, The nature of life. London 1961.
C. W. Williams, Where in the world? New York 1963.
L. Wittgenstein, Philosophische Untersuchungen/Philosophical investigations. Oxford 1956.

Chapter V

Chr. Argyris, Personality and organization. New York 1957.
K. Axelos, Marx, penseur de la technique. Paris 1961.
G. Balandier et al., Changements techniques, économiques et sociaux. Etude théorique. Paris 1959.
N. Berdiaeff, Der Mensch und die Technik. Lucerne 1943.
H. Bergson, Les deux sources de la morale et de la religion. Paris 1932.

A. A. Berle, The 20th century capitalist revolution. New York 1954.
K. Boulding, The organizational revolution. New York 1963.
P. Brandt, Schaffende Arbeit und bildende Kunst. 2 Vols. Leipzig 1927.
J. Brun, Prendre et comprendre. Paris 1963.
C. G. Carus, Das Maschinenwesen im Lichte der Physiologie. In: Lebenserinnerungen und Denkwürdigkeiten. 4 vols. Leipzig 1865.
F. Dessauer, Philosophie der Technik. Bonn 1927.
H. Diels, Antike Technik. Berlin 1914 (1919²).
E. J. Dijksterhuis, R. J. Forbes, Overwinning door gehoorzaamheid. Zeist 1961.
F. M. Feldhaus, Kulturgeschichte der Technik. 2 vols. Berlin 1928.
Ch. Frémont, Origines et évolution des outils. Paris 1913.
A. Gehlen, Die Seele im technischen Zeitalter. Hamburg 1957.
M. J. Herskovits, Man and his works. New York 1949.
E. Kapp, Grundlinien einer Philosophie der Technik. Braunschweig 1877.
F. Klemm, Technik. Freiburg-Munich 1962.
W. Kuhns, The post-industrial prophets: Interpretations of technology. New York 1971.
J. G. March, H. A. Simon, Organizations. New York-London 1959.
R. Mayntz, Soziologie der Organisation. Hamburg 1963.
D. McGregor, The human side of enterprise. New York 1960.
L. Mumford, Technics and civilisation. London (1934) 1962⁸.
L. Mumford, The myth of the machine. The Pentagon of power. New York 1970.
K. P. Oakley, Man the tool-maker. London 1950².
J. H. Oldham, Work in modern society. Richmond 1962².
P. M. Schuhl, Machinisme et philosophie. Paris 1938.
A. Tilghers, Homo faber. Paris 1929.
J. Vuillemin, L'être et le travail. Paris 1949.
W. H. White, The organization man. New York 1957.

Chapter VI

P. Berger, T. Luckmann, The social construction of reality. New York 1966.
D. J. Boorstin, The image. Middlesex 1963².
S. Chase, The tragedy of waste. New York 1925.
L. Coser, The functions of social conflict. London 1956.
J. C. Eccles, The neurophysiological basis of mind. Oxford 1953.
H. Ch. Elliot, The shape of intelligence. The evolution of the human brain. New York 1969.
E. Fromm, The sane society. New York 1955.
J. K. Galbraith, The affluent society. London 1958.

J. K. Galbraith, The new industrial state. New York 1968.
A. Gehlen, Zeit-Bilder. Zur Soziologie und Ästhetik der modernen Malerei. Frankfurt a.M.-Bonn 1965².
F. H. George, The brain as a computer. London-New York 1961.
N. Goodman, Language of art. An approach to a theory of symbols. Indianapolis-New York 1968.
C. T. Hardwick, B. F. Landuyt, Administrative strategy. New York 1961.
D. O. Hebb, The organization of behavior. New York-London 1949.
E. R. Hilgard, G. H. Bower, Theories of learning. New York (rev. ed.) 1966.
G. Katona, The powerful consumer. New York 1960.
E. Kaufmann, Architecture in the age of reason. Cambridge, Mass. 1955.
G. Kepes (ed.), Sign, image, symbol. New York 1966.
A. Koestler, The act of creation. London 1964.
T. S. Kuhn, The structure of scientific revolutions. 2nd ed. Chicago 1970.
A. Leroi-Gourhan, La geste et la parole. I. Technique et langage. II. La mémoire et les rythmes. Paris 1964.
A. R. Luria, Higher cortical functions in man. (trans. from Russian). London 1966.
A. Maslow, Religion, values and peak-experiences. Athens, Ohio 1964.
W. S. McCulloch, W. Pitts, A logical calculus of the ideas immanent in nervous activity. In: Bull. Math. Biophys. 5 (1943) 115-133.
G. H. Mead, Mind, self and society. Chicago 1934.
M. Mead, Male and female. New York 1949.
R. K. Merton, Social theory and social structure. Glencoe 1949.
O. H. Mowrer, Learning theory and behavior. New York 1963.
G. Murphy, Human potentialities. London 1957.
G. Myrdal, Beyond the welfare state. New Haven 1960.
F. C. S. Northrop, Philosophical anthropology and practical politics. New York 1960.
F. C. S. Northrop (ed.), Ideological differences and world order. New Haven 1949.
V. Packard, The hidden persuaders. New York 1957.
G. Pask, An approach to cybernetics. London 1961.
J. Piaget, Biologie et connaissance. Paris 1967.
D. Riesman, Abundance for what? Garden City 1964.
J. Robinson, Economic philosophy. London 1962.
J. P. Schadé, D. H. Ford, Basic neurology. Amsterdam-London-New York 1967.
G. Scherhorn, Bedürfnis und Bedarf. Sozialökonomische Grundbegriffe im Lichte der neueren Anthropologie. Berlin 1959.
D. A. Sholl, The organization of the cerebral cortex. London 1956.
K. Steinbuch, Automat und Mensch. Berlin 1961.
R. H. Tawney, The acquisitive society. New York 1920.

W. H. Thorpe, O. L. Zangwill (eds.), Current problems in animal behaviour. Cambridge 1961.
J. Tinbergen, Lessons from the past. Amsterdam 1963.
T. Veblen, The theory of the leisure class. New York (1889) 1962[8].
M. Wertheim, Productive thinking. New York 1954.
M. Young, The rise of meritocracy. London 1962.
E. Zahn, Soziologie der Prosperität. Munich 1964.

Chapter VII

L. Armand, Plaidoyer pour l'avenir. Paris 1961.
R. Atkinson, Sexual morality. London 1965.
S. de Beauvoir, Pour une morale de l'ambiguité. Paris 1947.
K. Boulding, The meaning of the twentieth century. New York 1964.
K. Britton, Communication. New York-London 1939.
K. Britton, The conscience of the city. Cambridge, Mass. 1968.
J. K. Feibleman, Moral strategy. An introduction to the ethics of confrontation. The Hague 1967.
G. Goyder, The responsible company.
J. Habermas, Erkenntnis und Interesse. Frankfurt a.M. 1968.
L. A. Hart, Law, liberty and morality. London 1963.
T. W. Hutchinson, Positive economics and policy objectives. London 1964.
K. Jaspers, Philosophie II. Existenzerhellung. Berlin 1932.
K. W. Kapp, Toward a science of man in society. The Hague 1961.
E. Katz, P. F. Lazarsfeld, Personal influence. New York 1955.
R. C. Kwant, Het arbeidsbestel. Utrecht-Antwerp 1956.
D. M. MacKinnon et al., God, sex and war. London 1963.
H. Marcuse, One-dimensional man. Boston 1964.
E. J. Mishan, Growth: the price we pay. London 1969.
G. E. M. Moore, Principia ethica. Cambridge 1959.
E. Morin, L'esprit du temps. Paris.
C. Morris, Signs, language and behavior. New York 1955[2].
R. Niebuhr, Moral man and immoral society. New York 1960[2].
P. Overhage, Experiment Menschheit. Die Steuerung der menschlichen Evolution. Frankfurt a.M. 1967.
P. J. Roscam Abbing, Ethiek van de geldbesteding. Nijkerk (undated).
A. Roth, Husserl's ethische Untersuchungen. The Hague 1961.
D. de Rougement, Penser avec les mains. Paris 1936.
C. W. Sherif, M. Sherif, R. E. Nebengall, Attitude and attitude change. Philadelphia-London 1965.
D. J. de Solla Price, Science since Babylon. New Haven 1962.
C. L. Stevenson, Facts and values; studies in ethical analysis. London 1964.

G. R. Taylor, The biological timebomb. London 1968.
B. Ward, R. Dubos, Only one earth. London 1972.
J. Wild, Human freedom and social order. Durham, N.C.-London 1959.
G. Wolsterholme (ed.), Ciba-symposium: Man and his future. London 1963.

Chapter VIII

T. W. Adorno et al., The authoritarian personality. New York 1950.
K. Axelos, Vers la pensée planétaire. Paris 1964.
R. Barthes, Système de la mode. Paris 1967.
G. Bastide (ed.), Sens et usage du terme structure dans les sciences humaines et sociales. The Hague 1962.
R. F. Behrendt, Der Mensch im Lichte der Soziologie. Stuttgart 1962.
E. Benveniste, Problèmes de linguistique générale. Paris 1966.
E. Bloch, Das Prinzip Hoffnung. 2 vols. Frankfurt a.M. 1959.
E. Brunner, Gerechtigkeit. Zurich 1943.
M. Buber, Pfade in Utopia. Heidelberg 1950. (Eng. trans. Paths in Utopia. Boston 1958).
A. Camus, L'Homme révolté. Paris 1951.
O. Ducrot et al., Qu'est-ce que le structuralisme? Paris 1968.
M. Foucault, Les mots et les choses. Paris 1966.
J. Fourastié, La grande métamorphose du XXe siècle. Paris 1961.
J. Fourastié, Essais de morale prospective. Paris 1967.
D. Gabor, Inventing the future. New York 1964.
J. W. Gardner, Self-renewal: the individual and the innovative society. New York 1964.
R. Jungk, Die Zukunft hat schon begonnen. Stuttgart 1952.
R. Jungk and H. J. Mundt, Der Griff nach der Zukunft. Munich 1964.
L. Kolakowski, Der Mensch ohne Alternative. Munich 1961.
H. Kraemer, World cultures and world religions. London 1960.
E. Levinas, Totalité et infini. The Hague 1961.
F. Lindenfeld (ed.), Radical perspectives in social problems. New York 1968.
Th. Luckmann, The invisible religion. The problem of religion in Modern society. (2nd ed. transl. from the German) New York-London 1967.
K. Mannheim, Ideologie und Utopie. Frankfurt a.M. 1952.
H. Marcuse, Ideen zur einer praktischen Theorie der Gesellschaft. Frankfurt a.M.
A. H. Maslow, Toward a psychology of being. New York 1962.
P. B. Medawar, The future of man. New York 1960.
W. G. Muelder, Foundations of the responsible society. New York 1959.
A. Müller-Armack, Diagnose unserer Gegenwart. Gütersloh 1949.
J. H. Oldham, A responsible society. The church and the disorder of society.

London 1948.
G. Orwell, Animal farm. New York 1945.
C. A. van Peursen, Wirklichkeit als Ereignis. Freiburg-Munich 1971.
J. Piaget, Le structuralisme. Paris 1968.
G. Picht, Mut zur Utopie. Munich 1969.
K. R. Popper, The poverty of historicism. London 1961.
A. Rapoport, Strategy and conscience. New York 1964.
A. Robida, Le vingtième siècle. Paris 1879.
E. Rosenstock-Huessy, Die europäischen Revolutionen und der Charakter der Nationen. Zurich-Vienna (rev. ed.) 1951.
A. Schaff, Marxismus und das menschliche Individuum. Vienna-Frankfurt a.M.-Zurich 1965.
W. Schapp, Philosophie der Geschichten. Leer 1959.
G. Schiwy, Der französische Strukturalismus. Mode, Methode, Ideologie. Hamburg 1969.
H. Scholz, Mathesis universalis. Darmstadt 1969^2.
R. Seidenberg, Analysis of the future. Chapel Hill 1961.
R. Shaull, Encounter with revolution. New York 1954.
A. Strauss, Mirrors and masks. The search for identity. Glencoe 1959.
P. W. Taylor, Normative discourse. Englewood Cliffs 1961.
P. Thévenaz, La condition de la raison philosophique. Neuchâtel 1960.
H. van de Waal, Th. Würzenberger, W. Froentjes, Aspects of art forgery. The Hague 1962.
P. Winch, The idea of a social science. London 1958.
L. Wittgenstein, Bemerkungen über die Grundlagen der Mathematik/Remarks on the foundations of mathematics. Oxford 1956.

Illustrations: list of sources

The names are followed by the numbers of the appropriate illustrations.

ABC Press, Amsterdam, 89, 100 (photo Erich Lessing), 102
ACL, Bussel, 129
Alinari, Fratelli, Florence, 121
Anton, Ferdinand, Munich, 21, 36
Associated Press, Amsterdam, 119
Bayer, Arnhem, 66
Berner Kunstmuseum, Berne, 79
Bibliothèque Nationale, Paris, 98
Brands, G., Waardenburg, 20
Clairefontaine et la Guilde du Livre, Lausanne (photo Michel Huet, from Afrique Africaine), 29
Detroit Institute of Arts, 13
Galerie Maeght, Paris, 60
Gemeente Museum, The Hague, 33, 114–117, 132
Glasgow Museums & Art Galleries, 12
Groeneveld, Ary, Rotterdam, 58, 59
Held, André, Ecublens, 16, 19, 37, 53, 62, 78
Henneman, J., Amsterdam, 125
Holle Verlag, Baden-Baden, 22, 23, 25, 35, 42, 55, 64, 65, 77, 81, 104
IBM, Amsterdam, 74, 105
Ichac, Marcel, Paris, 108
Inter Foto Service, Rijswijk, 63, 122
Klingeren, Architectenbureau F. v., Amsterdam, 82, 83, 84
Musée du Louvre, Paris, 61
Museum of Modern Art, New York, 9, 99, 130
Museum voor Volkenkunde, Leyden, 32
NVSH, Stichting, Uitgeverij, The Hague, 96
Oorthuys, Cas, Amsterdam, 118
Orion Press, Tokio, 112
Rapho, Paris, 10, 45
Rijksmuseum, Amsterdam, 11, 103
Rijksuniversiteit, Groningen, 25
Scala, Florence, 46
Spectrum, Uitgeverij Het, Utrecht, 87, 95
Stedelijk Museum, Amsterdam, 50, 123
Stenfert Kroese N.V., H. E., Leyden, 67
TELEAC, Utrecht, 109
UNESCO, Paris, 7, 75
Universiteits Bibliotheek, Amsterdam, 17
Vaderland, Het, The Hague, 1
Versnel, J., Amsterdam, 51
Victoria and Albert Museum, London, 90

The rest of the illustrations have come from the publisher's own archives.

Index to the illustrations

The subject headings are followed by the numbers of the appropriate illustrations.

Advertising 2, 54
Art: Architecture
  Africa 27, 29
  Japan 64, 65
  India 45
  Greece 28
  Baroque 44
  Modern 63, 66, 84
Photo and film 51, 80, 82, 96, 108, 118
Painting
  Prehistory 15, 73, 76
  Mexico and Ancient America 10, 21, 36
  Egypt 37, 78, 97
  Near East 7
  China 3, 34, 104
  Japan, Korea 41, 110
  Greek 8
  Middle Ages 11, 128, 131
  Renaissance 35, 113, 121
  Baroque 13, 42, 46, 103, 120
  Modern 9, 12, 16, 19, 33, 50, 53, 62, 79, 99, 114–117, 123, 125, 126, 130
Sculpture
  Prehistory 26
  Africa, Melanesia 22, 23, 25
  Etruscans and Greeks 61

  Middle Ages 81
  Modern 47, 58, 59, 60
Cartoons 38, 39, 106, 111
Countries
  Brazil(-ia) 2
  China 34, 104
  Egypt 37, 78, 79
  France 53
  Germany 35, 54
  Great Britain 3, 4, 52, 101
  India, Ceylon 45, 89, 91
  Italy 17, 100
  Japan, Korea 41, 64, 65, 110, 112
  Mexico 36
  Netherlands 58, 59
  Persia 32
  Russia 131, 139
  Sumer (Babylonia) 7, 31
  Switzerland 108
  United States 63, 122
Education 103, 104, 105, 109
Ethics 47, 118, 122, 128
Fashion 2, 127, 135
Hunting, agriculture, fishing 76, 77, 89, 90
Industry 52, 56, 91, 101
Politics 1, 119, 122, 130, 139, 140
Recreation 77, 98, 108, 112
Religion 7, 11, 12, 20, 27, 29, 39, 54, 119, 122, 132, 141
Sciences
  Mathematics 99, 111
  Physics 5, 100

Biology 40, 49
Medical sciences 85, 86, 87, 93, 94, 95, 102, 103
   Psychology 80
   Social sciences 14, 67, 109
   Literature 104
Sexuality, eroticism 26, 42, 47, 96, 97, 98, 129
Technology 48, 55, 56, 57, 63, 69, 73, 74, 102, 105
Traffic, trade 17, 18, 56, 68, 71, 72, 92
Urban building 34, 83, 84, 101, 137, 138

Subject index

Aggression, 10, 209
Ahimsa, 191
Alternatives, 49, 181, 208–210, 211, 222
Archetypes, 146
see also: Primal symbols
Art, 30, 73, 89, 92, 109–110
Atman, 65
Authentic(-ity), 79
Axiom, 92, 222

Being, 12, 33, 51, 53, 82
Biochemistry, 158, 198, 229
Biological sciences, 115, 119, 197, 209
Biomedical, 198
Body, 42, 65, 99, 114–120, 191
Brahman, 65, 70
Burning (self-inflicted death by), 180, 218

Capital, 68, 197
Caste, 68
Central nervous system (CNS), 116, 158–169, 231, 232, 236
Classes, 68, 176
Conflict, 89, 209, 222
Cookery, cooking, 10
Creative (-ivity), 148–158, 219
Critical, 11, 198, 211, 217, 226
Cultural policy, 7, 8, 11, 235, 236
Cybernetic(-s), 115, 124, 147, 158

Dance(-r), 8, 38, 42
Death, 43f, 170, 176, 179
Democracy, 201, 211
Development, 8–11, 116–124
Distance, 12, 54, 59, 187

Energy (-technology), 121–124
Eotechnology, 121, 123
Eroticism, 8, 43, 46, 73, 110–111, 176, 179–182, 230
Ethics, ethical, 54, 185–197, 200–211, 219, 221, 229–232
Evaluation, 9, 11, 23, 190, 199, 217, 232
see also: Value
Evolution, 10, 119, 126, 137
Existentialism, 80
Exploration, urge to, 175, 176, 179

'Face to face' contacts, 207
Fashion, 8, 226–227
Fecundity (mystery of), 39, 43, 170
Feudal, 68, 176
Fire, 192
Functional, 12, 15, 78–103, 180–182, 211

Genetic(-s), 9, 197
Gods, 42, 43, 53, 59, 65, 67, 100–102
Greece, 50–54, 71

Heredity, 143, 198

Humanity, 11, 28, 68, 147, 186
see also: Man
Hunting, 8, 132

Ideal (-ism) (-istic), 14, 62, 90
Identity, 13, 41–43, 66, 97, 109, 219, 220, 234
Immanent, 10, 19, 45, 189, 200, 210, 230, 235
India, Indian, 21, 54, 67, 191, 220
Individual (-ism), 13, 71, 72
Information (-technology), 125–131, 145–148
Interaction, 135, 200–207, 231, 232
Interpreting, 216, 233, 234
Inventiveness, 148–158, 222, 228, 236

Learning (-processes), 136, 142–148, 168–182, 219, 236
Life and death, 8, 43, 51, 201, 202
Logic, 30–31, 92, 160–163, 214, 222

Machine, 74, 112, 121–131
Magic, 14, 45–49
Man, 20–22, 41–43, 65–67, 97–102, 131–141
see also: Humanity
Manipulation, 110, 216, 236
Marriage, 39, 170, 208
Mathematics, 91, 92, 189, 204, 222
Meaning (-ful) (-less), 23, 24, 91, 169, 233
Medical sciences, 109, 136, 197, 201, 207
Memory, 116, 121, 125, 158
Metaphysics, 14, 50, 61–62, 63, 81
Monism, 53, 70
Myth (-ical), 12, 29–45, 63, 175, 187

Nature, 33, 61, 74, 90, 191
Norm, 20, 68, 197, 208, 210, 217
Nyaya-Vaisesiha, 52, 70

Object, 33, 59, 66, 80
Ontology (-ical), 12, 50–69, 170, 175–177, 187
Ontophany, 33, 60
Operational (-ism), 13, 103–111, 216, 236
Organization, 131–141, 181

Participation, 12, 32, 190, 210
Perspective, 66–67, 235
Phenomenology, 82, 90, 97
Pluralism, 63, 70
Policy, 11, 23, 180, 210, 211, 232, 235
see also: Programme, Strategy
Positivism, 14, 15, 40, 81
Powers, 12, 20, 42, 43, 187, 192, 215, 216, 235
Primal symbols, 146
Primitive, 30, 33, 44, 170, 191
Principium contradictionis, 34
Profane, 42, 60
Programme, 16, 142, 180, 222–228
see also: Policy
Prosperity, 175, 177, 181

Quaestio facti (iuris), 9, 16

Recreation, 7, 91, 208, 209
Relation, 12, 83
Responsibility, 16, 23, 28, 197, 210, 216, 230
Restructuring, 11, 148–158, 168, 230
Revolution (-ary), 153, 155, 169, 233
Rule, 10, 153–157, 209, 214, 219, 222, 225, 231

Sacral, 60
Sciences, 14, 61, 64, 93, 175, 187, 190–200, 222, 228f, 231
Secularization, 102
Selection (-ive), 197, 207
'Sensitivity', 157, 216, 219

Servomechanism, 125
Sign, 146, 233
Signal, 119, 136, 146
Socio-mythical, 41, 66
Solipsism, 72
Soul, 42, 65, 176
Strategy, 11, 23, 24, 168, 199, 236
see also: Policy, Programme
Subject, 33, 59, 66, 80
Substance, substantialist, 13, 65, 69–77, 80
Symbol (-ism), 32, 40, 146–153, 232
System, 133–136, 147, 213

Technology, 68, 112–131, 188
Telepathy, 116
Telephony, 115, 119
Television, 203, 220
Theology, 14, 62, 67, 101
Thesis (anti-) (syn-), 13, 14

Transcendence, 10, 19, 20, 40, 189, 200, 208, 211, 218, 230, 235
Tribe (-s), 40, 41
Trigger-mechanism, 163–165, 217–219

Urban architecture, 89, 156, 204, 211, 227, 228
Utopia, 15, 69, 208, 209, 227

Value, 74, 81, 102
see also: Evaliation
Veda, 48, 52
Venus, 47, 73
Verelendungstheorie ('descent into misery'), 197
Visualizing, 202, 203

Walfare, 177, 181, 189, 197
Wellbeing, 179, 182, 197

Name index

Anaxagoras, 60
Archimedes, 155, 191
Aristotle, 54, 59, 60, 61, 64, 93
Augustinus, 63, 64, 69
Baaren, Th. P. van, 45
Bacon, Francis, 69, 188
Bellini, G., 66
Benedict, R., 31
Benveniste, E., 212
Bergson, H., 116
Blake, William, *196*, 214
Botticelli, S., 73, *106*
Boucher, François, 73, *106*
Braque, Georges, 98, *118*
Breuer, M., 89
Bridgman, P. W., 104
Buytendijk, F. J. J., 99
Caesar, 63, 214
Caillois, R., 33
Carnap, R., 93
Carpaccio, Vittore, 66, *87*
Carus, C. G., 114
Cassirer, Ernst, 93, 143, 146
Castagno, Andrea del, 20, *38*
Chen-Chu-Chung, 66, *87*
Chiang Yee, *18*
Chirico, Giorgio del, *172*, 189
Chomsky, N., 213
Comte, A., 14, 15
Coomeraswamy, A. K., 116
Copernicus, 155
Cork, 101, *101*
Dali, Salvador, 20, *38*, 110, *128*

Delvaux, Paul, *223*, 230, 232
Descartes, René, 51, 53, 63, 64, 69
Dewey, J., 84, 146
Dilthey, W., 16
Dobzhansky, Th., 21, 143
Doré, Gustave, *172*, 192
Durkheim, E., 40
Dijksterhuis, E. J., 62
Eccles, J. C., 165
Edme, Gabriel, *178*
Einstein, A., 97
Eliade, M., 33, 39, 40, 44, 45
Escher, M. C., 67, *86*, 98
Fischer, K., 188
Ford, D. H., *166*, *167*
Foucault, M., 212
Fowlie, J., *171*
Fränkel, H., 43, 54
Galbraith, J. K., 177
Galilei, Galileo, *172*, 192
Giacometti, A., 110, *128*
Glasenapp, H. von, 48
Gombrich, E. H., 12
Groot, Hugo de, 71
Grünbaum, A. A., 16
Harder, R., 71
Hawkes, Jacquetta, 22
Hegel, G. W. F., 13, 14, 15, 70
Heidegger, M., 84
Heisenberg. W., 94
Henneman, J., *205*, 225
Heraclitus, 54, 65
Herbart, J. F., 82

Hercules, 13, *36*
Hiriyanna, 52
Hobbes, 71
Hofer, Carl, *196*, 221
Holt, Friso ten, 234, *235*
Hume, D., 68
Husserl, E., 82, 97
Huygens, Chr., 23
Hydén, 165
Jaeger, W. H., 54
Jakobson, R., 212
James, E. O., 34
Jaspers, K., 16
Jensen, A. E., 39
Jerome, 20
Kant, I., 10, 51, 53, 62, 64, 68, 77, 93, 221
Kapp, E., *113*, 114
Kerényi, K., 59
King, Martin Luther, *196*, 218
Klages, L., 113
Klee, Paul, 146, *150*, *152*, 156
Klingeren, F. van, *152*, 156
Kluckhohn, C., 11, 31
Kneulman, C., *224*, 234
Koestler, A., 155
Kravtshenko, A. I., 233, *233*
Lam, Wilfredo, 42, *57*
Lamettrie, J. O. de, 74
Langer, S., 146
Lavelle, L., 116
Leenhardt, M., 41
Leeuw, G. van der, 34, 44, 47
Leibniz, G. W., 63, 65, 214
Levinas, E., 220
Lévi-Strauss, C., 31, 43, *43*, 44, 45, 170, 213
Lévy-Bruhl, L., 14, 30
Linnaeus, C., 212
Lorenz, K. Z., 209
Marett, R. R., 48
Marx, Karl, 69, 89, 197
Mascherini, Marcello, 83, *108*, 110

Matisse, Henri, 46, *47*
Mauss, M., 47
McCulloch, W. S., 165
Mead, Margaret, 31, 44
Merleau-Ponty, M., 32
Meyer, F., 119, 124, 137
Michelangelo, 214
Miró, J., 13, *36*
Mondriaan, P., *194*, 213
More, Thomas, 69
Müller, F. Max, 30
Mumford, L., 115, 121
Nestlé, W., 50
Newton, I., 23, 53, 61
Nietzsche, F., 77
Northrop, F. C. S., 166
Oorthuys, Cas, *195*, 221
Otto, W. F., 40, 42, *59*
Pabst, G. W., *151*, 153
Pask, G., *167*, 168
Pavlov, I. P., 167
Peirce, Ch. S., 84
Pettazzoni, R., 45
Piaget, J., 94, 99, 213
Picasso, P., 39, *206*, 221
Pitts, W., 165
Plato, 23, 51, 53, 59, 60, 62, 63, 64, 65, 68, 176
Plose, *95*
Plotinus, 53, 59, 62
Polanyi, M., 99
Polybius, 69
Preuss, K. Th., 45
Pufendorf, 71
Rapoport, A., 94
Rembrandt, 8, *173*, 197
Reni, Guido, 82, *108*
Ricoeur, P., 32, 53
Robida, A., *206*, 226, 227, *227*, *228*, *229*, 230
Rodier, 8, *18*
Rousseau, J. J., 19, 29
Russell, B., 71

Ruysdael, Jacob, 22, *38*
Saint-Exupéry, A. de, 112
Sankara, 70
Sartre, J. P., 84, 221
Schadé, J. P., 159, *160*, *166*, *167*
Schelling, F. W. von, 30
Scholz, H., 214
Schopenhauer, A., 53, 72, 176
Schrödinger, E., 132
Simpson, G. G., 21
Sin Yoon Bok, *184*, 208
Skinner, B. F., 104
Snell, B., 34, 42, 65
Socrates, 23, 60, 65, 68
Solon, 54
Spencer, H., 77
Spengler, O., 113
Spinoza, B., 63, 69, 70, 188
Steinbuch, K., 121, 167
Straus, E., 99
Tacitus, 69
Thévenaz, P., 62

Thierry, H., *133*, 134
Thomas v. Aquino, 62, 64
Toft, M., *171*
Uccello, Paolo, 132, *149*
Utamaro, Kitagawa, 73, *106*
Vaihinger, H., 63
Venturelli, José, 233, *233*
Versnel, Jan, 89, *117*
Vesalius, A., 158, *159*
Vinci, Leonardo da, 66, *194*, 213
Voltaire, 69
Waal, H. van de, 226
Wach, J., 47
Waddington, C. H., 21, 143
Wagemaker, Jaap, 89, *117*
Whitehead, A. N., 146
Wilson, G., *190*
Wittgenstein, L., 27, 71, 84, 97
Wright, Frank Lloyd, 110, *129*
Young, M., 181
Zadkine, Ossip, 96, *127*
Zuccari, Taddeo, *196*, 214